O Lord, all my longing is known to you;
My sighing is not hidden from you.
My heart throbs. . . .
But it is for you, O Lord, that I wait;
It is you, O Lord my God, who will answer.

Psalm 38:9-10a, 15 (NRSV)

So far as I am concerned, to die in Jesus Christ is better than to be a
monarch of earth's widest bounds. He who died for us is all that I
seek: he who rose again for us is my whole desire. . . . Leave me to
imitate the passion of my God.

Ignatius of Antioch, *Epistle to the Romans*

PRACTICING PASSION

Youth and the Quest for a Passionate Church

Kenda Creasy Dean

William B. Eerdmans Publishing Company
Grand Rapids, Michigan | Cambridge, U.K.

© 2004 Wm. B. Eerdmans Publishing Co.
All rights reserved

Wm. B. Eerdmans Publishing Co.
255 Jefferson Ave. S.E., Grand Rapids, Michigan 49503 /
P.O. Box 163, Cambridge CB3 9PU U.K.

Printed in the United States of America

10 09 08 07 06 05   9 8 7 6 5 4 3

Library of Congress Cataloging-in-Publication Data

Dean, Kenda Creasy, 1959-
Practicing passion: youth and the quest for a passionate church /
Kenda Creasy Dean.
p.   cm.
Includes bibliographical references and index.
ISBN-10: 0-8028-4712-9 (pbk.: alk. paper)
ISBN-13: 978-0-8028-4712-6
1. Church work with youth. 2. Theology.   I. Title.
BV4447.D395   2004
259'.2 — dc22

2003068566

www.eerdmans.com

In memory of

Kenneth B. Creasy
1932-1992

and in honor of

Juddean Ferguson Creasy Kauble

Passionate teachers

CONTENTS

CONTENTS

SECTION THREE

PRACTICING PASSION

ACKNOWLEDGMENTS

This book began as a dissertation but then took on a life of its own (as passion is wont to do, I suppose). I am deeply indebted to Princeton Theological Seminary for approving and funding my sabbatical leaves to work on this project, to the Valparaiso Project on the Education and Formation of People in Faith, and to the Louisville Institute for additional resources that allowed me to refine my research on youth and practices. I am grateful also to the John Wesley Fellows, who funded part of my dissertation research; to the wonderful people at Wesley Theological Seminary, especially G. Douglass Lewis and David McAllister-Wilson, who gave me happy sanctuary to finish this book (for the third time); and most of all to my colleague and friend Richard R. Osmer, who shepherded this project through its original incarnation and who offered wise and welcome counsel as I tried to turn it into something — dare I say? — more useful.

Many generous friends served as an informal, good-humored, and vastly underpaid editorial board for the early manuscript(s). To thank them is to say too little: Dorothy Bass, Ellen Charry, Robin Maas, Don Richter, Dayle Gillespie Rounds, Amy Scott Vaughn and the students in my Ph.D. seminar "Practical Theology, Popular Culture, and Adolescents"[1] all gave perceptive and (very) honest feedback at many points in the manuscript's evolution. I especially cherish the input of James E. Loder, whose incomparable passion guided my thinking on many points, and who "slipped the surly bonds of earth" just as I was typing the final pages. This

---

1. Shannon Bachelor, Mark DiGiacomo, Larisa Hamada, Michael Langford, Theresa Latini, Ajit Prasadam, and Marti Reed Hazelrigg — practical theologians all, whose insights I cherish, whose ministries I admire, and whose passion I love.

project would never have been completed without the incredible assistance of Blair Bertrand (Canadian patriot, research assistant extraordinaire, and practical theologian and youth ministry scholar in his own right). Blair became resident expert on focus groups and videography, and he spent the better part of his seminary career faithfully trailing the scent of hundreds of fugitive footnotes until they finally gave up and turned themselves in.

There are many others whose significant contributions are less immediately obvious. I especially treasure the candor of many thoughtful young people who offered their wisdom in focus groups. I am deeply indebted to Ron Foster, whose pastoral intuition helped hone the final draft and whose unceasing prayers saw me through the desert; to Mark Burrows, who kindled my interest in — and offered resources for — understanding passion through the eyes of the medieval church; and to Jon Pott and David Bratt, my liberating and unbelievably patient editors who would not let me quit. Most of all, I thank God for the enduring blessing of my family. Let me introduce you: our tender teen Brendan, who makes me think deeply and laugh loudly in spite of myself, and whose basement band will forever linger in my brain as the soundtrack for this project; our intrepid "tween" Shannon, whose generous spirit and headlong love of life I so admire; and most of all Kevin, keeper of my heart and guardian of my soul, without whom I simply cannot imagine life being any fun. Their embrace during this project was my lifeline — and if their self-giving love is the least visible to you, it is the most visible to me.

The person who lingers behind the central thesis of this project is my father, Kenneth B. Creasy: coal miner's son, politician, educator, and unapologetic fan of Ohio State football, his wife, and his daughters. His death one day ten years ago took from the world the most passionate person I have ever known. Dad never understood faith but deeply understood the peculiar quality of love that this book explores; he argued with the church but never with Dostoyevsky — and this gives me hope. If I owe what I know of the Passion of Christ to my mom, I owe what I know of the passion of life to my dad. Their marriage was a microcosm of the way God brings these things together to turn the world upside down. I offer this book to the memory of my father and to the honor of my mother: God has blessed me with passionate teachers.

PARABLE OF A PARENT

God said to Abraham, go kill me a son.
Abe said, Man, you must be puttin' me on!

Bob Dylan, "Highway 61"

Teenagers are heat-seeking missiles. They're drawn to fire.
They yearn for experiences that will channel their passions.
And by and large they are not detecting many signs of life in
the church.

Cuyler Black[1]

My God, how I burned with longing to have wings to carry
me back to you . . . although I had no idea what you would do
with me!

Augustine, reflecting on his youth[2]

1. Cuyler Black, "Jesus, Britney and Thermodynamics," *Fellowship Magazine,* June 2001. Black is a youth minister in Ridgefield, Connecticut.
2. Augustine, *Confessions,* trans. R. S. Pine-Coffin (Harmondsworth, U.K.: Penguin Books, 1961), 59.

I wonder if I would like Abraham better if I weren't Christian. The rabbis used midrash to dust off Father Abraham's more questionable qualities, but we Christians have to contend with the patriarchal portrait in Genesis, which is hardly the kind you want hanging on your family tree. Here is a man with a disconcerting slippery side and an extremely dubious approach to women and parenting. Heartless enough that he banished Hagar and first-but-slave-born Ishmael, but then to virtually sacrifice Isaac? That was the Bible story that most infuriated me. *This* was a story of passionate faith? No amount of searching the text or teaching or preaching it ever quelled the rage that mounted when I read that Abraham bound Isaac to an altar, automoton-like, following the divine dictum that he present his child as a burnt offering to God. What kind of parent would do such a thing? What kind of God would *ask* such a thing?

And then my son turned twelve.

Now, it seems, there are only two choices. Brendan could come of age alone, as scores of his pubescent peers will do, heading into the wilderness of adolescence to face decisions — many with irreversible consequences — once reserved for adults. I know he can't survive this alone. He has youth, smarts, and vigor, but few skills of resistance, and precious little experience exercising wisdom over whim. Consumer culture would surely eat him alive. Its greedy teeth marks show already.

The other option is to accept God's invitation: "Take your son, whom you love, and offer him as a burnt offering on one of the mountains that I shall show you" (Genesis 22:2). I can climb this coming-of-age mountain with Brendan just so far, knowing that very soon I will run out of ways to protect him. He will figure this out, of course. Isaac did: "Father!" Isaac said to Abraham in the middle of their fated walk. "The fire and the wood are here, but where is the lamb for a burnt offering?" (Genesis 22:7). I might respond like Abraham and say something wise and faithful, like "God will handle it." Then again, I might not. I might build an altar and then at the last minute start shrieking, "No! Run! Go back! God's going to get you!" — sounding like the panicked woodsman who couldn't quite bring himself to cut out Snow White's heart for the evil queen.

Surely God does want Brendan's heart, the way God desires the heart of every adolescent. But is God really the evil queen in this story? Snow White found refuge with seven doting dwarfs; Kierkegaard imagined slightly more conventional alternatives for Isaac.[3] Yet if Brendan were

---

3. Søren Kierkegaard, *Fear and Trembling*, trans. Alastair Hannay (London: Penguin Books, 1985).

to run, where would he go? Back to the shelter of childhood? He could try, but he'll soon learn that no adolescent can be a child again, no matter how immature he acts. Forward, then, to adulthood? A rather optimistic plan, given the fact that no one today knows where, exactly, adulthood actually begins. To his peers? Maybe. But they're lost in this wilderness too — although we can still hear their voices, most of them, calling out through the media that tempt them off this holy mountain. He could come back to his parents — well, I guess not. Anyway, we're not home. We're along for Brendan's adolescent journey too, which means facing the fact that very soon we are either going to have to give him up or give him over to God.

Given the options, I'm banking on God.

And so his dad and I find ourselves these days hammering away at an altar, made of practices of faith and a fellowship of believers we've been attending to over the years — the combustible stuff of Christianity, faith fuel that ignites in the presence of holy fire. It frightens me that I might try to take things into my own hands, as Abraham tried to do, just before the angel stopped him. Whether Brendan will be as compliant as Isaac remains to be seen. I have my doubts. But for better or worse, one of these days we will arrive at a sacred place, and I will lay him down on this altar of faith. And when that day comes — when the car keys, the career plans, the dates, and the decisions are his, not ours — his dad and I will offer him up to God, who (we actually believe this) has a plan.

It's terrifying.

The Cost of Good Intentions

It's easier on us than on Abraham, of course. Those of us on this side of the cross have read the last chapter first; we know that God has already provided the Lamb. I dare to think that even Abraham, a primitive man in primitive times, miscalculated God's intentions about blood sacrifices. The Hebrews looked back on the story of Abraham and Isaac and saw a God who forbade child sacrifice — a courageous and countercultural conviction in their day, and in ours. The angel of the Lord called to Abraham in the nick of time: "Do not lay your hand on the boy! Now I know that you fear God, since you have not withheld your son, your only son, from me." And Abraham looked up and saw God's unspeakable grace: a ram, stuck in the thicket by its horns, and he offered it as a burnt offering instead (Genesis 22:11-13).

It would be another two thousand years before God gave up on the

xiii

ram-in-the-bush plan and came, once and for all, as the Lamb in the Passion of Jesus Christ. Too many sheep tangled in the shrubbery got overlooked; too many children got sacrificed on society's pious good intentions. Who knows how many angels God has deployed over the centuries to stop us before it's too late: "Do not lay your hand on these children!" Most of the time we have ignored them, sacrificing young people to violence, poverty, pornography, greed, and other false gods who thrive on the blood of children. We're still doing it.

The word "altar" comes from a Latin word that means "to burn up." There is no doubt: God desires our burnt offerings, above all, the offering of a burning, passionate heart. After all, this is how God loves us, with love so profound that God willingly suffers on our behalf — so profound, in fact, that God incorporates us into God's own passion on the cross.[4] I suppose every adult is an Abraham of sorts, someone God calls to accompany precious children to an altar of freedom somewhere, to that place that seems "in the distance" when they are small and scrubbed and new in the world. But, like Abraham, we arrive too soon. And now we must give them up, and either turn them loose or bind them to something sacred — and hope.

Combustible Youth: Keepers of Holy Fire

From the dawn of time, people have described passion in terms of fire to distinguish it from cuddly sentimentalism. Passion devastates. It is "to die for." And it is not to be denied — which is precisely why it leads us to God. Most of us spend our lives looking for ways to rekindle the passion of youth: the burning desire to be engulfed by love, to be ignited by a purpose, to radiate light because the love of another shines within us.

Because adolescence is shot through with passion, young people number among God's most combustible creations. Human experience calls forth religious questions, and developmental psychologists have implicitly organized the lifecycle, to a greater or lesser extent, around them. Human beings are created to seek God — *homo religiosus*. Young people, who by definition must figure out how to be human, may not know that

---

4. See Robert Jenson, "An Ontology of Freedom in the *De Servo Arbitrio* of Luther," *Modern Theology* 10 (1994): 247-52. "When God 'enraptures us' *(nos rapiat)*, he frees us by sharing with us his own freedom, his *liberium arbitrium*. Human freedom . . . is nothing less than participating in God's own triune rapture of freedom" (p. 252).

their quest for "a love worth dying for" is a quest for the Love who died for them. What compels them to search at all is God's gift of passion, the deep human longing for authentic love — a longing present in each of us, but acute during adolescence. For good or for ill, the fire in their loins and the fire in their souls are intimately connected — and, as my late colleague James E. Loder liked to observe, "Spiritual heat is hotter than sexual heat every time."

The truth is that I don't want Brendan to run away from this sacred place, though I understand if he does. I *want* God to get him, desperately. I want God to snatch him up, to seize his life, throw a match on his heart and set him ablaze with faith. And soon: those other gods are circling — Madison Avenue, MTV, Harvard, Hollywood, and others — threatening to drop him on some precarious precipice of their own making. Binding him to the altar of a combustible church is as close to God's fire as I can get my son. He and Jesus will have to take it from there. But I have brought him to this sacred place — and yes, I *want* him to be a burnt offering. I want God to engulf his life with passion: reckless hope, incandescent faith, and all-consuming love.

And so, up this mountain we trudge, my twelve-year-old and me, headed for that place in the distance that God has shown us. The morning is quiet, with birds.

INTRODUCTION

Youth Ministry Is Not Just about Youth[1]

*I think of the young novice in the desert who went to the elder,
the holy man of God, and said, "Father, according as I am
able, I keep my little Rule, and my little fast, my prayer, meditation, and contemplative silence; and, according as I am
able, I strive to cleanse my heart of thoughts. Now, what more
should I do?" The elder rose up in reply and stretched out his
hands to heaven, and his fingers became like ten lamps of fire.
He said: "Why not be totally changed into fire?"*

A desert saying[2]

*It is not just that humans long for God. God also longs for
humans.*

Jürgen Moltmann[3]

The highest passion in a human being is faith.

Søren Kierkegaard[4]

1. Thanks to Steve Bailey, whose unceremonious (but pastoral) leap on the Lakeside Pier saved these handwritten notes from soggy oblivion in Lake Erie.

2. William McNamara, *Mystical Passion: The Art of Christian Loving* (Rockport, Mass.: Element Books, 1991), 4.

3. Jürgen Moltmann, *The Trinity and the Kingdom* (Minneapolis: Fortress Press, 1993), 43. Quote changed to inclusive language.

4. Søren Kierkegaard, *Fear and Trembling*, trans. Alastair Hannay (London: Penguin, 1985), 145.

INTRODUCTION

Someone once told me, "Every adult is a junior high kid with wrinkles." If that is true (and so far, I would have to say that it has been a pretty fair assessment), then no book on youth ministry is really just about "ministry with youth." It is about *ministry,* about being the *church* in which God calls young people to play an irreplaceable and irrepressible part. That is why youth ministry — ministry by, with, and for people between the onset of puberty and the enduring commitments of adulthood[5] — cannot be reduced to keeping or capturing young people in the pews. Adolescents are searching for something, for some*one,* "to die for," to use Erik Erikson's haunting phrase:[6] a cause worthy of their suffering, a love worthy of a lifetime and not just a Sunday night. In short, they are searching for passion, even — maybe especially — in church. Teenagers will not settle for a God who asks for anything less. If we are honest, neither will we.

The Passion of Christ is good news to adolescents, not because Jesus suffers, but because Jesus *loves* them with such wild, passionate hope that even death on a cross cannot stop his determination to win them. Adolescents do not want to suffer, but they do desperately want to love something *worthy* of suffering, and to be so loved. The Christian story both authenticates adolescent passion and turns it inside out, redeeming, redirecting, and redefining it with a more profound Passion still: the suffering love of Jesus Christ. As a result, youthful passion serves the church both as a sign of the *imago dei,* and as an energy source of enormous potential. By acknowledging the Passion of Christ, adolescent passions give way to faith; and, fueled by the energy of fierce love, this faith inevitably leads to ministry.

---

5. I will use the term *youth* as it is popularly understood, as a rough equivalent to the term *adolescent,* which includes young people who, in the early twenty-first century, are engaged in the various psychosocial tasks associated with identity formation. (Ages vary substantially according to cultural and developmental circumstances, but in North America *early adolescence* is frequently viewed as roughly ages 10-14; *middle adolescence* as roughly ages 14-18; and *late adolescence/young adulthood* as the broad and highly variable span between the ages of 18-30. Outside North America, it is common to consider someone a "youth" until marriage or until both parents have died.) The word *teenager* is more specific, and more specifically derived from the American context, usually referring to youth between the ages of 13-19. In this project, I use the phrase *young people* or *youth* to include youth in all phases of adolescent development. Some ministries employ the term *student* to embrace the spectrum of ages implied by adolescence, but I have avoided the term only because it carries class assumptions (namely, that all young people are students, which is true only among certain socio-economic classes). When I speak of adolescents, youth, teenagers, or young people, my intention is to offer an aerial view — commonalities that can be viewed from a distance — rather than individualized portraits.

6. Erik H. Erikson, *Identity, Youth, and Crisis* (New York: W. W. Norton, 1968), 233.

The Passion of Adolescence: Problem or Promise?

One of the most riveting stories of 2002 came to a climax in July of that year:

> ASSOCIATED PRESS (July 15), Alexandria, Va. — John Walker Lindh, the American captured in Afghanistan fighting for the Taliban, pleaded guilty Monday to two charges in a surprise deal with prosecutors that spared him from life in prison.[7]

John Walker Lindh grew up in the tolerant, multicultural insouciance of the San Francisco area, played basketball in the driveway, listened to hip hop and rap music, and converted to Islam at sixteen, after reading *The Autobiography of Malcolm X* for a high school assignment. Mentored by local Islamic teachers who encouraged his newfound faith, Lindh traveled to Yemen after graduation to study the Qur'an, and wound up as a self-confessed *jihadi* — a fighter of holy wars — in an al-Qaeda training camp in Afghanistan. The rest quickly became history; in the war against terrorism following September 11, 2001, CIA agents discovered Lindh among Taliban prisoners of war, brought him home, and charged him with ten counts of treason. Lindh confessed to carrying two hand grenades and supplying services to the Taliban in exchange for two ten-year prison sentences.

He was twenty-one years old.

Lindh's story is a recent version of an oft-told tale: the ill-fated marriage of youth and passion, a union whose alchemy begets radicals and reformers, poets and prophets, mystics and martyrs, despots and defenders of the faith. Religion has always depended upon the passion of youth to enact its ideals. In passion, desire meets will, and since young people possess extravagant quantities of both, society has long viewed adolescent passion as dangerous — too risky to allow, much less encourage, unless something truly radical is at stake.

Yet something crucial is lost in this defensive posture against adolescent passion, a loss that distorts the "to die for" core of Christian faith. After Anselm, medieval scholars tended to truncate divine passion into Jesus' suffering during Holy Week. But there was another view of divine passion that remained visible in the practices of popular piety, whose imprint can be seen in the teachings of the Cappadocians in the East, and in

---

7. Larry Margasak, "Lindh Pleads Guilty; Avoids Life in Prison," The Associated Press (AP-NY-07-15-02).

3

the pastoral writings of reformers like Bernard of Clairvaux in the West. This view promoted the entire Christ-event as the manifestation of God's passion. To these pastoral leaders, God's willing vulnerability in the self-giving love of the Incarnation was a divine posture *culminating* in death on the cross, not synonymous with it.[8] Love always involves suffering on behalf of the beloved; desire longs for what lies painfully out of reach. Yet Christianity's perspective on passion makes love the *reason* for willing vulnerability — and, specifically, for *God's* chosen vulnerability on the cross.

Losing It for Jesus

It is an obvious question: If adolescents and Christianity are both so full of passion, then why aren't young people flocking to church? Maybe it is because the church, like the greeting card industry, has largely sanitized love of suffering, leaving Christianity with a mealy-mouthed niceness that fails to ring true to young people who know in their bones that love and heartache go together. Or maybe it is because the church — and specifically, the mainline Protestant church[9] — has not been completely forthcoming

8. Among those are John and Charles Wesley, whose soteriology substantially influences my thinking on this subject. John Wesley's sermons and "Notes on the New Testament" do not address passion as explicitly as the later theologians cited here; however, the passion of God as self-giving love is a frequent theme in Wesleyan hymnody, which is widely regarded as the *de facto* doctrinal summary of "the people called Methodist."

9. The phrase "mainline Protestant church" is increasingly problematic in our current climate of fading denominationalism. In this study, the term "mainline Protestant" represents the largest Protestant denominations in the United States affiliated with the National Council of Churches during the past century (e.g., United Methodists, Presbyterians [PCUSA], Lutherans [ELCA], Episcopalians, American Baptists, United Church of Christ, Disciples of Christ). Many points raised here also apply broadly to American Catholics and smaller denominations (e.g., Nazarenes, Mennonites, Missouri Synod Lutherans) whose demographic makeup is similar to the denominations listed above. These groups are "mainline" in the sense that their members tend to describe themselves as mostly white and middle class and therefore wielded the most social power throughout the twentieth century. The use of the phrase "mainline church" in this study reflects denominational perspectives more than those of individual congregations. While individual congregations often hold views that vary greatly from "official" denominational stances, many (if not most) congregations in a denomination bear out the denominational imprint to a greater or lesser degree. Variations (not contradictions) in the denominational agenda are especially likely to occur in congregations where racial or cultural identity is at stake. For example, William Myers's ethnographic research in youth ministry suggests that black mainline churches are likely to

about sacrificial love where teenagers are concerned, oblivious to the connection between the passion of youth and the passion of faith. On the whole, we have been reluctant to claim "passion" as love worthy of sacrifice, even when the love involved is God's. Meanwhile, Christian passion has encountered serious competition from global culture, which routinely offers distorted views of passion that range from sex to *jihad*. Severing passion from the self-giving love of God inevitably yields catastrophe, whether the "to die for" object of passion is a boyfriend or a plan to blow up the World Trade Center.[10]

What fascinated us about John Walker Lindh, I think, was less our shock over his Al-Qaeda connections than our inescapable sense that we knew this young man. Didn't he grow up down the street from us? How do we connect the dots between the gentle teenager who played basketball in the driveway and Abdul Hamid, the *jihadi* with a tangled mass of dark hair and an affected Arab accent who came home to charges of treason? Lindh grew up in what is arguably the most tolerant place in America. He attended an elite alternative high school that encouraged students to design their own curriculum. His parents allowed him to choose his own ideological boundaries — and he did, with a vengeance. He did not just convert to Islam; he became a disciple of the least tolerant, least self-directed, most exacting, most oppressive form of Islam in the Middle East.

In some ways, Lindh's story could be told as a triumph for youth ministry. Significant adult mentors during his late teens ushered him into practicing faith communities that confirmed his intuition that faith calls for a radical way of life. Religion became deeply important to him in ways youth pastors usually hope for. It influenced his lifestyle (he turned down his father's offer of an air conditioner as offensive to Allah, though he accepted 1200 dollars to travel to a cooler place) and his vocational direction (he meticulously devoted himself to studying the Qur'an). He was more than willing to suffer for his faith; as a *jihadi*, he was ready to die for it. In short, John Walker Lindh discovered what every teenager is hard-wired to seek: an object he deemed worthy of passion. And he invested his all in it.

---

prioritize cultural identity over denominational agendas when presenting the gospel to youth (see William R. Myers, *Black and White Styles of Youth Ministry* [New York: Pilgrim Press, 1991]). These mainline congregations may constitute exceptions to the historical and theological trends described here.

10. Karen Breslau and Colin Soloway, "He's Really a Good Boy," *Newsweek*, 9 December 2001, available from www.msnbc.com/news/666792.asp?cp1=1; accessed 7 December 2001.

So upon closer inspection, the dots do connect, and rather predictably. If adolescents search for something and someone to whom they can pledge their troth, the object of this devotion must be worthy of their lives, nothing less. Passion asks something of young people; in fact, it asks *everything* of them.[11] This does not mean that youth invest their passions wisely. On the contrary, inexperience is an investor's worst enemy, and most of us have some notoriously bad investments in our emotional portfolio, especially during adolescence. The landscape of human experience is littered with the consequences of "looking for love in all the wrong places," the relics of to-die-for faith placed in the hands of too-small gods who would not or could not die for us. Yet if the Hebrew scriptures exhorted the faithful to "choose life" (Deut. 30:19), Jesus taught that choosing life requires *losing* it for his sake (Matt. 10:29; Luke 17:33). If commitment to Jesus Christ is not, ultimately, a life and death investment, then young people will invest their God-given passion elsewhere.

A Crisis of Passion

Every stage of the life cycle brings certain human characteristics to the fore; in adolescence, one of these qualities is passion. Although the brain's frontal lobes governing reason and judgment continue to develop into adulthood, by adolescence the emotional centers of the brain are well on their way to maturity, giving teenagers their propensity for leading with their hearts. In other words, the adolescent brain is wired for passion; young people feel it in their bones, proclaim it in their hopes and their hormones, act out its power and herald its promise for the imprecise art of human life. This is the mission of the young, for the world, and perhaps above all for the church.

Consequently, young people are among God's most forthright, frustrating, and often unwitting prophets, reminding us that salvation is at stake, for they will not give up on true love until they find it, or until consumer culture numbs them into a kind of lobotomized compliance, whichever comes first. Whether they discover the true source of passion — whether they ever connect their desire for love with the life, death, and res-

---

11. The *Didache* (c. 60 CE), the earliest Christian curriculum we know, poses the basic issue of faith in Jesus Christ directly: "There are two ways, one of life and one of death, and there is a great difference between the two ways." *Didache, The Apostolic Fathers: An American Translation,* trans. Edgar J. Goodspeed (New York: Harper and Brothers, 1950), 11.

urrection of Jesus Christ or with the church at all, for that matter — largely depends on whether the church bears witness to a love more true than those available in popular culture. And that, of course, depends on whether the church practices the passion we preach.

The adolescent quest for passion reveals a theological aneurysm in mainline Protestantism: *We are facing a crisis of passion, a crisis that guts Christian theology of its very core, not to mention its lifeblood for adolescents.* Teenagers are quick to point out the oxymoron in passionless Christianity, quick to smell danger in suppressing their emotional range, quick to question faith that fails to register on the Richter scale, and quick to abandon a church that accommodates such paltry piety.[12] Not only does a church without passion deform Christian theology, it inevitably extinguishes the fire behind Christian practice as well. In short, without passion, Christian faith collapses. And young people know it — which may be why most of them are not spending much time in church.

Vanishing Adolescents

The hemorrhage of adolescents from mainstream Protestantism began in the late 1950s, and by century's end had swelled to a full-fledged ecclesial crisis.[13] Between 1976 and 1996, the number of twelfth graders attending weekly religious services in the United States declined eight percent, though the number of high school seniors who said that religion is "very important" in their lives increased slightly during the same period.[14] Today, about half of North American adolescents say they attend religious services in an average week (only two in five adults say the same). Just where these youth attend is not altogether clear, since pastors routinely

12. This understanding will be contrasted to the early church's understanding of *apathaeia,* or dispassion, in Chapter Two.

13. See Wade Clark Roof and William McKinney, *American Mainline Religion* (New Brunswick, N.J.: Rutgers University Press, 1987), 153-55; see also Kenda Creasy Dean, *A Synthesis of the Literature on, and a Descriptive Overview of, Protestant, Catholic, and Jewish Religious Youth Organizations in the U.S.* (Washington, D.C.: Carnegie Council on Adolescent Development, 1991), 21-22.

14. George H. Gallup, Jr., *The Spiritual Life of Young Americans: Approaching the Year 2000* (Princeton, N.J.: George H. Gallup International Institute, 1999), 11; also, George Gallup, Jr., and Michael Lindsay, *Surveying the Religious Landscape* (Harrisburg, Pa.: Morehouse, 1999), 14-15. Data on high school seniors' patterns of worship is from the Monitoring the Future survey, cited by the National Study of Youth and Religion in 2002 and available from http://www.youthandreligion.org/news/3-1-2002.html; accessed 7 December 2002.

question these statistics (young people never seem to be attending *their* churches at anything close to a rate of fifty percent). What *is* clear is that adolescents have little patience for institutional forms of religious expression, causing some mainline Protestant denominations to flatly cite their "inability to retain young people" as a chief factor in their decline.[15]

Although adolescents distanced themselves from churches of all theological traditions through the late twentieth century, mainline Christianity's theological disposition proved especially conducive to an adolescent exodus. The First and Second Great Awakenings, arguably North America's first religious youth movements (youth constituted their primary audience as well as their primary source of leadership), bequeathed a lasting evangelical legacy to youth ministry. Even in today's liberal, Catholic, and Orthodox theological traditions, youth ministry's existential methods, broad tolerance for affect, and concern for "saving" young people (physically as well as spiritually) shades it with evangelical hues.[16]

Yet early in the twentieth century, mainline Protestants broke ranks with American evangelicals over liberal theology, eschewing evangelical purity movements in favor of a social gospel that emphasized "doing good" over "being good" — and divested themselves of the soteriological urgency of youth ministry's revivalist beginnings. Justifying this shift on civic as much as on theological grounds, Christian formation in these traditions de-emphasized doctrine in favor of relevant social action. While liberal Christianity helped youth demythologize Christian tradition with the laudable aim of spurring them toward critical reflection, mainline Protestant young people soon found themselves unable to supply their activist roles with the theological content their forebears took for granted. Critical thinking became one of the enduring spiritual gifts of liberal Christianity, but the methods of modern rationalism also tended to cleanse faith of messy intangibles — an approach that required major renovation

15. See William H. Willimon and Robert L. Wilson, *Rekindling the Flame: Strategies for Vital United Methodism* (Nashville: Abingdon, 1987), 42; Richard R. Osmer, "Challenges to Youth Ministry in the Mainline Churches," *Affirmation* (1989): 1-25; Milton J. Coalter, Jr., John M. Mulder, and Louis B. Weeks, "A Re-forming Agenda," *Presbyterian Survey* 82 (July/August 1992): 12-13; also, Gallup, Jr., and Lindsay, *Surveying the Religious Landscape,* 14-15.

16. George Whitefield's first preaching tour in America took place when he was twenty-three years old. See Quentin Schultze et al., *Dancing in the Dark: Youth, Popular Culture, and the Electronic Media* (Grand Rapids: Eerdmans, 1991), 18. Joseph Kett points out that even the YMCA (1844) — often cited as the first "official" Protestant youth ministry — sponsored frequent youth revivals, and carried three requirements for membership: an evangelical creed, personal piety, and "evangelical enthusiasm"; see Kett, *Rites of Passage: Adolescence in America 1790 to the Present* (New York: Basic Books, 1977), 73-74.

of doctrines like incarnation, atonement, and other teachings tied explicitly to God's mystery and grace.

The result was a more intellectually palatable church, but one that had been gutted of its most radical and transcendent faith claims, the very claims young people need in order to anchor an organizing worldview. For youth, ridding faith of radicalness and transcendence amounted to castration, and rendered Christianity impotent for reordering the self. With nothing left "to die for" in Christian teaching, it became increasingly unclear whether or not Christianity offered something worth *living* for. Mainline churches began to lose track of faith's claim on identity and, consequently, on youth in the process of identity formation. Without a truth capable of transcending lesser commitments of the self, Christianity became just another side dish in the postmodern cafeteria of personal choice.

Theology: The Weakest Link

Today, the escalating risks facing American young people point to mainline churches' failure to substantially alter the culturally-driven course of young people's lives — either for youth allegedly "in" the church or, more critically, for those outside of it.[17] By the late twentieth century, youth ministry analysts had launched a cottage industry of lament, blaming youth ministry's failures on everything from insufficient leadership training and lack of denominational support to sociological cycles and the invasion of secular culture.[18] The literature flourished, but on the whole, youth ministry did not.

17. Research consistently identifies significant levels of at-risk behavior even among churchgoing youth; while many studies note that religious involvement reduces the degree of this at-risk behavior in teenagers, the presence of *any* caring community in young people's lives, religious or otherwise, seems to have a similar effect. Among unaffiliated youth (those absent from religious communities), at-risk behavior is, simply put, rampant. A number of studies converge on this point; see Joy Dryfoos, *Adolescents At Risk: Prevalence and Prevention* (New York: Oxford University Press, 1990). For levels of risky behavior among churchgoing young people, see Peter L. Benson and Carolyn H. Elkin, *Effective Christian Education: A National Study of Protestant Congregations* (Minneapolis: Search Institute, 1990), and Peter L. Benson, *The Troubled Journey* (Minneapolis: Search Institute, 1993). Both found that significant involvement in community organizations, including churches, mitigates high-risk behavior, but does not eliminate it.

18. See Mark H. Senter III, *The Coming Revolution in Youth Ministry* (Wheaton, Ill.: Victor Books, 1992); see also Kenda Creasy Dean, *A Synthesis of the Literature on, and a Descriptive Overview of, Protestant, Catholic, and Jewish Religious Youth Organizations.* Based on

Something remarkable was missing from all of these explanations. Nowhere did we suggest that *theology* may be partly responsible for the church's diminishing influence on young people. While youth ministry has routinely capitalized on the passions of adolescents, little (if any) attention has been given to connecting them to the Passion of Christ. Most congregations confine divine passion to Holy Week, and view adolescent passion as a hormonal rite of passage, not as the fingerprint of God. Prevailing wisdom suggests that passion, like algebra and acne, should be endured, not exegeted. Churches routinely praise youth ministry while exiling it to a fellowship group in the church basement. Outreach to young people beyond the congregation normally threatens established ways of "doing church," and consequently seldom occurs beyond carefully circumscribed weeks during the summer. The sign potential of adolescence — the possibility that young people might point to something fundamental about who God is, and about who God created us to become — has often been completely overlooked.

Adolescent Passion:
The Universal Symptom of Being Human

Passion is a symptom of adolescence, but it is also a symptom of being human. Young people have always served as barometers of the human condition, indicators of rising and falling pressures on the human psyche.[19] As

---

extensive interviews with representatives from the ten largest American Protestant denominations, leaders of the three branches of American Jewry, and youth staff of a variety of national Catholic youth organizations, this same study found that the lack of leadership training was the most commonly cited problem for religious youth organizations.

19. This was true even before adolescence became widespread in the twentieth century. See Erik H. Erikson, *Young Man Luther* (New York: W. W. Norton, 1958); see also Aaron H. Esman, *Adolescence and Culture* (New York: Columbia University Press), 1990. Esman describes how rites of passages in pre-modern cultures dramatize the culture's "claiming" of young people; Erikson's work limits adolescence in pre-modern societies to a few privileged and gifted young people, who uniquely embody the stresses and strains of their particular moment in history — and were sometimes considered mad for doing so (cf. *Young Man Luther* [New York: W. W. Norton, 1959]). This phenomenon (including the perception of adolescence as a form of madness) became generalized in modern adolescence. Johan Fornas explains, "Young people's biological, psychodynamic, socially and culturally-conditioned flexibility . . . [give] them a strong, seismographic ability to register deep but hidden social movements and to express these in the clear language of style." Johan Fornas, "Youth, Culture and Modernity," in *Youth Culture in Late Modernity,* ed. Johan Fornas and Goran Olin (London: Sage, 1995), 1.

Christian educator Michael Warren has put it, there are no so-called "youth problems" that are not, in fact, *human* problems found among all age groups, "now come to roost among the young."[20] This does not relieve us of the need to adapt ministry for young people; ministry is always a particular enterprise. Yet because adolescence itself is a modern invention that weds social location with psychological development, young people inevitably "act out" — acutely — what is required for being human in their particular moment in history. As one young person told me, "Adolescence is, like, you know, the human condition on steroids."

As a result, the signature assumptions of global culture — radical pluralism, a heightened awareness of risk, and a view of life as a journey in which the self is continually "under construction" — are writ large across the experience of contemporary youth.[21] In 1993, a *Rolling Stone* headline asserted: "If the symptoms are rapid increases in teen deaths from murder, suicide and car crashes, alcohol and drugs. . . . The Disease Is Adolescence."[22] But adolescence is not the "disease." Rather, young people reveal *society's* fault lines, including violence, despair, technological dependence, and poverty, precisely because they are so sensitive to the tremors of culture.

In other words, if you want to account for a people, look at their young. Poised at the fulcrum of human development, youth must renegotiate past identifications in order to secure a foundation for future developmental tasks. Like metal filings in the presence of a magnet, youth orient themselves toward a culture's peculiar seductions, and align their desires with the most powerful force that seems to desire them. This alignment is in the service of identity formation, as adolescents try to measure their inner sense of self against various external standards, searching for fit.[23]

20. Michael Warren, "Youth and the Evangelization of American Culture" (address given at a symposium at Wesley Theological Seminary, Washington, D.C., March 9, 1990).

21. By "postmodern," I mean here a cultural shift away from modern rationalism, not a philosophical school of thought. Friedrich Schweitzer and Richard R. Osmer identify radical pluralism, awareness of risk, and view of life as a journey as distinctive features of postmodern culture that can be observed in the thinking of large numbers of adolescents in response to globalization. See Richard R. Osmer and Friedrich L. Schweitzer, *Religious Education between Modernization and Globalization: New Perspectives on Germany and the United States* (Grand Rapids: Eerdmans, 2003), 49.

22. Douglas Foster, "The Years of Living Dangerously," *Rolling Stone,* December 9, 1993, 55.

23. "The adolescent search for a new and yet reliable identity can perhaps best be seen in the persistent endeavor to define, to overdefine, and to redefine oneself and each other in often ruthless comparison; while the search for reliable alignments can be seen in

Eventually, adolescents select those external standards to which they wish to conform, but first the external standards choose them. And in a world that presents the developing self with such a dizzying array of options, the task of choosing between them can be paralyzing.[24]

Barometer Falling

Perhaps we should have seen this coming. In the 1950s Erik H. Erikson (and virtually all developmental theorists after him) declared "identity" the attainable goal of adolescence, and "identity formation" the developmental "crisis" that young people must resolve. Erikson, whose work has influenced Protestant theology, practical theology in particular, more than any other developmental theorist, thought adolescence required a *moratorium* — a socially-sanctioned "time-out" from adult roles and commitments in which young people could construct an integrated self that both responded to their historical context and cohered across time and social roles. This sense of self, or identity, was borrowed in part from social institutions and significant others whose established selfhood helped anchor young people's developing psyche.

Yet practically before the ink was dry on Erikson's theory of identity formation, identity-bearing social institutions like families, schools, and religious communities grew noticeably weaker, and a new institution, the electronic media (embryonic in Erikson's time but monstrous in ours) started to make fragmentation look normal. As the diffuse egos of American youth came to personify the diffuse nature of American community life generally, the "moratorium" Erikson considered essential to modern adolescence began to evaporate.[25] The line demarcating adolescence

the restless testing of the newest in possibilities and the oldest in values. Where the resulting self-definition, for personal or for collective reasons, becomes too difficult, a sense of role confusion results: the youth counterpoints rather than synthesizes his sexual, ethnic, occupational, and typological alternatives, and is often driven to decide definitely and totally for one side or the other." Erik H. Erikson, *Insight and Responsibility* (New York: W. W. Norton, 1964), 92.

24. This is the psychosocial context in which the adolescent must establish inner coherence, or a sense of identity. Erikson calls the "key problem" of identity "the capacity of the ego to sustain sameness and continuity in the face of changing fate. . . . Identity connotes the resiliency of maintaining essential patterns in the processes of change." Erikson, *Insight and Responsibility*, 96.

25. This scenario led sociologist Peter Berger to comment, "Modern man . . . is ever in search of himself. If this is understood, then it will also be clear why both the sense of 'alien-

from adulthood faded; adolescents played adult roles prematurely, and adults played adolescent roles immaturely. Today, channel surfing, split screens, hyperlinks, and hundreds of other momentary investments seem to challenge Erikson's notion of an integrated identity while simultaneously underscoring his original insight: Adolescents *do* internalize the struggles of their historical moment, which is precisely why personal integration eludes so many young people in contemporary culture. Today, this process is often replaced by sequential, momentary commitments of the self, making identity less a matter of integration than accumulation, accomplished in the thick of adult demands rather than apart from them. The protected moratorium that Erikson envisioned — a place youth could safely "dangle," uncommitted, while constructing an identity that responded creatively to their moment in history — seems as far away as Mayberry.

If a barometric reading of adolescence illuminates the nature of identity in American culture generally, it also reveals youth ministry's real potential for the church, because addressing the "problem" of youth simultaneously addresses the "problem" of being human. Changing atmospheric pressure surrounding adolescence challenges many standard assumptions of ministry, and of youth ministry especially, that have been in place for more than a century. For example:

- *"Adolescence is a deficient form of adulthood."* On the contrary, if youth serve as barometers of culture, we can no longer view youth as incomplete adults, people who are "missing something" that the institutional church must "supply." Rather, social institutions, including the church, often ask adolescents to "give up" something — namely, the drive for inner coherence disclosed by passion — in order to be socialized into institutions that are themselves diffuse.
- *"Christian youth programs solve problems youth face."* Not necessarily. If the church fails to offer a theological alternative to secular views of passion, Christian "youth programs" cannot significantly relieve young people who are in distress. In fact, they may actually contribute to adolescents' sense of fragmentation by reinforcing cultural views of passion that contradict the unifying Passion of the cross.
- *"Youth ministry's primary purpose is to ensure the church of tomorrow."* This has never been the case. If the church's identity crisis is indica-

ation' and the concomitant identity crisis are most vehement among the young today." Peter Berger, *The Homeless Mind* (New York: Random House, 1973), 94.

13

tive of a larger crisis in American institutional life, youth ministry's potential lies not only in reclaiming young people for the *church,* but in reclaiming young people *period* — for whom "salvation" from the violence, suicide, drugs, alcohol, and poverty alluded to in *Rolling Stone* has become a literal necessity.

* *"Youth ministry is primarily about youth."* Untrue. Theologically, youth ministry is primarily about Jesus Christ, and about the church's witness to the self-giving love of God. While youth ministry contextualizes this gospel for young people, a barometric reading of adolescence suggests that youth ministry has something to teach us about being the church for *all* people, whose muffled passions need redemption as urgently, if not as overtly, as teenagers' do.

Alternative Imaginations

By the late twentieth century, it had become evident that teenagers were capable of conceiving ministry in ways that extended far beyond the youth room. When young people gathered for worship and ministry with their peers, often in settings segregated from the congregation at large, they self-consciously "did church" differently than their elders. As a result, youth ministry consistently challenged dominant ecclesiologies in American Protestantism by embodying alternative images of the church. Despite the dismal statistics, something often "goes right" in youth ministry, and legions of clergy, professional church staff, and Christian activists point to the encouraging presence of a youth minister during their teenage years as a decisive factor in their vocational choice. Over time, this proved significant. As these young people became adults, they carried their youthful ecclesial imaginations with them. They did not simply imagine youth ministry; they imagined the *church* — and in so doing they subtly expanded the reach of youth ministry beyond teenagers themselves.

For example, many visible leaders of today's "alternative" congregations — where pastors intentionally refashion styles of worship, patterns of polity, and forms of nurture to attract Baby Boomers and their progeny — admit strong roots in youth ministry. A quick scan through their proliferating publications shows that, by and large, these leaders simply adapted their visions (and methods) of youth ministry to address the adults these youth inevitably became.[26] A 1994 report to the Lilly Endowment con-

26. Two visible examples include Bill Hybels, Senior Pastor of Willow Creek Com-

ceded, "What has become clear . . . is that youth ministry is ultimately about something much more than youth ministry. . . . These [Christian youth] movements are redrawing the ecclesial map of the United States."[27] In other words, the predicament of adolescents is intimately linked to the predicament of the *church,* and the transformation of one implies the transformation of both.

The Transforming Potential of Passion

In this book, I suggest that the passions of young people serve as signs of a deeper, human longing for love that is most fully addressed by the Passion of Christ — a Passion that mainline Protestants have failed to share fully or faithfully with young people. Christ's Passion transforms adolescent desire into sacrificial love that finds expression in the witness of the church and is made visible in the practices of Christian community that shape human relationships according to a "cruciform pattern" of self-giving love. The Holy Spirit employs these relationships to infuse the world with Christ's redeeming Passion. Jesus enters the world in these practices again and again — only this time, through us.

Practical theologian James E. Loder described this process as "existential transformation," a transformation in which the "experience of Nothingness" — our potential for "nonbeing" or death — is negated.[28] For

---

munity Church, and Ed Dobson, Senior Pastor of Calvary Church in Grand Rapids, Michigan. Anecdotal testimony to the connection between "seeker"-oriented pastors and youth ministry abounds in church-growth literature. The following is typical: "I am a former 'youth evangelist.' For most of my years in ministry I spoke to junior high and high school students and young adults. . . . When I came to Grand Rapids I had a desire to start something in the community similar to the old Youth for Christ Rally" (Ed Dobson, *Starting a Seeker Sensitive Service* (Grand Rapids: Zondervan Publishing House, 1993), 23. One respondent to Kimon Howland Sargeant's Seeker Church Pastor survey noted, "Most of the people in the boomer generation in the ministry . . . were seriously affected by Young Life, Campus Life, Campus Crusade — one of those high school or college ministries. So really their loyalties were much more towards a paraministry structure and then converted back into the church." Kimon Howland Sargeant, *Seeker Churches: Promoting Traditional Religion in a Nontraditional Way* (New Brunswick, N.J.: Rutgers University Press, 2000), 153.

27. Ronald White, "History of Youth Ministry Project" (unpublished mid-project report submitted to Lilly Endowment, Indianapolis, Indiana, August 20, 1994), 7.

28. Loder describes the experience of nonbeing in terms of the "abyss" we confront for the first time as adolescents, a confrontation that calls us into transformation (James Loder, *The Logic of the Spirit* [San Francisco: Jossey-Bass, 1998], 204). For Loder, transformation only takes place by "the self-confirming impact from the presence of a loving other,"

our purposes, this human experience of "nothingness" or "nonbeing" is portrayed in identity-diffuse contemporary American adolescents, for whom an integrated self has become particularly elusive. Without a coherent identity, adolescents feel constantly at risk of disintegrating, of becoming nonexistent — literally, of being a "nobody." They intuit that this disparate self is "not right," but they lack the resources to justify it. So they resort to myriad anesthetics to numb the pain of falling apart: achievement, substance abuse, consumerism, serial relationships — the list is endless. Every salve eventually wears off, revealing the fragile self anew.

Christian theology, on the other hand, posits a new, re-centered self in light of the cross. Instead of being divided by unconverted "passions," the new self identifies with Christ's Passion; in the words of Jürgen Moltmann, "Christian identity can be understood only as an act of identification with the crucified Christ."[29] When this happens, adolescents find themselves in a new place; the new self is "in Christ" (Eph. 1:4-11). Christ makes them new, not by making them complete, autonomous individuals, but by grafting them onto one Person whose Body includes young people but is not defined by them. Our identity in Christ depends not on our rituals, practices, or moral standards, but only on God's identification with us

---

regardless of developmental stage (Loder, "Negation and Transformation: A Study in Theology and Human Development," in *Toward Moral and Religious Maturity,* ed. Christiane Brusselmans et al. [Morristown, N.J.: Silver Burdette, 1980], 169, 173). According to Loder, apart from this self-confirming impact of a loving other, identity formation is doomed to be incomplete. The Passion of Christ introduces the self-confirming presence of the Divine Other who loves ultimately, that is, who unifies the adolescent's disparate self by taking it to the cross. From there the young person "rises again" as a new self who is wholly transformed in the resurrected Lord. This self is the divine gift of our true identity — the self God created in us, but which was masked and corrupted by the defenses necessary to our ego formation. Womanist theologian Jacqueline Grant describes the formation of "somebodiness" over against "nobodiness" as the goal of youth ministry for African American adolescents, and bases her analysis on the dehumanizing history of African Americans. Her basic premise may also describe the developmental (but not necessarily the historical) experience of adolescents generally. See Charles Foster and Grant Shockley, *Working with Black Youth: Opportunities for Christian Ministry* (Nashville: Abingdon Press, 1989), 55-76.

29. The complete quote reads as follows: "Christian identity can be understood only as an act of identification with the crucified Christ, to the extent to which one has accepted the proclamation that in him God has identified [God's] self with the godless and those abandoned by God, to whom one belongs oneself. If Christian identity comes into being by this double process of identification, then it is clear that it cannot be described in terms of that faith alone, nor can it be protected against decay by correct doctrinal formulae, repeatable rituals and set patterns of moral behavior." Jürgen Moltmann, *The Crucified God* (Minneapolis: Fortress, 1993), 19.

in the Incarnation. This divine-human identification is the work of salvation, in which humanity is "justified" or made right, re-centered by Jesus who restores us through acts of witness that proclaim his life, death, and resurrection until he comes again.

So What Do We Mean by "Passion"?

In ancient literature, *pathos* (Latin, *passio,* "to suffer") meant to submit, to undergo an experience, to be completely affected or overcome.[30] Hellenistic culture maintained that gods were incapable of suffering, because a god, by definition, cannot be overtaken. Only once in the New Testament does the term *passion* describe the suffering of Jesus Christ (Acts 1:3); in keeping with the Greek view of "the passions" as dangerous, disruptive forces that interrupt the clarity of reason, Christian scriptures overwhelmingly paint human passions as disorderly appetites in dire need of conversion, examples of "our former ignorance" (1 Peter 1:14) before Christ transforms our fickle human desires into holiness.[31] The medieval university banished passion to the monastery, and the gap between affect and the academy widened as the Enlightenment stamped "reason" across the intellectual landscape. Even the romantic Rousseau sought to erase "passion" from the student Emile, and Kant distinguished the "rational" love found in Scripture from the "pathological" love of the passions. In short, most Western philosophy has insisted that our ability to reason links us to the gods, while our inability to control our passions binds us to the beasts.[32]

Yet as Moltmann points out, passion's "long history of use" in Judaism and Christianity changed the word by providing it with a new context of meaning.[33] The ancient Hebrews' experience of God was as One pas-

---

30. Moltmann points out that what Christianity proclaimed as *agape* (or as *philia* or *eros,* for that matter — terms used for the "love" of God and believer in the biblical Greek) were seldom translated as *pathos,* though all of these terms carried connotations associated with Christ's suffering love (*The Crucified God,* 270). For a fascinating look at the confusion of passions, see the movie *Chocolat,* directed by Lasse Hallstrom (Miramax Home Entertainment, 2001), in which a passion for chocolate serves as a metaphor for other passions, including the passion of love and the passion of Christ viewed as an ethical standard for human relationships.

31. For references to passion typical of the New Testament position, cf. Acts 14:15; Gal. 5:24; Col. 3:5; 1 Thess. 4:5; James 5:17.

32. Robert C. Solomon, *The Passions* (Garden City, N.Y.: Anchor Press/Doubleday, 1976), 11.

33. Moltmann, *The Crucified God,* 270.

sive in the face of death, a suffering born out of God's concern for the beloved. Abraham Heschel calls this the "ultimate significance of *pathos*":

> *Pathos* in all its forms reveals the extreme pertinence of man to God, His world-directness, attentiveness, and concern. God "looks at" the world and is affected by what happens in it; man is the object of His care and judgment. The basic feature of *pathos* . . . is a divine attentiveness and concern.[34]

This ultimate attachment and concern distinguishes prophetic from pagan experience, maintains Heschel. Pagans view existence as experiencing being, while prophets view existence as experiencing concern. Judeo-Christian history "associated passion with love out of freedom for others and those who were different, and taught an understanding of the meaning of *the suffering of love* from the history of the passion of Israel and of Christ."[35] Heschel sees this divine *pathos* revealed by God's personal (subjective) relationship to Israel and humankind, by God's mysterious transcendence that condescends to know us, and by the experience — as we turn toward God — of recognizing God's turn toward us.

Adolescents instinctively hold a similar view of passion as they search for a love that will unleash their humanity, a love that is born out of ultimate concern for them. Like prophets, teenagers recognize passion in communities where God's fidelity, transcendence, and communion with them take human form. For Israel and Christians alike, passionate love includes but transcends desire alone; love involves longing, but it also involves suffering in the more arcane sense of willing passivity and chosen vulnerability. In a decisive break from their pagan neighbors, Christians and Jews proclaimed a passionate deity, a God who desires love, who suffered betrayal by God's beloved, and who submitted to being "overcome" by love in order to suffer our return. In contrast to the Greeks, who sought to subdue passion with reason or avoid it through denial, Christians proposed passion as God's solution to evil. Thus, the early Christians viewed the willingness to suffer and die in Jesus' name, morally or physically, as a creative, dynamic force that led to new birth. To use the terms of modern psychology, salvation led to identity, and Christians maintained that the revealed route to this identity was through the suffering love of Jesus Christ.

Christians, therefore, came to view passion not simply as an emotion

---

34. Abraham Heschel, *The Prophets,* 2 vols. (New York: Harper & Row, 1962), vol. 2, 263. Emphasis and gender language in the original.

35. Moltmann, *The Crucified God,* 270.

but as the experience of being willingly "undone" by divine love. Passion, literally, is God's undoing. Out of love for God's creation, the divine self is poured out into human form (Phil. 2:6-11) and undergoes death on the cross. Yet in this passionate act of self-giving love, God provides the means for our undoing as well. In Jesus' death, God "undoes" our "undoing" from sin. Our negation is negated; our nobodiness gives way to our status as God's beloved: "Once you were not a people, but now you are God's people, once you had not received mercy, but now you have received mercy" (1 Peter 2:10). In identifying with the One who is God's undoing, you and I — not to mention the youth in our care — are undone and refashioned into new creations.

The Active Passivity of Christian Passion

Christians, therefore, proclaim a double meaning for passion. Passion connotes "suffering" in the sense of being unwillingly overwhelmed by a powerful experience, as well as being willingly overtaken by great emotion, especially the voluntary "suffering" of great love. As Moltmann puts it, "The word 'passion,' in the double sense in which we use it, is well suited to express the central truth of Christian faith. Christian faith lives from the suffering of a great passion, and is itself the passion for life which is prepared for suffering."[36] The connecting thought is passivity — a theological twist that distinguished the passionate God of Jews and Christians from the gods of classical culture:

> Suffering is what comes upon one, against one's will. It is something of which one is a passive victim. Thus suffering is a mark of weakness and God is necessarily above suffering. But, for the Greeks, one is also passive when one is moved by passions and emotions. To be moved by desire or fear or anger is to be affected by something outside of the self, instead of being self-determining. Again, this is [considered] a weakness and so God must be devoid of emotion. To suffer or to feel is to be *subject* to pain or emotion and the things which cause them. God cannot be subject to anything.[37]

36. Moltmann, *Trinity and the Kingdom,* 22-23; see also Richard Bauckham, *Moltmann: Messianic Theology in the Making* (Basingstoke, Great Britain: Marshall Morgan and Scott, 1987), 102.

37. Bauckham, *Moltmann,* 102.

Jews and Christians alike maintained that God *can* be affected by God's creation, and in fact *desires* to be moved by the love of God's creatures. While God's love is not motivated by self-seeking desires and anxieties — God's passion is not synonymous with human passion — divine freedom allows God to choose a *pathos* that lies beyond either the incapacity for suffering or fateful subjection to it. This "third form of suffering," observes Richard Bauckham, is the "voluntary laying oneself open to another and allowing oneself to be intimately affected by him, that is to say, the suffering of passionate love."[38]

The church, therefore, came to teach many passions. The suffering Passion *of* Christ inspires a life of passion *for* Christ, by which the disordered passions (or desires or appetites) of being human become realigned with the holy passion (or self-giving love) of God.[39] To simplify, we can think of "passion" in a way reminiscent of Heschel and Moltmann, as *loving something enough to suffer for it.* The "suffering" implied here is the willingness to place that which we love on Abraham's altar, our willing surrender of ego in actions that give witness *(marturia)* to the self-giving love of God. "Dying to self" in the biblical sense restores one's true identity as God's beloved. Normally, the God-given self remains buried beneath the humanly constructed ego that we have created by grasping. Yet the self intended by God is revealed when we "die" to the grasping ego and give ourselves over to a life conformed to the self-giving love of God, evidenced in the passion of Jesus Christ.

Human passion, in other words, is imprinted with the divine passion even when human desires run amuck. While "the passions" (plural) have historically described unconverted human desires or appetites, *passion* (singular) reflects a deep yearning to love and be loved authentically, a universal human longing to be united with the One who makes "something out of nothing" — whose love can negate adolescents' overwhelming sense of negation. Passion also impels young people, often in ways that go unrecognized, to keep looking for "true love" even when human love fails them. Since adolescents seek a caliber of love no human can possibly sustain without disappointment, the discovery of the one Love who really *is* worthy of sacrifice, who really *does* love us selflessly and extravagantly — the Love who never disappoints, who will not let them down, and who will not go away — is a discovery that reorders the self. For adolescents whose

---

38. Moltmann, *Trinity and the Kingdom,* 23; also see Moltmann, *Crucified God,* 230.

39. I capitalize *Passion* when I am referring specifically to the event of the incarnate self-giving of God in Jesus Christ; otherwise I employ the lower case.

identities are works in progress, this discovery is the pearl of great price. By seeking out the *one* Love that matters above all others, passion unites lesser commitments of the self and weaves the shards of identity into something approaching an integrated whole.[40]

Passion, then, is not primarily about suffering, but about love — the love God gives, and the love God longs to have returned. Christian passion transcends youthful sentimentality by insisting that true love reflects the image of God and consists essentially of choosing to act on behalf of one's beloved. This, after all, is how God loves us — with a love so profound that nothing, not even death, can dissuade God from pursuing us. Divine desire manifests itself on the cross, the focal point of Jesus' Passion. Passion suffers not because of emotional fervor, but because *true love inspires willing sacrifice.* Made in the image of a God who passionately seeks us, we are created to seek God passionately and sacrificially as well.

Couldn't We Just Hold a Car Wash?

If we seek God's transformation for adolescents — and if we hope to convince them that Christianity is worth the trouble — the mainline church must reclaim passion, and specifically God's passion in Jesus Christ, as fundamental to our identity. This will require a more self-conscious theological awareness for youth ministry than we currently possess. It will also shift youth ministry's emphasis away from sociology, psychology, anthropology, educational theory — not to mention car washes and lock-ins — towards theology, and especially practical theology, that form of theological reflection concerned with Christian actions. This is not to say that youth ministry as practical theology never needs car washes or lock-ins, only that these youth activities — like all church activities — are harnessed for a larger purpose: to enlist young people in the mission of God.

Practical theology takes as its "text" the contemporary situation as it calls forth acts of self-giving love that witness to Christ's passion. These acts of witness are the living artifacts of Christian tradition, culminating in worship as the ultimate expression of *marturia.* In worship, our lives become signs of God's passion as we take part in holy practices, human ac-

---

40. The psychological dimensions of this concept have been discussed by Robert Kegan, *In Over Our Heads: The Mental Demands of Modern Life* (Cambridge: Harvard University Press, 1994), 354.

tions that God uses to infuse creation with grace, wonder, and love.[41] Practical theology reflects on these practices, or acts of witness, to help the church more faithfully extend God's passionate love into the world. In this project, the Passion of Christ functions not as a controlling interpretive framework but as a theological "doorway" through which we may enter the world of the young, and through which they may enter the world of the church.

As a result, this book is written for people whom God has called for thoughtful ministry with adolescents — seminarians and senior pastors, people who teach Bible studies and people who lead youth groups, college professors and military chaplains, parents and mentors — practical theologians all, called to "translate" doctrine for the concrete task of forming young people in the name of Christ to become envoys of God. My guiding conviction is simply this: If the church is going to make sense to adolescents, then our ministry must be predicated on passion — the Passion of Christ, the passion of youth, and the passionate faith that is made possible when these two things come together.

Youth Ministry as the Art of Faithful Improvisation

Those of us who call ourselves practical theologians are more like experienced cooks than gourmet chefs. We cook like grandmothers, mixing meatloaf with our hands, substituting ingredients, estimating measurements, seasoning to taste — not because these are random choices, but because we draw upon family memory and accumulated wisdom to determine which choices "fit" the situation at hand while remaining faithful to the basic thrust of the family recipe. We are schooled in the art of faithful improvisation, which — to swap metaphors — makes practical theology

---

41. See Richard Osmer, *The Teaching Ministry of Congregations* (Louisville: Westminster/John Knox, forthcoming). Osmer observes that practices enable us to find our identities within the biblical narratives of God's relationship to the world — not by removing us from the world but by setting us apart as people who extend the ministry of the church into the world. The practices that witness to God's self-giving love are not confined to congregations, but practical theology helps congregations develop these practices in two ways. First, it provides them with a theory that can help assess how well they are carrying out the practices that witness to the transforming Passion of Jesus Christ. Second, practical theology helps congregations develop guidelines for what sociologist Pierre Bourdieu calls the "necessary improvisation" of practices that allows us to employ them more faithfully. See Pierre Bourdieu, *Outline of a Theory of Practice* (Cambridge: Cambridge University Press, 1977), 8.

much like a jazz riff. Practical theology is a disciplined performance marked by the freedom to respond to the moment at hand, which helps determine its shape. This book affirms such an "improvisational rationality," a way of thinking that (besides guiding cooks and jazz musicians) places Christian tradition in conversation with the messy particularities of ministry: particular people with particular needs in particular situations, all of which are informed by a particular gospel.

As a result, practical theology privileges the authority of Scripture and Christian tradition, but concedes their ambiguity because the Christian community is a lively, fluid context where the Holy Spirit still speaks. Admittedly, the innate "messiness" of practices requires disciplined theological reflection to tether it to tradition, the way a jazz singer requires technical precision and a sophisticated appreciation of musical theory to live in her bones and not just her brain. The gift of such discipline is the freedom to innovate, the ability to faithfully wander around a melody without losing track of it. Likewise, Christian tradition offers practical theologians the freedom to explore innovative forms of Christian life without losing our way home.

For this reason, I draw significantly upon Jürgen Moltmann's reflections on passion to anchor our discussion, guided by Moltmann's conviction that the measure of Christian identity is identification with the plumb line of divine passion. Because practical theology exegetes culture and the human subject as well, I also proceed from the methodological assumption that the world of today's adolescents, and adolescents themselves, may also be considered theological texts. This does not make them normative in matters of theological interest; where theological resources come into conversation with human sciences in this study, I explicitly privilege theology as the Christian community's well-worn record of human experience with God.[42] But I also maintain that the question of faith is built into the life cycle, and that this question is raised, even when unacknowledged, by the hu-

---

42. For various approaches to transformational method in practical theology, sometimes called a "Chalcedonian pattern," see Deborah van Deusen Hunsinger, *Theology and Pastoral Counseling: A New Interdisciplinary Approach* (Grand Rapids: Eerdmans, 1995); also James E. Loder and W. Jim Neidhardt, *The Knight's Move: The Relational Logic of the Spirit in Theology and Science* (Colorado Springs: Helmers & Howard, 1992). I follow Hunsinger more closely than Loder and Neidhardt, using what might be better described as a "revised" transformational method, since I grant more agency to the movement of the Holy Spirit in the ecclesial practices of the Christian community than Loder and Neidhardt do, and I assume an ongoing, mutual critique between doctrine and practice in the life of the Christian community.

man experience of passion that enlivens every adolescent — a deep desire for reliable Love that is ultimately satisfied by the passion of God in Jesus Christ.

Overview of the Project

Each of this book's three sections, therefore, advocates a theological awareness for youth ministry — for the sake of youth, obviously, but also for the sake of the church — that views the passionate identity of the Triune God as the norm for human identity, and that considers a "Trinitarian self" — an ego incorporated into the divine Passion — the result of redeemed human passion. Section One, *Shared Passions,* focuses on the theological resonance between the Passion of Christ and adolescents' experience of passion, especially in light of the now nearly universal adolescent experience of developing a self. Using socio-cultural and developmental theory as dialogue partners for practical theology, this section explores why theological interpretations of passion receded into the shadows of the modern church, stripping liberal Protestantism of much of its ability to influence adolescents.

Section Two, *Dimensions of Passion,* probes contemporary culture's distortion of three dimensions of *pathos* — fidelity, transcendence, and communion — and how this distortion has affected contemporary adolescents in the process of identity formation. The human hunger for fidelity, transcendence, and communion lies at the core of human identity, and therefore becomes acute when the ego is in flux. While youth ministry cannot "create" passion in young people, when adolescents experience steadfast, ecstatic, and intimate love in communities that practice Christ's Passion as fidelity, transcendence, and communion, the Holy Spirit uses these communities to awaken young people's awe, invite their wonder, and inspire their reach toward God and others through acts of costly love that both anchor the formation of faith and ground the transformation of the emerging ego.

Section Three, *Practicing Passion,* suggests a framework for youth ministry that draws on the historic practices of the Christian community as a "curriculum of passion." The memory of Christ's Passion has always been preserved in the practical piety of the Christian community, and these practices serve as a scaffolding for maturing faith. Theologian Miroslav Volf points out that practices are not something "added to" Christian beliefs; rather, practices inhere in beliefs — they are what Christian beliefs *do*. As Volf puts it, Christian identity takes shape in the midst of both belief-shaping practices and practice-shaped beliefs.[43] Consequently, every Christian practice embodies, to a greater or lesser degree, God's self-giving love in the life and death of Jesus Christ, forming us into "passion-shaped" people and communities of faith.

In Search of a Passionate Church

Theology that takes passion seriously offers a "portal" between Christianity and young people, a crucial link between the lived experience of adolescents and the historic practices of the Christian community. Clearly, young people are gripped by different passions than that of the cross; the ardor of youth pales beside the ardor of God. But there is a real connection between them as well. If the passion of adolescence provides the impetus for relationships, including a relationship with God, then the Passion of Jesus Christ provides the substance of that sought-after relationship, the content of faith and the *raison d'etre* for the church. If youth invest their passions elsewhere (and statistics overwhelmingly suggest that they do), then the church must receive this news as a judgment not on adolescents, but on us.

All of this suggests an obvious possibility: What if the passion of God makes a difference, not just for the way we approach Christian doctrine, but for the way we go about Christian ministry itself? What if mainline Protestantism's disappointing track record with young people (in and beyond the church) has not been primarily a failure of models, educational strategies, historical cycles, or institutional support, but a failure of theology? Is it possible that the "problem" facing youth ministry reflects all too accurately a *malaise* infecting mainline denominations generally: a flabby theological identity due to an absence of passion? That would be ironic. Most young people come to us brimming with passion. Could it be that, instead of fanning this youthful zeal into holy fire, we have more often doused it, dismissed it, or drowned it in committee meetings?

The theological challenge youth pose to the church is blunt: Are we who we say we are? Do we practice passion, transformed by a Love who never disappoints, and live by a faith so convincing that we stake our lives on it? Or are we just another sagging social convention, like Dracula, that needs young blood to survive? We are not the first people to wonder this

43. Miroslav Volf, "Theology for a Way of Life," in *Practicing Theology,* ed. Miroslav Volf and Dorothy C. Bass (Grand Rapids: Eerdmans, 2002), 250-51.

aloud. In 1934, the leader of the German youth delegation to the Universal Christian Council for Life and Work — a twenty-eight-year-old named Dietrich Bonhoeffer — suggested that the "problem" of youth would not be answered by youth ministry, but by theology:

> The future of the church does not depend on youth but only on Jesus Christ. The task of young people is not reorganization of the church but listening to God's Word; the church's task is not the conquest of young people, but the teaching of the Gospel.[44]

To Bonhoeffer, only the church mattered, not any church organization, Christian club, or youth group. For all their merits (and there are many) youth groups remain notoriously unreliable for the formation of *faith*. Faith, it turns out, is far more likely to take root in the contexts of families, congregations, and significant adult-youth relationships — communities where passion is practiced, where people are given to loving others sacrificially, and where we experience sacrificial love on our behalf.[45]

In short, God bestows the gift of faith in the practice of passion, as Christ's Passion meets us in relationships marked by the disciplines of costly love. Youth ministry must invite young people into communities that practice passion — not just any passion, but God's passion — through acts of worship and witness that invite us to love foolishly, and to suffer love's consequences as we seek after God's own heart. So this is where we begin: with a passionate God, and with young people searching for passionate love, hoping against hope that their search is not in vain.

44. Dietrich Bonhoeffer, *Gesammelte Schriften,* Band 3 (Munich: Chr. Kaiser Verlag, 1960), 292-93.

45. See Robert Wuthnow, "Religious Upbringing: Does It Matter, and If So, What Matters?" in *Christ and the Adolescent: A Theological Approach to Youth Ministry — 1996 Princeton Lectures on Youth, Church and Culture* (Princeton: Princeton Theological Seminary, 1997), 79; Benson and Elkin, *Effective Christian Education,* 38.

Section One

SHARED PASSIONS

Chapter One

SOMETHING TO DIE FOR

The Subversive Power of Passion

[The S.S. hanged two Jewish men and a young boy in front of the whole camp. The men died quickly, but the death throes of the youth lasted for half an hour.] "Where is God? Where is He?" someone behind me asked. . . . The two adults were no longer alive. Their tongues hung swollen, blue-tinged. But the third rope was still moving; being so light, the child was still alive. . . . Behind me, I heard the same man asking: "Where is God now?" And I heard a voice within me answer him: "Where is He? Here He is — He is hanging here on this gallows."

Elie Wiesel[1]

Love doesn't sound so dangerous until you've tried it.

Paul Wadell[2]

People who have not been in Narnia sometimes think that a thing cannot be good and terrible at the same time.

C. S. Lewis[3]

1. Elie Wiesel, *Night* (New York: Hill and Wang, 1960), 70-71.
2. Paul J. Wadell, *Becoming Friends: Worship, Justice, and the Practice of Christian Friendship* (Grand Rapids: Brazos Press, 2002), 30.
3. C. S. Lewis, *The Lion, the Witch and the Wardrobe* (Harmondsworth, U.K.: Penguin Books, 1966), 117.

S omehow I had missed the news that morning. I strode into my class on
April 26, 1999, to find a room of grim, silent seminarians staring back
at me. One by one they filled me in on news gleaned from CNN, the
Internet, *The New York Times.* A high school in Colorado. Two teenagers,
black trench coats, gunfire, bombs, a cafeteria under fire. Students hud-
dled in closets, calling CNN on their cell phones; one student, crazed with
fear, leapt from a window into the parking lot below. How many shot? No
one knew yet, but fifteen bodies still lay in the school, mostly in the library,
including those of the two boys who finally ended their killing spree by
committing suicide. All the victims were teenagers but one, a teacher: Dave
Saunders died while protecting his students.

For awhile, no one spoke.

"Where was God?" one young man finally asked, his voice cracking.
He said what the rest of us were thinking. We wept silent tears together.

There was one more thing, someone remembered. She had received
an email that morning, forwarded by one of the girls in her youth group.
According to some of the kids who witnessed the shootings, there had
been a girl in the school library. One of the gunmen asked her if she believed in God. When she said yes, he killed her.

Dying for Something Worth Dying For

The electric speed with which teenagers — not the press — circulated
"the Cassie Bernall story" made it urban myth within hours, long before
the media (who were presumably busy checking sources) reported it.[4] It
did something else, too: it transformed a massacre into a martyrdom. We
now know that many students witnessed to their faith during the Columbine High School tragedy, some in word, some in deed, and some at gun-
point. Cassie's "yes," in fact, may have belonged to classmate Valeen

---

4. The term "urban myth," as used here, does not disqualify the story attributed to
Cassie Bernall; rather, it refers to a story that "feels so true" to hearers that factuality becomes secondary. What is significant is that these stories, as Peter Lewis notes, "take on a serious tone and tap into some deep-seated fears and apprehensions people have about the
world and teach lessons about those shared fears and dangers." The *New York Times's* Peter H. Lewis examines the impact on such stories caused by the sheer speed that urban myths
can travel on the Internet in "Urban Myths," available at http://www.units.muohio.edu/
psybersite/cyberspace/folklore/index.shtml; accessed 7 December 2001. See Jan Harold
Brunvand, *The Choking Doberman and Other "New" Urban Legends* (New York: W. W.
Norton, 1984).

Schnurr.[5] But all of this was quickly beside the point. The lightning speed with which adolescents claimed Cassie's story as their own — and the tidal wave of public soul-searching that followed — revealed our collective hunger for a story of faith in the midst of profound evil, just as it revealed teenagers' desire for something heroic to redeem their lost innocence. If nothing else, Columbine brought a theological perception to public consciousness: Young people are dying for God, any way you look at it.

Cassie Bernall "put a teenage face on martyrdom."[6] The label became fixed the following summer, when Cassie's mother released her daughter's biography, an instant bestseller among teenagers.[7] Adolescents read Cassie's journey from troubled teen to Christian convert as the saga of someone who *had* found something to live for that was "worth dying for" — and she was one of their own. The question flooding Internet chat rooms and bulletin boards following the Littleton shootings was stark: "Would *you* die for your faith?" A Florida girl's response on an Internet bulletin board typified hundreds of others: "I haven't totally pledged all of my being to God. When I heard [Cassie's] story I realized she gave up everything. She DIED for Him. . . . Would I have done the same?"[8]

The Columbine story turns on the question of *passion*: the twisted passions of two lonely boys who thought they had nothing to live for, but also the holy passion of faith — fidelity, as Erikson called it: "a disciplined devotion," the strength of having something "to die for."[9] When young people ask, "Would *you* die for your faith?" what they really want to know is, "Is Christianity worth it? Is it worth staking a life on, and not just a Sunday night? Because if it's not — if God isn't worth *dying for* — then I'm outta here."

But listen closely. Behind these youthful ultimatums is a plea: Please,

---

5. My point is not to argue the quality of one student's courage or faith over another's, only to acknowledge the public perception of martyrdom associated with the tragedy. Valeen's courage was overlooked by early reports, as was the courage of John Tomlin, who invited classmate Nicole Nowlen to share his space under a table and then was murdered beside her, and Rachel Scott, whose serene spirituality and premonitions of a life called to witness touched students and journalists alike. There were many others.

6. David van Biema, "A Surge of Teen Spirit," *Time,* May 31, 1999, 58.

7. Misty Bernall, *She Said Yes: The Unlikely Martyrdom of Cassie Bernall* (Farmington, Pa.: Plough Publishing House), 1999.

8. Van Biema, "A Surge of Teen Spirit," 58. The phenomenon repeated itself four months later on September 15, 1999, when a gunman burst into a back-to-school youth rally at Wedgewood Baptist Church in Fort Worth, Texas, killing seven people, four teens and three adults.

9. Erik H. Erikson, *Identity, Youth and Crisis* (New York: W. W. Norton, 1968), 233.

please tell me it's true. True love is always worth dying for. Please tell me I'm worth dying for. Please tell me someone loves me this much and won't let me go, even if the Titanic sinks, even if the library explodes, even if the towers fall, even if the world ends. Please show me a God who loves me this much — and who is worth loving passionately in return. Because if Jesus isn't worth dying for, then he's not worth living for, either.

Theological Canaries

To suggest that youth are searching for something to die for, on the surface, seems irresponsible, if not downright dangerous. Adolescents are known for dying for the wrong passions, being co-opted by the wrong causes. Furthermore, the theological drift of the twentieth century has been to *minimize* the place of passion in Christian theology, thereby eliminating much of the tension between Christian faith and culture. Not that American teenagers don't believe in God; a staggering 95 percent of adolescents consistently say that they do.[10] They just don't believe God matters — or cares. At issue is not their conversion; adolescents convert as a matter of course. But to what, or to whom, will they be converted? Martin Luther King and Nelson Mandela won passionate followers, but so did Adolf Hitler and Osama bin Laden. Passion can be co-opted by evil as well as won by God — and by any number of deities in between.

By the end of the twentieth century, children's advocates had begun to think of postmodern young people as canaries in the mines, whose fading voices warn of an increasingly toxic cultural environment. Church and culture analyst Lyle Schaller predicted that "[making] this a better world for children" would constitute the number one social cause for Christian churches in the first half of the twenty-first century — as important to churches in our era as the abolition of slavery was for nineteenth-century churches, and as the Civil Rights movement became for churches of the twentieth century.[11] But Columbine legitimized a new issue in the public debate over children's well-being: theology. Until Columbine, theology rumbled beneath the surface of much American public policy, but lawmakers, educators, social critics, and even church leaders avoided explicit refer-

10. George H. Gallup, Jr., *The Spiritual Life of Young Americans: Approaching the Year 2000* (Princeton: George Gallup Institute, 1999), 3.

11. See Lyle E. Schaller, *Discontinuity and Hope: Radical Change and the Path to the Future* (Nashville: Abingdon, 1999), 226.

ence to religious faith as a factor in public health. The Columbine story, by contrast, was rife with unapologetic Christian testimony.[12] We could not tell this story without reference to God. Unfortunately, it took tragedy in an upscale, suburban high school where things like this "just don't happen" to force a public revelation: without something to die for, adolescents have nothing to live for, either.

Salvation is not an eschatological category for adolescents; it is a near and present hope.[13] Their newfound capacity for self-reflection also gives them new capacities for faith, hope, and dread. For the first time, youth recognize that they are dying a thousand deaths they cannot stop — a condition Christian tradition chalks up to sin, and developmental theorists attribute to identity diffusion. Either way, youth realize that they could live or they could die, and they do not want to live or die for nothing.

The Adolescent Menace to Society

The passion we associate with adolescence — the raw desire for an object for which we are "sold out," for which we would risk everything — is often viewed as a sign of trouble. After the Littleton shootings, Channel One (a TV station beamed into the nation's classrooms) and the National Association for Mental Illness posted a web page identifying symptoms of teen manic depression. The list included "unrealistic highs in self-esteem — for example, a teenager who feels especially connected to God."[14] The line between adolescence and mental illness has never been abundantly clear; Joan of Arc was accused of witchcraft, Victorian medical journals classified adolescence as a form of insanity, and by 1989 the fastest growing sector of the hospital industry was private psychiatric beds for teenagers.[15]

12. Even lawmakers had difficulty avoiding religious interpretations of the Columbine shootings. On May 27, 1999, Darrell Scott, the father of victim Rachel Scott, was invited by the House Judiciary Committee to testify against an N.R.A. position on gun registration, and stunned subcommittee members by saying: "No amount of gun laws can stop someone who spends months planning this type of massacre. The real villain lies within our own hearts. . . . The young people of our nation hold the key. There is a spiritual awakening taking place that will not be squelched!" Journalists noted that his remarks were not well received. (House Judiciary Committee Subcommittee on Crime, May 27, 1999).

13. See Kenda Creasy Dean, "Proclaiming Salvation: Youth Ministry for the Twenty-First Century Church," *Theology Today* 56 (January 2000): 524-39 for a more complete discussion of the significance of the doctrine of salvation for adolescents.

14. Walter Kirn, "The Danger of Suppressing Sadness," *Time,* May 31, 1999, 48.

15. See http://www.fordham.edu/halsall/source/nider-stjoan1.html (accessed 7 De-

James E. Loder writes, "Because of their totalism, their deep ideological hunger, their heightened awareness of their potential nonbeing, and their sense of urgency about the meaning of life, adolescents are especially capable of the kind of commitment and 'fidelity' in self-sacrifice that life in the Spirit calls for." Apart from a sense of identity, warns Loder, this commitment may come too easily and be misleading. But, he adds, "given clarity about the object of faith, Jesus Christ, and the transformational work of his spirit, the struggle to work out *who* one is only in relation to *why* one exists at all forges an identity of theological proportions."[16]

The problem is that an identity of theological proportions runs counter to the expectations of society, and therefore it actually *impedes* our ability to succeed by the standards of contemporary culture. Consumer culture depends upon ideologies of self-fulfillment, and upon the electronic media's ability to convince teenagers to buy into them (literally). But young people who identify with Christ's Passion enact self-*giving* love, the kryptonite that undoes ideologies of self-fulfillment. Youth who bear witness to the suffering love of God subvert the ideologies on which consumer culture stands, as the life, death, and resurrection of Christ becomes a filter through which youth begin to recognize efforts to co-opt their passion for the market. Alas, human society has a long history of suppressing subversives, even when they are our own children. And so we demand that passionate youth contain themselves, put limits on their passion, relinquish their desire for full humanity so they may succeed in a culture where limited, partial, and fragmented selves rule the day. But there is a price. For passion will not be boxed, and the tension created by tamped-down desire inevitably seeps through the seams in mutant forms or bursts the dam altogether, only intensifying society's desire to keep adolescents "under control."

So it is true: Adolescents who develop Christian identities really *are* menaces to society. An adolescent who knowingly shares in the freedom of God, who participates in the life, death, and resurrection of Jesus Christ, inevitably unmasks culturally accepted forms of domination, greed, and fear. This makes her dangerous to the dominant culture, and to human institutions like the church that depend upon these deceits to function. Faith founded on passion — from Joan of Arc to Martin Luther, Eric Liddell to Cassie Bernall — always exposes our cultural underwear and reveals our

cember 2001); Joseph Kett, *Rites of Passage* (New York: Basic Books, 1977), 231; Nina Darnton, "Committed Youth," *Newsweek*, July 31, 1989, 66-72.

16. James E. Loder, *The Logic of the Spirit* (San Francisco: Jossey-Bass, 1998), 248.

stripped-down emperors, even the Christian ones. Christian identity in young people reminds us, often awkwardly and overtly, that self-fulfillment without self-abandonment is a sham. Selfish desire is patently *not* worth dying for. True passion has a price.

The Church's Invitation to Oddity

Every culture is predicated on the expression of some passions, the exploitation of others, and the denial of still others. The very fact of living in human society requires passion to be artificially curtailed — starting from the time we are young. "It is a regrettable fact of our cultural situation," writes sociologist Peter Berger, "that capitulation to permanent dishonesty is often interpreted as a sign of 'maturity.' By contrast, the intellectual passions of rebellion are seen as simply a symptom of 'immaturity.'" For Berger, adolescence represents the "one moment in an individual's biography when questions of truth and authenticity are at least glimpsed," but this becomes neutralized when we pass off adolescents' rebellious passions as just "sowing wild oats." Adulthood, says Berger, "becomes a more or less comfortable settling down with the half-truths or even the organized delusions which are embodied in the various social institutions."[17]

Berger maintains that adolescents' passionate refusal to accept a "comfortable settling down with half-truths" is a sign not of immaturity, but that the young person has reached a crucial decision point. Religious faith comes into play at the very point that this passion comes to the fore; in fact, Berger observes, Christianity *by definition* must be interpreted in light of "intellectual passion." Growing more "mature" — i.e., capitulating to social dishonesty — stands in direct contradiction to the passion of faith, so "maturation" holds no advantage in the formation of Christian identity. Notes Berger, "The Christian faith itself forbids its being interpreted as the religious rationalization of a process of 'maturation.'"[18]

The decision facing adolescents (and by implication, the rest of us), then, is whether to capitulate to the kind of dishonesty Berger describes as part and parcel of socialization. Just as the passions of human existence become explicit during adolescence, society clamps down on them. And since adolescents have to learn how to function in society, they have little

17. Peter L. Berger, *The Noise of the Solemn Assemblies: Christian Commitment and the Religious Establishment in America* (Garden City, N.Y.: Doubleday, 1961), 10.
18. Berger, *Noise of the Solemn Assemblies,* 10.

choice but to relinquish their nascent search for passion in the name of "growing up," repressing the inner compass that directs them toward coherence, wholeness, and holiness.

As we will see, when youth ministry finds its moorings in the practices of Christian community — practices that have the force of the cross behind them — it challenges the social forces that clamp down on passion. Consequently, Christian practices *heighten* the tension between youth and their culture, and mark them as people who belong to a community "set apart." From the perspective of a culture of self-fulfillment, whether in the first or the twenty-first century, imitating Christ is unavoidably dangerous. In the words of Madeleine L'Engle, for Jesus the "rules don't hold," which accounts for his continuous appeal (especially for teenagers) as well as his deep subversiveness:

> Read the Gospels. Read what this guy was really like. He had a strong personality, he told jokes, his friends were all the wrong people, he liked to go to parties. He didn't start a lepers' rights movement, he just healed lepers in his path. He was far more severe about people who were judgmental than he was about people who committed adultery. Love was always more important than anything else. All of his miracles were done on the Sabbath. God should have said, "Jesus, tone it down a bit. Be a little more tactful!"[19]

Acts of passion enact love in light of the cross, not in light of human fulfillment — a love that is never "toned down" for the sake of propriety. No wonder holy love looks foolish; it *is* foolish. Through the historic practices of the Christian church, young people are invited into an odd and holy life that imitates and participates in a life and death commitment: the life, death, and resurrection — or Passion — of Jesus Christ.

The Heresy of Wholesomeness

But what if the Passion of Christ were to fade from the center of Christian theology, leaving the historic practices of the Christian community without a visible referent? What if the Christian risk factor — the cross — were to fade from the forefront of Christian education, which has traditionally "housed" youth ministry in the life of the church? This was precisely the

19. Quoted by Robert Wuthnow, *Creative Spirituality: The Way of the Artist* (Berkeley: University of California Press, 2001), 142.

scenario that faced mainline Protestant youth ministry in America at the end of the twentieth century. In the absence of an adequate Christology — namely, one that retained a central place for the passion of God — the practices of faith that once celebrated our "oddity" as Christians easily became domesticated as vehicles of wholesomeness. Bereft of ultimate life-and-death significance, churches found themselves unable to invest their practices with urgency, regardless of the amount of enthusiasm they employed.

Meanwhile, in keeping with postwar trends of age segregation that increasingly characterized American institutional life, twentieth-century church educators began to separate youth from the broader Christian community.[20] Adults met in the sanctuary; youth met in the "youth room." Adults worshipped on Sunday mornings; youth did devotions on Sunday nights. Adults took part in mission; youth held service projects. Adults heard sermons; youth heard "talks." In short, young people increasingly seemed "set aside" more than "set apart" for holiness. The more disconnected youth ministry became from the worshipping community as a whole, the less often youth took part in the practices by which centuries of Christians imitated the Passion of Christ. Slowly, youth ministry devolved into a wholesome extracurricular activity with no real analog in the adult Christian community.

Of course, an argument might be made that young people's estrangement from congregational life may have fueled a hunger for long forgotten forms of spiritual discipline, jettisoned by mainline Protestants so long ago that they now seem exotic. At the turn of the twenty-first century, for instance, contemplative prayer enjoyed a minor comeback among Christian teenagers (and Protestants generally), as did medieval disciplines like walking the labyrinth, saying the rosary, praying with icons, and doing, wearing, or singing anything "Celtic." To date, however, these practices lay beyond the common life of most mainline Protestant congregations, and for the most part the pattern of distancing young people from the practices of the broader Christian community intensified

20. The American high school, universally available to American youth following World War II, became the first petri dish for a true "peer culture" in America. Advertisers quickly learned the economic rewards that came from target-marketing this particular age group. By the end of the twentieth century, peer culture was so complete as to constitute "a tribe apart" in which adults and youth rarely interact. For a number of views that support this thesis, see Thomas Hine, *The Rise and Fall of the American Teenager* (New York: Avon Books, 1999); Patricia Hersch, *A Tribe Apart* (New York: Ballantine Publishing Group, 1998); and Kett, *Rites of Passage*.

throughout the twentieth century. As a result, youth ministry learned to justify itself on the basis of educational goods (teenagers "learn" about faith), political merit (teenagers become good citizens of the church), or psychological value (teenage peer groups maximize adolescent development) — but not on the basis of the mission of the church. Predictably, by the turn of the twenty-first century, youth ministry often looked less like ministry and more like a civic responsibility that seemed neither odd nor dangerous. Discipleship flattened out into a pragmatic wholesomeness, and Christianity became one more decent thing to do, if you have time for that sort of thing.

What Happened to Passion?

Not surprisingly, the most serious theological critiques of passion in Christian education flowed from mainline Protestantism — also the home of Christian Endeavor, the Religious Education movement, and Young Life, the three early twentieth century movements that decisively shaped youth ministry in mainline Protestantism as we now know it. All three movements were born in the American middle class and constituted bids for respectability that gutted the church of passion's strangeness in an effort to imbue youth ministry with middle class ideals. Christian Endeavor spawned the wildly popular "youth club" model that swept every major Protestant denomination in the late nineteenth and early twentieth centuries to prepare converted youth for participation in the American church establishment.[21] The Religious Education movement — liberal theology's brief but massive program of educational reform in the early twentieth century — cheerfully pilfered the progressive education movement and imposed an often unwelcome degree of professionalism on the chaotic landscape of mainstream Protestant education.[22] Young Life, one of the

21. Between 1880 and 1893 alone, the Sunday Schools of the United States and Canada gained nearly five million members, primarily in Midwestern small towns, thanks to large numbers of people who streamed from makeshift revivals into congregational life. Christian Endeavor emerged as Protestantism's most effective tool for shifting from revivalism to the structured life of an institutional church. See Kett, *Rites of Passage,* 191.

22. The Religious Education movement's reforms for youth — tremendously influential at denominational headquarters — were never well received locally. The optimism and rationalism of professional educators rang hollow to rural congregations, accustomed to the harsh unpredictability of agricultural life; in both urban and rural areas "the methods of progressive education — the experience-centered approach with stress on problem-solving and

two major parachurch youth movements of the 1940s, grew out the Reformed orthodoxy of Jim Rayburn, a Presbyterian minister who believed that the adult-youth relationship (more than the church fellowship group) served as the context for Christian conversion, and that the Apostles' Creed (more than liberal theology) provided the theological grounding necessary for vital faith.[23]

Of these influences, only Young Life self-consciously fostered adolescents' identification with the Passion of Christ. Yet Young Life located its ministries *outside* of congregations (and outside of the broader intellectual discussion on youth ministry generally), which gave salvation an individualistic spin and considerably truncated the range of Christian practices available to students. Furthermore, Young Life's explicitly relational methods tended to capitalize on the socializing forces of the high school, sometimes reinforcing norms of passion (e.g., popularity) that contradicted the passion of the gospel. Christian Endeavor, assuming a clientele of already-converted youth, originally inherited some of the theological leanings of American revivalism, but was quickly swept into the mainstream church's middle-class agenda as church fellowship groups became the hoped-for antidote to "trouble in River City." In fact, much of Christian Endeavor's popularity stemmed from the fact that *because* it assumed the prior conversion of its members, it concentrated on method over content — making it easy to adapt to any theological climate.[24]

The Religious Education movement, on the other hand, openly scorned passion and its connotations of excess.[25] True to their modern

---

attention to students' needs — required a sophistication and commitment of time" not feasible for volunteers. Robert W. Lynn and Elliott Wright, *The Big Little School* (New York: Harper & Row, 1971), 75. In sum, "these reformers . . . succeeded more at the theoretical level than at the level of local church practice." Michael Warren, *Youth, Gospel, Liberation* (New York: Harper & Row, 1987), 8.

23. The other was Youth for Christ, which emerged as an arm of American fundamentalism. See Mark Senter III, *The Coming Revolution in Youth Ministry* (Wheaton: Victor Books, 1992), 107-20.

24. Both John Dewey, hero of American progressivism, and Francis Clark, founder of Christian Endeavor, spoke at the first Religious Education Association national convention in 1903. See Proceedings of the Religious Education Association Convention (1903), 60-65, 44-51.

25. Many of the founders of the Religious Education movement devoted their professional careers to decrying revivalistic pressure on adolescents to convert. At the same time, they fixated on adolescent conversion — redefining it as a psychological, not a theological, phenomenon. Not a little projection was involved on the part of these theologians; many of them found in liberal Protestantism a refuge from the "failed" conversions of their own

sensibilities, progressive religious educators de-emphasized divine passion and found the affective dimensions of human passion particularly odious, unpleasant reminders of revivalism's emotional manipulation. Curriculum reformers replaced lurid illustrations of Christ's suffering, popular in nineteenth-century Sunday School literature, with more benign images of a kindly Jesus who kept company with children and sheep. Religious educators tended to view Christ's suffering not only as an unfit topic for children but as an unfit topic for Christians. Salvation was seldom considered an act of sacrifice and was only marginally considered an act of God; the cross's primary benefit was to inspire humans to get along.[26] By the 1920s and 1930s, the goals of the nascent field of youth ministry in mainline churches had become virtually indistinguishable from the goals of professional educators and public education — a realm wholly indifferent to the influence of Christian theology.[27]

---

youth. G. Stanley Hall's 1904 tome *Adolescence* (New York: D. Appleton and Company, 1908) officially inaugurated this age of psychology, and Hall — like his contemporary, Christian educator George Albert Coe, and many others — spent much of his academic career coming to terms with the absence of a conversion experience of lasting worth during his own youth.

26. Leading the liberal charge at the turn of the century were educators like George Albert Coe, who viewed passion as a weakness, a sorry reminder of the blood, sweat and tears evoked by manipulative revival preachers. Coe's early work prophesied that the serene educational methods of professional educators would replace passion with the more reasonable emotions of a "mature mind." The result would be a "wholesome atmosphere" in the church and nation, and the emotions present would be "social emotions," which are "gentle and pervasive rather than explosive." In place of atonement, Coe heralded "salvation by education," in which the oddity of Christian life was replaced by a facile marriage of democracy and Christian charity. George Albert Coe, *The Religion of a Mature Mind* (Chicago: F. H. Revell, 1902), 249ff.

27. Christian educator William R. Myers points out that during this period, many Anglo, middle-class, mainstream congregations surrendered their more organic shape to the emerging schooling, therapeutic, and marketing metaphors employed by the controller of age-graded growth: the public high school. Many black congregations avoided this pattern, as did other congregations where insufficient social power or money prohibited the hire of professional educators, or where racial or cultural identity remained a preeminent concern. Still, these cultural metaphors left an indelible imprint on mainline Protestant Christian education. See William R. Myers, *Black and White Styles of Youth Ministry* (New York: Pilgrim Press, 1991), 175.

The Most Wasted Hour of the Week

As it turned out, the Religious Education movement, though a monument to modern optimism and a triumph of good intentions, was a house built on theological sand. Ill-equipped either philosophically or theologically to address social tides beginning to define the twentieth century, the Religious Education movement lost momentum as two world wars, the Great Depression, and Adolf Hitler finally exposed liberal theology's feeble doctrine of sin and cheap good news. The neo-orthodoxy of Karl Barth and the Christian realism of the Niebuhr brothers arose to proclaim a costlier gospel: an evangel that self-consciously embraced the suffering of the cross. Yet while these movements largely supplanted theological liberalism elsewhere, they failed to substantially alter the direction of American youth ministry.[28] Christian education in the United States proved remarkably resistant to theological change and continued to turn to social science and progressive education, not theology, for its intellectual moorings.

A number of factors account for this. Americans had long established personal experience as part of the civic canon, and preferred to distill their theology from the practice of Christian life than from the sweeping doctrinal systems espoused in Europe. A God conceived as "wholly Other" seemed like a direct affront to can-do American pragmatism,

28. Liberal theology posed a number of theological problems for American youth ministry. Christian educator William Myers notes the vulnerability of white churches in particular: (1) While the *immanence* of God necessarily accentuated God's presence in the midst of life, churches often assumed that theological language could be equated with "managerial" (middle class cultural) language. When congregations shrank from a theological language distinct from cultural language, they offered youth no theological distance from which to critically reflect on God's presence in the midst of life. (2) The use of *growth* as a metaphor for understanding the ushering in of God's kingdom tended to equate American middle-class existence with membership in God's kingdom. In other words, youth ministry that brought youth up under the governing images of American success became easily confused with bringing them up as faithful Christians. (3) The liberal emphasis on the *goodness* of humanity, necessary historically to counter the nearly morose revivalistic preoccupation with human depravity, was also theologically risky. When youth over-identified with personal and social goodness, what Myers calls a "we-are-good" enclave mentality developed: "our class is good, our race is good, our church is good, our God is good." (4) Finally, while the pursuit of the "historical Jesus" subjected the church to the rigors of theological scholarship, it also implied that little children already possessed the kingdom of God, rendering sin and redemption obsolete. Liberal theology, according to Myers, tended to mutate Jesus into "a kind of benevolent 'Mr. Chips' who has a one-sided view of child development." In response, youth ministry sought to maintain youth in their child-likeness, rather than to transform them into mature Christians. See Myers, *Black and White Styles of Youth Ministry,* 178-79.

which factored prominently into youth ministries predicated on defending teenagers against urban corruption and fortifying the church against membership losses. Even Young Life, which drank deeply from neo-orthodox wells, relied upon affiliative models of nurture and socialization throughout the twentieth century. By the 1930s child-rearing trends in the U.S. had replaced categories of "sin" with the more progressive, child-centered category of "risk" — implying that young people required protection, not atonement. Liberal education was already Americans' primary weapon against the European class system, and after World War II, most Americans considered universal access to public education essential to democracy, if not to Christianity — making them reluctant critics of liberal education's principles and methods, even if it put youth ministry theologically at odds with the rest of the congregation.

Yet without the suffering love of Jesus Christ, no compelling distinction existed between the goals of Christian youth ministry and secular education, steeped in various doctrines of self-actualization. As the sacred and secular youth agendas became increasingly blurred, institutional religion's contribution to adolescents came into question. By 1957 *Life* magazine declared Sunday School "the most wasted hour of the week."[29] Within a decade, the theological rallying cry of young people had become the death of God, not the Passion of Christ.

Atoning for a Passionless Church

When the Passion of Christ recedes in Christian theology, Christianity's ability to challenge the dominant culture's ideologies of self-fulfillment with sacrificial love recedes along with it. Whether we define Christ's Passion broadly (as God's reconciling work through the entire spectrum of the Incarnation, the approach taken by this project), or narrowly (as God's reconciling work in the Good Friday event itself), the Passion of Christ stands inconveniently at the heart of the doctrine of atonement, an area of theological reflection that came under fire in the twentieth century, especially from mainstream theologians who feared its use as a sanction for oppression and abuse. Understandably, the most vocal critics of atonement theory in this regard have come from feminist theology. Womanist theologian Carter Heyward, for example, states emphatically: *"A christology of passion has no place in atonement"* and with Beverly W. Harrison calls

29. Wesley Shrader, "Our Troubled Sunday Schools," *Life,* February 1957, 100-114.

Anselm's doctrine of atonement "the sadomasochism of Christian teaching at its most transparent."[30]

In fact, the mainline church has never settled on a single interpretation of God's atoning work in Jesus Christ, and recent streams of scholarship have begun to track the doctrine's cultural mutations while acknowledging divine suffering as an aspect of divine-human reconciliation.[31] Given the idealized but marginalized status of youth in American society, it would be ludicrous to reclaim church teachings that ghettoize them. The biblical story of Christ's Passion reveals Jesus' solidarity with suffering, not his legitimization of it. After all, the objective of faith is not to suffer in Christ's name, but to *love* in Christ's name — and the decision to love always implies a willingness to suffer alongside the beloved. The source of God's passion is extravagant delight in creation, which leads to the divine decision to suffer death in our stead. Church historian Roberta Bondi observes,

> The early church does not teach that the most basic quality of God's love is a suffering self-sacrifice. What first engages God with us is not a duty or need or self-sacrifice or obligation or the need to be right or

30. Carter Heyward, "Suffering, Redemption, and Christ," *Christianity and Crisis* 49 (December 11, 1989): 384. Emphasis in original. See also Beverly W. Harrison and Carter Heyward in *Christianity, Patriarchy, and Abuse: A Feminist Critique* (New York: Pilgrim Press, 1989), 153. Rita Nakashima Brock calls the Christian understanding of atonement "divine child abuse," a condition that so pollutes our understanding of God that grace becomes an experience of relief for not being punished, not an experience of forgiveness. See Rita Nakashima Brock, "And a Little Child Will Lead Us: Christology and Child Abuse," in *Christianity, Patriarchy, and Abuse: A Feminist Critique,* ed. Joanne Carlson Brown and Carole R. Bohn (New York: Pilgrim Press, 1989), 51-52; see also Joanne Carlson Brown and Rebecca Parker, "For God So Loved the World?," in the same volume, 1-30. The precise role of the cross in relationship to women's suffering varies according to social location; see, for example, Thelma Megill-Cobbler, "A Feminist Rethinking of Punishment Imagery in Atonement," *Dialog* 35 (Winter 1996): 14-20; Jacquelyn Grant, in *White Women's Christ and Black Women's Jesus* (Atlanta: Scholars Press, 1989); Shawn Copeland, "Wading Through Many Sorrows," in *A Troubling in My Soul: Womanist Perspectives on Evil and Suffering,* ed. Emilie Townes (Maryknoll, N.Y.: Orbis, 1993); and Chung Hyun Kung, *Struggle to Be the Sun Again* (Maryknoll, N.Y.: Orbis, 1990).

31. See S. Mark Heim, "Christ Crucified: Why Does Jesus' Death Matter?" *Christian Century,* March 7, 2001, and "Visible Victim: Christ's Death to End Sacrifice," *Christian Century,* March 14, 2001; Pamela Dickey Young, "Beyond Moral Influence to an Atoning Life," *Theology Today* 52 (October 1995): 344-55; Leanne Van Dyk, "Do Theories of Atonement Foster Abuse?" *Dialog* 35 (Winter 1996): 21-25, and *The Desire of Divine Love: John McLeod Campbell's Doctrine of the Atonement* (New York: Peter Lang, 1995); and Susan Bond, *The Trouble with Jesus* (St. Louis: Chalice Press, 1999).

good but delight in us as the beloved. . . . Delight makes the lover extravagantly eager to make sacrifices for the beloved. The cross, which is the occasion for God's own terrible pain, is very real, but it is God's delight in and desire for us that calls God to do it.[32]

Joy, not suffering, provides the proper perspective on passion. "The theology of the divine passion is founded on the biblical tenet, 'God is love' (1 John 4:16)," Jürgen Moltmann writes.[33] God's love, given and received in the trinitarian dance between Father, Son, and Holy Spirit, is the wellspring of passion; sacrifice is secondary, a means to restore self-giving mutuality to creation by incorporating us into God's own *pathos*. The pain of love is real, as every broken-hearted teenager knows. But it is secondary to the delight of loving, and of being loved, which is what makes passion worth the risk — for God and for us.

Who Gets the Kids?

By the end of the twentieth century, youth ministry in the mainline Protestant church found itself embroiled in a theological custody dispute. Where the church interpreted Christ's Passion solely in terms of Jesus' sufferings during Holy Week, youth ministry tended to equate divine passion with justification, overlooking the scope of the Incarnation as an enactment of the *pathos* of God. Practically, this often meant approaching young people as objects of mission, potential converts whose salvation would avert eternal damnation. This approach had the advantage of theological urgency, since churches tended to enthusiastically support youth ministry when they perceived heaven and hell were at stake. But it had the disadvantage of straitjacketing grace. Salvation easily became seen as young people's "decision" for Jesus, instead of as the salvific work of God in Christ's life, death, and resurrection. Meanwhile, the church did little to

32. Roberta C. Bondi, *To Pray and to Love: Conversations on Prayer with the Early Church* (Minneapolis: Fortress, 1991), 121-22.

33. Moltmann, *The Trinity and the Kingdom* (Minneapolis: Fortress Press, 1993), 57. Given Moltmann's Western view of personhood, in which God "has" relationships rather than "is" a relationship, the choice of John's ontological language (God *is* love) is surprising. In my view, it is a fortuitous choice, making his definition of personhood less vulnerable to charges of tritheism (a view that Moltmann clearly did not intend). God *is* love — contra Moltmann's own analysis. This is the position of the Eastern church, which views God as inseparable from God's relationality, either *ad intra* or *ad extra*.

account for Jesus' saving grace in terms that made sense to young people weaned on cultural pluralism and empirical science, leaving them to navigate the gap between faith and culture with whatever resources they already possessed.

On the other hand, where the church downplayed the significance of the cross in a bid to seem scientifically relevant or culturally open, youth ministry often managed to avoid the concept of atonement (and its pesky theological companion, sin) altogether. Without a doctrine of sin, divine-human reconciliation was unnecessary, allowing ministry to convert divine passion into a form of righteous energy directed toward human reconciliation instead. This approach made Christianity seem intellectually viable, and tended to promote an acceptance of "otherness" and participation in social transformation. But youth ministry so conceived also tended to replace costly grace with a cheerful, facile optimism that reduced redemption to human betterment — with sacrificial love nowhere in the picture.

Neither of these approaches struggled with the real desires of adolescents: their desire not only for blessing, but for redemption; their need not only to hope for the future, but to be forgiven in the present; their acceptance not only of Christian love, but of Christian oddity as the practices of faith mis-shape them for the culture of self-fulfillment. At the end of the twentieth century, neither "conservative" nor "liberal" approaches to youth ministry seriously addressed Christ's Passion and its potential for reordering human identity through a relationship of sacrificial love between God and humanity, mediated through the Christian community's acts of worship and witness. Meanwhile, adolescents — ever in search of a significant other who can assist in constructing the self — instinctively steered a different course. Youth insisted on passion's embodiment in persons and communities that enact costly love (which may or may not be the church, as gangs and terrorist groups illustrate).

Yet this communal embodiment of passion is precisely the vocation to which the church is called. The "passionate life" of God *can* be enacted by people and communities shaped by God's self-giving love as we take part in Christ's life, death, and resurrection for the sake of the world. The disciplines that "imitate Christ" bear witness to costly love. They embody the cruciform pattern of self-giving love that characterizes Christian communities. Jesus enters the world through such communities, imbuing their practices with the sanctifying grace that makes the imitation of Christ possible.

Beyond Xerox:
Mimesis and the Imitation of Christ

The concept of "imitating Christ" is a staple of youth ministry, long adapted by adults who value its potential for moral formation. Take "W.W.J.D." bracelets, for instance. An enterprising youth pastor had bracelets made for her youth group retreat (the entire phrase "What Would Jesus Do?" wouldn't fit), and the idea quickly spread to evangelicals who saw it as a useful motto for contemporary purity movements, like the "True Love Waits" campaign that asked youth to sign pledge cards promising virginity until marriage. Follow-up research found that true love did *not* wait until marriage for most of these adolescents, but it did wait *longer;* on average, pledge-signing teens postponed sexual intercourse eighteen months longer than their non-pledging peers.[34]

Although the W.W.J.D. phenomenon is now widely associated with American evangelicalism, the phrase's 1896 prototype, from Charles Sheldon's *In His Steps* — also written originally for youth — actually grew out of the social gospel of liberal Christianity (testimony to youth ministry's potential for theological rapprochement).[35] Both W.W.J.D. and *In His Steps* present Jesus as an ethical role model, but neither fully represents the meaning of "the imitation of Christ." True to its social gospel roots, W.W.J.D. viewed the imitation of Christ as a moral delivery system, a way to encourage young people to follow Jesus' example by copying his behavior. But besides the fact that few of us stop to think about what might happen if youth actually *did* copy Jesus' behavior (think about those tables in the temple for a minute), what is at stake in "imitating Christ" is not mim-

---

34. A study published in the *American Journal of Sociology* reports teenagers who publicly pledge to remain virgins until marriage delay having sex by about eighteen months in comparison with their non-pledging peers. Among those who make such promises, about 50 percent remained virgins until age 20. Among non-pledgers, 50 percent were no longer virgins at age 17. The study admits that multiple factors contribute to the decision of when to have sex, but Columbia University sociologist Peter Bearman maintains these statistics convey "pure pledge effect." The study also notes that when pledgers break their promises and do have sex, they most often do so without any form of contraceptive, since it would be illogical for a student who has pledged abstinence to carry a contraceptive. Peter Bearman and Hannah Bruckner, "Promising the Future: Virginity Pledges and First Intercourse," *American Journal of Sociology* 106:4 (January 2001): 859-912.

35. Mainline Protestant youth actively participate in the W.W.J.D. movement, although these youth are more apt to see it as an opportunity for testimony, a relatively non-threatening way to proclaim their affiliation with the Christian community, than as a standard for moral purity.

icry, but *identification* — becoming one with Christ through the cross, as he engrafts our lives onto his.

If we are going to recommend the imitation of Christ to young people, we would be wise to know what we are asking them to do. The Greek term *mimesis,* which we translate as "imitation," means actually acquiring what the other has, or becoming what the other is.[36] John's Gospel, for example, underscores the need to identify with Christ by repeatedly using the word *kathos* in Jesus' exhortations to his followers: "As I . . . so you" (cf. John 15:9, 17:18). Although in English *kathos* means "as," suggesting a rough equivalency or similarity, in Greek the connotation is stronger: "exactly as" or "to the exact same degree and extent." The Bible portrays *mimesis* as the route to holiness, sanctification, "perfection." *Mimesis* does not just imagine the object it imitates; it enacts it, embodies it, becomes it. Unlike its Latin counterpart *imitatio,* which suggests simulation or copying, *mimesis* means identifying with the original, and involves *methexis,* or participation. In other words, Christians do not "ape" Jesus' life, death, and resurrection; by God's grace, we are *incorporated into them.* We become part of them, and in so doing they begin to define us.

So far, so good. The problem comes when we reduce the imitation of Christ to its Xerox potential, imitating Christ selectively, or assuming that "what Jesus did" is self-evident, forcing a one-to-one correspondence between first-century ethics and our own. In some cases, churches "imitate Christ" by insisting on replicating one aspect of Jesus' humanity (youth ministries that privilege Jesus' maleness, for example, by eliminating women from pastoral leadership, or that urge lifestyles patterned exclusively on the Sermon on the Mount). In other cases, churches privilege one portrait of the life of Christ over another, urging young people's participation in a particular writer's vision of Christ at the expense of the multidimensional portrait offered by Scripture as a whole. Still other churches interpret "imitation" to mean the replication of first-century values, even when Jesus' social context bears little resemblance to our own, and it is likely that young people will encounter any number of situations in which we simply do not know what Jesus would do. The point is that "the imitation of Christ" is a *theological,* not a sociological, literary, or historical, move. Our identification with Jesus depends not on what we do to "copy" Jesus, but on what God did to identify with us.

36. The most thorough treatment of the concept of mimesis available is Erich Auerbach, *Mimesis: The Representation of Reality in Western Literature,* trans. Willard R. Trask (Princeton, N.J.: Princeton University Press, 1953).

Consequently, youth ministry that aspires to "imitate Christ" must recognize the risk involved, for young people and for the church. "Imitating Christ" entails more than moral formation; it means participating in the self-giving love of God, manifest in the life, death, and resurrection of Jesus in which God identified with us.[37] The objective of the holy life is *conformity* to God in Jesus Christ, whose self-giving love enables our own. After all, what if young people actually *do* do what Jesus does? What if an adolescent we know actually *does* identify with the God of the cross, and therefore *does* love something truly, with the kind of passion that exposes all lesser loves, including the greedy, self-fulfilling ones on which human society stands? *Mimesis* of Jesus Christ does not create "good teenagers" or "wholesome youth programs." It creates radicals and prophets — people who reveal the root of cultural deceits with the searchlight of Christ's love, and who unmask avarice, violence, rivalry, and smallness, exposing them like the Wizard of Oz behind the curtain. And like the Wizard, the ideologies of self-fulfillment can no longer intimidate once the humbug has been revealed.

Mimetic Desire: Subtle but Sinful

Imitating Christ *should* be the objective of youth ministry, for *mimesis* is crucial to identity formation theologically as well as developmentally. If the Trinity is "*the love which arouses us to full personhood* by inciting in us a response to (and participation in) *the personhood of Jesus the Word incarnate*," then, as theologian Mark A. McIntosh proposes:

> One's own provisional personhood comes to blossom as one enters into the particular patterns of self-giving enacted by the Son and the Spirit as they come forth into Trinitarian life.... It is not just a question any more of emulating Jesus in the Spirit but of realizing the fullness of one's life by discovering that one in fact has *come into being* in enacting his life.[38]

The imitation of Christ, then, depends upon the self-giving love of divine passion in two ways. First, God gives of God's own self, extending the di-

---

37. Some scholars have argued that conformity, not imitation, is the proper lens for understanding the mimesis necessary to Christian formation. See Robert Tannehill, *Dying and Rising with Christ* (Berlin: A. Töpelmann, 1967).

38. Mark A. McIntosh, *Mystical Theology* (Oxford: Blackwell, 1998), 158, 179-80. McIntosh illustrates this perspective with the writings of the Flemish Beguine Hadewijch.

vine Self to us in Jesus Christ. But we also "come into being" as we enact the life, death, and resurrection of Christ — what McIntosh calls the "particular patterns of self-giving" of God.[39]

Unfortunately, *imitatio* also has a negative side. Human sinfulness militates against patterns of self-giving — God's and ours — which makes imitating Christ an ambiguous business, especially for adolescents. Social conformity and holy *imitatio* are easily confused; society routinely metes out approval and belonging to those who identify with those in power, just as it scapegoats those who do not. Young people's need to identify is stronger than their ability to discern what or who is worth identifying with. French philosopher Rene Girard calls this unfiltered need to identify *mimetic desire,* which is passion's seamy underside, the shape of sin that makes human passion so easily co-opted by false gods. According to Girard, an existential "lack" — an inner sense that something is missing — leads us to look to a model who seems to possess a greater fullness of being, whether or not he or she actually does.[40] Adolescents, especially, are prone to identify with any "self" nearby who seems halfway appealing, whether or not that "self" is an integrated one, whether or not it is a product of any number of virtual worlds. As the young person patterns himself after the model, he begins to love whatever the model loves, to desire whatever the model desires, in order to acquire a similar fullness of being.[41]

Girard is more helpful as an expositor of cultural ritual than as a theologian, but his theory helps us understand why society goes to such great lengths to quash adolescent passion and how Christian faith helps young people resist pressure to conform to culturally acceptable solutions to mimetic desire. Only those who have known true love can discern between self-giving passion and the self-fulfilling desires that masquerade as love.[42] The Passion of Christ transforms the passions of adolescents by di-

---

39. McIntosh, *Mystical Theology,* 158.

40. See Rene Girard, *The Scapegoat,* trans. Yvonne Freccero (Baltimore: The Johns Hopkins University Press, 1986). Charles K. Bellinger's "The Crowd Is Untruth: A Comparison of Kierkegaard and Girard," *Contagion: A Journal of Violence, Mimesis, and Culture* 3 (1996): 103-19 made me aware of the substantial ways in which Kierkegaard anticipated Girard, and whose retrieval on these issues invests Girard with needed theological substance.

41. See Rene Girard, *Violence and the Sacred,* trans. Patrick Gregory (Baltimore: The Johns Hopkins University Press, 1977), 145-46.

42. Girard, therefore, critiques vicarious atonement, maintaining that the crucifixion was our doing, not God's: "Neither the Son nor the Father should be questioned about the cause of this event, but all [humankind], and [humankind] alone." Rene Girard, *Things Hidden Since the Foundation of the World,* trans. Stephen Bann and Michael Metteer (Stanford: Stanford University Press, 1987), 213. Inclusive language added.

recting them to an object of such utter integrity, an object capable of such true love that it reveals mimetic desire for what it is — a distortion of passion. Mimetic desire describes our ravenous hunger for wholeness, so gluttonous that we willingly stuff ourselves with fragmented identities and false gods to substitute for the one Love "worth dying for." It seeks self-fulfillment because something seems to be missing, turning adolescents into defective puzzles whose "lack" makes them voracious consumers of anything they might cram into the void. Christian passion, on the other hand, reaches beyond the self to others, not because something is missing, but because we realize we are so full of God's love that we cannot contain it all. In Christ's death on the cross, Jesus' identification with a young person exposes her true identity as God's beloved, a recognition so life-giving that she cannot keep it to herself.

The value of Girard's theory for youth ministry is that it unmasks the mimetic desire that often passes for passion, and indeed that global consumerism markets to adolescents *as* passion, but that in reality lusts for what only self-giving love can provide: a love so true, so utterly fulfilling, so overabundant that it cannot be held.[43] Mimetic desire is the primary mani-

---

43. In Disney's version of *Beauty and the Beast* (Disney, 1991), we note that Belle is the beloved "object" of both her father Maurice and his enemy, the brute Gaston. (The term "object" is used here in the psychological, not the material, sense.) According to Girard, societies organized around mimetic desire are inherently unstable because rivalry over the same object of desire leads to violence. And so, when Gaston realizes that Maurice has no intention of forcing Belle to marry him, the traditional order of village life — in which beautiful women cow to handsome men who desire them — is threatened. Gaston knows nothing of self-giving passion; he understands love as self-fulfillment, which allows him to perpetrate domination, viciousness, and violence in the name of "love." Belle's refusal to marry Gaston endangers provincial life by threatening to expose it for the inhumane house of cards it really is.

To prevent social disintegration, says Girard, societies band together against a common enemy — a scapegoat — and blame the potential loss of the object of desire on *them* instead of on each other. Ironically, the scapegoat becomes the savior, because in uniting against the scapegoat, society coheres — though at a price. The scapegoat mechanism can never be revealed. In *Beauty and the Beast,* Maurice, Gaston, and the villagers band together to kill the Beast. After all, isn't this social tension the Beast's fault? Identifying a common enemy is a time-honored method of fostering social unity, and the village eagerly unites to kill the scapegoat, a pursuit undertaken with so much vigor that it masks the real threat to village life: the violence Gaston inflicts in order to get what he wants. Meanwhile, Belle's love has begun to transform the Beast, whose increasing identification with Belle — and participation in common civil practices alongside her — provide the means for his transformation. Scapegoating the Beast may save social coherence, but love saves the Beast, exposing his true humanity so that he is no longer a viable scapegoat. Although Gaston mortally wounds the Beast, he cannot kill the human being who dwells within the Beast — a human

festation of self-fulfilling "love." It is the antithesis of Christian passion: it is "all about me" — self at all costs, even if the selves borrowed for this purpose are co-opted, fractured, ephemeral ones. Real passion, on the other hand, impels young people to search beyond mimetic desire for a love that is true, to keep searching for a model who is worthy of mimesis. Mimetic desire causes us to seek our identities in the hall of mirrors of human society, where every self is just a reflection of another, but true passion refuses to rest until the young person looks behind the hall of mirrors of human society to find the true gaze of One who knows her for who she really is.

The imitation of Christ offers young people a route to formation *in* Christ, as they identify with Jesus in the historic practices of Christian community. But it also invites their transformation *by* Christ, as Jesus envelops adolescents in his Body, the Church. Ministry that invites young people to participate in Christian practices is more than a massive "what would Jesus do?" project. The imitation of Christ invokes the principle of *pathos:* a willing surrender of ego — a *loss* of self — through acts of worship and witness that help young people become who God created them to be in the first place: people created for passion, engrafted into the life, death, and resurrection of Jesus Christ. In the practices that imitate the Passion of Christ, God incorporates youth into Jesus' own Passion: his desires become their desires, and his story becomes their story.

Amputated Christianity:
Life without Religious Affections

When Christian theology cannot embrace God's suffering love as its focal point — or, worse, when it denies passion as the crux of Christian identity — the church has no basis on which to challenge the culture's claim on

---

being whose true identity is revealed by Belle's unconditional love that allows her to identify with him (and vice versa). This is the formula that "breaks the spell" in all fairytales, restoring true humanity to those caught in the matrix of sin that has led to deceit, dishonor, and disguise. True love "breaks the spell" in Girard's theory of mimetic desire as well. But for Girard, Jesus Christ represents the only source of true love, the one person capable of exposing the deceits underlying human culture. The gospel narratives do what human society tries *not* to do: they reveal the scapegoat mechanism by telling the story from the point of view of the victims, not the persecutors. Had Gaston told the story of *Beauty and the Beast,* we would have an entirely different tale on our hands. Only those who experience love's transformation can point to transformation's source. (For a more contemporary, if decidedly more complex, rendering of the same themes in contemporary film, see *The Matrix* [Warner Bros., 1998]).

young people. Passionless Christianity has nothing to die for; it practices assimilation, not oddity. Passionless Christians lead sensible lives, not subversive ones; we are benignly "nice" instead of dangerously loving. We become a race of amputees, cutting off passion — that divinely appointed impetus toward the Other — in order to fit in with all the other limbless Christians who are incapable of reaching out. Every now and then we feel a phantom pain, an impulse toward suffering love. But for the most part, we have learned to live without the capacity to extend ourselves.

Those leaders commonly associated with religious affections in Christian history — Bernard of Clairvaux, Catherine of Siena, Martin Luther, Jonathan Edwards, John and Charles Wesley, to name a few — were subversives in the sacred sense. They deftly straddled the lines of discourse between the intellectual conversations of their day and the prayers, liturgies, hymns, and sermons that explicitly connected the passions of being human with the redeeming *pathos* of God. In short, they believed that the more we align ourselves with the life and death of Jesus Christ — his Passion — the more we find ourselves integrated into the life of God, and the more readily we reach out to those who suffer.

The stakes, of course, are very high. Passionate youth disclose the church's enculturation; they unravel human passions that have been co-opted by selfish love. So we have learned to brace ourselves against adolescent passion and all that goes with it. Sociologist Talcott Parsons referred to each new generation of youth as a "barbarian invasion" — the dominant culture must either conquer them, or be conquered by them.[44] Knowing that the basic fabric of our culture is at stake, social institutions — even religious ones — conspire to suppress youthful passion. And for the most part, they succeed. When the church abandons the language of passion, we not only collude with consumer culture in scapegoating the young as society's "barbarians" — after all, isn't this social tension their fault? — we also encourage their turn to popular culture as the source of their identity. In popular culture, the language of passion, if not its substance, is at least audible, distorted though it may be.

Mimesis and True Identity

The crucified God confronts teenagers with radical fidelity, infinite transcendence, and genuine communion, dimensions of Christ's Passion that

44. Talcott Parsons, *The Social System* (Glencoe, Ill.: Free Press, 1951), 208.

both expose and redeem the violence that accompanies socialization into the values of a dominant culture. Unless Christian theology retains a central place for the Passion of Christ — and unless the Christian community engages youth in practices that identify with Jesus' suffering love — youth looking for something "to die for" will, inevitably, look elsewhere. In the absence of a Christian vocabulary of passion, youth will turn to the broader society to interpret their passions for them, where consumer culture is only too happy to oblige.

As we will see in Chapter Two, the mainline Protestant church — and not just the culture — has created a conundrum for young people that is not only theologically irresponsible; it is developmentally lethal. The dilemma facing young people searching for something "to die for" is that a unified sense of identity depends upon finding it, for youth as well as for the church as a whole. Yet when mainline Protestants downplay the Passion of Christ, we rob youth of the climactic scene of their own life stories. We not only jeopardize their ability to identify with the church; we jeopardize the church's ability to identify with Jesus. Identity is at stake — for adolescents, and for us.

Chapter Two

THE WORLD'S GREATEST LOVER

The Unifying Power of Passion

My God, I choose all. I do not want to be a saint by halves. I am not afraid to suffer for You. I fear only one thing — that I should keep my own will. So take it, for I choose all that You will.

Therese of Lisieux[1]

The teenagers I know are both cynical and harshly passionate. What they want is so big, it's hard to get your eye around it at first. Who would've thought that teenagers talking about sex would end up talking about their souls? For that's what they're talking about, isn't it? Not body heat but life everlasting. Not the adventure of skin on skin, but a dinner table in the skies. They have none of our ambivalence — independence vs. love, distinction vs. belonging. Their struggle is with the world — will it let them lose their loneliness? And how? They want something bigger than themselves to live for, something steadier and stronger than one-on-one love, something I long for and loathe, something eradicating — a "we" in their lives, a family feast that never ends, a tribe of friends, God's will.

Kathie Dobie, editor, Pacific News Service[2]

1. Therese of Lisieux, *The Autobiography of St. Therese of Lisieux: The Story of a Soul*, trans. John Bevers (New York: Bantam Doubleday Dell, 1957), 26. She was only twenty-four when she died (1873-1897).

2. *Mother Jones* (January/February 1995), available at http://www.motherjones.com/mother_jones/JF95/dobie.html; accessed 7 December 2002.

He came to his own people, but they didn't want him.
But whoever did want him, who believed he was who he claimed
and would do what he said,
He made to be their true selves,
their child-of-God selves.
These are the God-begotten,
not the blood-begotten, not flesh-begotten, not sex-begotten.

Eugene Peterson, *The Message,* John 1

Nobody wants to be in love more than a teenager. Augustine observed of his own youth: "The single desire that dominated my search for delight was simply to love and be loved."[3] In the movie *Don Juan de Marco* (1995) — the story of a delusional twenty-one-year-old who thinks he is "the world's greatest lover" — Don Juan explains to his psychiatrist,

> There are only four questions of value in life, Don Octavio: *What is sacred? Of what is the spirit made? What is worth living for? And what is worth dying for?* The answer to each is the same: Only love.

And he is right. The answer *is* love — though, not unlike many of his real-life peers, Don Juan's concept of love has been distorted by cultural norms, not to mention some serious abandonment issues. An ideology that reduces love to sexual passion is simply too narrow to function as an overarching worldview, so Don Juan solves the problem by becoming disturbingly, if charmingly, delusional. Yet the movie's pivotal scene occurs when his psychiatrist decides that it is better for Don Juan to remain in his fictitious, love-infused world than to return him (with the dubious help of medication) to the "real world" of broken relationships and infidelity.

True, it's only a movie. Yet every adolescent longs for a center that holds, a sacred core to the fractured soul. Passion reveals the human desire to construct a self in relationship to a reliable "other" — just as passion revealed God's desire to show the divine self in relationship to us in Jesus Christ. Our identities take shape in relationships that mirror back to us "who we are" and the kind of person we are becoming, but not just any relationship will do. Ultimately, identity requires the self-confirming pres-

---

3. Augustine, *Confessions,* trans. Henry Chadwick (Oxford: Oxford University Press, 1991), 24.

ence of reliable love. The intuition that we can be "loved into being" by another impels us to *keep* looking for this reliable love, even when lesser loves disappoint. And when we do find it, this authentic love reorders our view of the world and our place in it.

The Church's Problem with Passion

Passion is the point at which adolescent experience and Christian theology intersect. The passion of God and the passions of youth are different passions, to be sure; in the Passion of Christ, God comes to us, and in the passions of being human we reveal our (sometimes well-disguised) longing for God. Even when human passion fails us, our deep longing for union with an "other" causes us to continue seeking these identity-conferring relationships. This desire is so potent that it inspires sacrifice, so profound that it draws us beyond ourselves toward that which inspires us, so large that we become larger with it. The ambiguity of the classical phrase *le desir de Dieu* is intentional; the French preposition *de* suggests that the desire *of* God for human relationship is simultaneously our desire *for* God.

The Christian community, therefore, came to describe passion in terms of the suffering of desire, and specifically God's desire for us. Christians inherited the Hebrew belief that God can be infinitely supple without compromising omnipotence; the medieval church, for instance, saw no contradiction in describing God as a smitten lover, comparing the passion of faith to the passion of falling in love.[4] Nor did Christians see a contradiction between divine power and divine vulnerability. Passion "burns" — it has firepower, it illuminates and devastates simultaneously. At the same time, passion requires vulnerability, passivity, a willingness to ignite, for vulnerability is the condition for love's transformation.

For adolescents, however, the vulnerability required by passion poses a significant problem. Unlike God, adolescents *do* risk annihilation when they become vulnerable to another. Adolescents' "desire for desire" — their mimetic need to identify — allows them to readily come under another's spell. They convert easily and uncritically. They "overdo" things: they overidentify, invest their passion in unworthy objects, go to the life-or-death limit for gods unable to love them back. In other words, adolescents acutely embody the human predicament before God. Created for

4. Erotic interpretations of divine love formed the backbone of much mystical theology. See Mark A. McIntosh, *Mystical Theology* (Oxford: Blackwell, 1998).

love, we succumb to sin; designed to seek Christ, we turn to flirtatious idols; intended for self-giving, we give in to self-fulfillment. Like the rest of us, young people confuse their passions with God's passion — which is why, from the beginning, the church had to reckon with a dilemma: if passion is an attribute of God, then how are we to contend with the unruly passions of human beings?

Celebrating Our Oddity:
Pathos in Human Communities

Ancient Hebrew society viewed *pathos* as a personal quality of divine love, embodied by the community of faith and not only by individuals. The Jews described Yahweh in very personal terms, using images such as friend and lover; the Hebrew word for love *(ahav)* means to be filled with desire and delight and passion for the one we love, to long for the presence of the beloved.[5] Old Testament scholar Walter Brueggemann claims that this caused Jews to prize Torah, the story of God's longing, over the more restrained wisdom literature, allowing biblical tradition to defy Western philosophical trends by consistently favoring "the impossibilities of passion" over the more disciplined perspective of reason. Education in ancient Israel, notes Brueggemann, was "education in passion" — nurture into a distinct, passionate community that knew itself to be at odds with the dominant culture. "This nurture in passion," writes Brueggemann, "is concrete and specific, as indeed passion must always be. . . . It is a nurture that produces adults who know so well who they are and what is commanded that they value and *celebrate their oddity* in the face of every seductive and powerful imperial alternative."[6]

Education in passion led to particular *practices* in the public life of the people of Israel that directed community life toward the God of *pathos*. These practices recounted the ways in which God had remained the faithful lover of Israel, and preserved and promoted the Jews' distinctiveness as

5. Throughout the Old Testament, God longs for a love relationship with the people of Israel. In the Hebrew scriptures, Yahweh empathizes with the Israelites, is on friendly terms with leaders and prophets, becomes involved in their joy and suffering, is moved by the plight of the unfortunate, and displays laughter, sorrow, joy, wrath, and even repentance. J. Massyngbaerde Ford, *Redeemer, Friend and Mother: Salvation in Antiquity and in the Gospel of John* (Minneapolis: Augsburg Fortress, 1997), 24-26.

6. See Walter Brueggemann, "Passion and Perspective: Two Dimensions of Education in the Bible," *Theology Today* 42 (July 1985): 180, 173.

a people by heightening — not minimizing — the tension between the Jews and Hellenistic culture. By practicing passion, the people of Israel maintained their "oddity" in an imperial culture, defining themselves as people who actively submitted to Yahweh's love and care.

As children of the Exodus, Christians also turned to spiritual practices to sculpt a distinctive identity for the church. Like the Israelites, Christians employed practices as a way to live out the story of God's faithfulness. But Christians also believed that God used the practices of human communities to impart divine power and grace for the present transformation of the world as well — a process that amounted to the spiritual "realignment" of human communities. The church viewed the practices of faith as the Holy Spirit's chosen vehicle for conforming human passions to God's passion in order to construct a "new creation" around the core of divine love, and to redirect human desire toward the One whose love we truly seek.

The Discipline of Detachment:
Practicing Realignment

Admittedly, Christians over the centuries have been notorious for seizing spiritual practices as weapons designed to bludgeon human passions into submission. Less newsworthy but more orthodox views held that human passions were dynamic, God-given impulses, presently distorted by sin and therefore prone to wandering off after the wrong things. Eastern scholars Evagrius and Isaac the Syrian considered the passions impulses "to be purified, not killed; to be educated, not eradicated; to be used positively, not negatively."[7] In the Western church, Thomas Aquinas — while subordinating emotion to reason at every turn — stressed that the passions were not inherently evil, and could lead to virtue.[8] In other words, spiritual practices did not eliminate human passion, but refocused it on its proper object: God. Especially among inexperienced Christians, spiritual disciplines became the tools that loosened young people's grip on lesser loves so they could freely accept and respond to the passion of God. These disciplines "detached" human passion from sinful objects that corrupted

7. St. Nikodimos of the Holy Mountain and St. Makarios of Corinth, *The Philokalia*, vol. 3, trans. and ed. G. E. H. Palmer, Philip Sherrard, and Kallistos Ware (London: Faber and Faber, 1984), 361-62.

8. Thomas Aquinas, *Summa Theologica*, trans Fathers of the English Dominican Province (Benziger Bros., 1947), first part of the second part, question 24, articles 1-4.

the self, and realigned human desire with God's desire, manifest in the Passion of Christ.[9]

The Eastern church heralded this state of detachment as *apatheia* — literally, an "absence of *pathos*" — a state in which the believer "burns" with desire for God. The route to such purification, wrote John Climacus (579-649) in *The Ladder of Divine Ascent*, is *dispassion*: detachment from the lesser passions that free us to be our "true selves," making us free to love others and to love God with new energy. Contemporary Orthodox theologian Kallistos Ware notes that the dispassionate heart is characterized by suffering love; it is a heart on fire with love for God, humans, and all creation.[10] Conceptually, the "dispassioned" heart burns with holy desire and therefore imitates God's own suffering love. Having redirected human passions toward Christ, the "dispassioned" heart is anything but "unpassionate" as it is redefined by the self-giving passion of God.

To be sure, the vocabulary of detachment, dispassion, and *apatheia* had risks; extremists abound in the church as in the world (especially among the young and the zealous). Ecclesiastical authorities bent on eradicating passion quickly learned, though not quickly enough, that quashing youthful passion outright often had the effect of creating martyrs, which frequently ignited public passions further (not all of them holy) and had the circular effect of confirming church authorities' opinions that passion was, indeed, the devil's tool. Some practices — penance, for example — easily devolved into abuse. Not surprisingly, *apatheia* and its related terminology confused rank and file believers, and Christian dispassion was often misconstrued as stoicism. The Western church rarely emphasized *apatheia* (some scholars found it heretical, others merely impractical), preferring the disciplined will to the dispassioned heart as the path to holiness.[11] Yet whether used to discipline the will or the emotions, spiritual

9. Enlightenment writers called the route to detachment *abandonment* — the casting off of outward, worldly cares and inward, spiritual needs through disciplines that continually focus on Christ: "By continuing to do this over a long period of time," advised Jeanne Bouvier de la Mothe Guyon (1648-1717), "your heart will remain *unattached....* How do you practice abandonment? You practice it daily, hourly, and by the moment." See Jeanne Guyon, *Experiencing the Depths of Jesus Christ* (Gardiner, Maine: Christian Books Publishing House, 1975), 31-35.

10. Kallistos Ware, introduction to John Climacus, *The Ladder of Divine Ascent*, Classics of Western Spirituality, trans. Colm Luibheid and Norman Russell (Mahwah, N.J.: Paulist Press, 1982), 32.

11. A related concept is indifference as freedom from "inordinate attachments" described by Ignatius Loyola, *Spiritual Exercises*, Classics of Western Spirituality, ed. George

practices "loosened" human passions from sinful objects, liberating the true self for its created purpose: the passionate pursuit of God.

The church's problem with passion, then, was never passion, but *sin:* adolescents, like the rest of us, love the wrong things. The divided self instinctively seeks the perfection of divine love, but in all the wrong ways, for sin wreaks havoc on the divine imprint, leading teenagers to invest their God-given passion in objects that cannot suffer love on their behalf. These objects cannot give them the love they seek, and because they think they want to gratify their own appetites, they remain unfulfilled.[12] So they suffer: greed, envy, rage, ambition, lust ("the passions" classically considered) overtake them. Human passions career out of balance, distracting the heart and overwhelming the will. In the absence of a unifying passion — a love so profound that it reorders every other human desire — the young person's fragile ego falls apart.

The Atomized Self: Falling Apart at the Seams

As the information age pelts adolescents with new role expectations (simultaneously allotting less time to each role), psychologists have begun to observe profound changes in the human psyche.[13] Postmodern people routinely experience their "selfhood" as atomized, diffuse, fleeting. Identity is no longer "achieved" in the way Erikson proposed, because the self is more or less in a state of continuous construction and reconstruction — which means there is no "self" for adolescents to surrender to God, passionate or otherwise.

Of course, this is nothing new. The adolescent ego, by definition, is a work in progress. With the onset of formal operational thought — the abil-

---

Ganss, S.J. (Mahwah, N.J.: Paulist Press, 1991), 129-30, which made the language of indifference common in mystical and ascetic circles of the seventeenth century, representing a disciplined state of the will that leads to an alertness to God in history.

12. Robin Maas, *Living Hope: Baptism and the Cost of Christian Witness* (Nashville: Discipleship Resources, 1999), 42. Maas bases her comments on 1 Peter 1:13–2:3.

13. "Social saturation furnishes us with a multiplicity of incoherent and unrelated languages of the self. For everything we 'know to be true' about ourselves, other voices within respond with doubt and even derision. This fragmentation of self-conceptions corresponds to a multiplicity of incoherent and disconnected relationships. These relationships pull us in myriad directions, inviting us to play such a variety of roles that the very concept of an 'authentic self' with knowable characteristics recedes from view. The fully saturated self becomes no self at all." Kenneth J. Gergen, *The Saturated Self: Dilemmas of Identity in Contemporary Life* (New York: Basic Books, 1991), 6-7.

ity to think about thinking[14] — the young person recognizes for the first time a "proliferation of me's": the "me" at home is different from the "me" at school, and the "me" who is in love with Shannon is different from the "me" who plays in a band with my friends.[15] Integrating all the "me's" is a daunting task under any circumstance, but for young people new to the quick-change artistry required by multiple demands on the self, integrating the "me's" represents a full-time, and often overwhelming, job.

What *is* new for postmodern youth is the growing assumption that this fluctuating self is normative; maturity is no longer necessarily a goal of adolescence. In consumer culture, purchasing power — not an integrated identity — is the ticket to full franchise.[16] Increasingly, adults function with serial selves instead of integrated ones. Adolescence itself has become a life*style* as well as a life*stage,* an equally viable choice for fourteen- and forty-year-olds. In a universalized youth culture, everyone from toddlers to middle-aged adults wants to be a teenager, a phenomenon that forces young people to turn to increasingly marginal "alternative" cultures for self-definition. All of this means that, for postmodern teenagers, maturity is not the outcome of adolescence, but an optional accessory. Predictably, when teenagers are neither expected nor encouraged to pull themselves together, they tend to "fall apart" instead.[17] In the absence of adults mature or available enough to offer them sustained forms of nurture, postmodern young people become competent *briccoleurs* — inveterate "borrowers" who cobble together "selves" at a moment's notice from the resources at hand. They "wear" their identities lightly, like t-shirts; they have drawers full of them, ready to change whenever style or temperature dictates.

Such a concept of self represents a kind of identity Erikson barely an-

14. Jean Piaget called the onset of "formal operations" (beginning at ages 11-15) the beginning of conceptual reasoning. Formal operational youth search for truths, construct proofs, use metaphors, attempt to build logical systems, argue formally and universally. This manner of thinking is necessary to establishing an identity that is separate from the family but retains significant connections to strongly defined groups. At this point, Piaget believed, the child's cognitive structures are like those of an adult.

15. Robin Maas, "Will the Real Me Stand Up?," *Living Light,* Spring 1993, 39.

16. Thirty-one million teenagers spent 141 billion dollars in the United States in 1998, according to industry-leading Teen Research Limited, available at http://www.teenresearch .com/

17. The Carnegie Corporation study *A Matter of Time* (Washington, D.C.: Carnegie Council on Adolescent Development, 1992) reported that American teenagers are significantly "at risk" simply because they become fourteen. At any given time, according to the study, half of American 10-14 year olds are at risk, and one in four are in imminent peril (pp. 25-42).

ticipated. Child psychologist David Elkind dubbed it the "patchwork self":[18] a patternless mosaic of borrowed slivers of influence, loosely held together so that new influences easily displace old ones. As Robin Maas put it, "When we don't know what we really think and feel, we will 'borrow' thoughts and feelings from those around us who seem more competent and in control, or whom we admire or even fear, and then substitute their thoughts and feelings for our own."[19] The "patchwork self," therefore, is an extremely fluid — and fragile — construction. Rather than engage in the difficult and time-consuming chore of integrating the "me's," the self created by *briccolage* is neither internalized nor integrated. It possesses no guiding core, no unified center, no guiding narrative, no organizing truth. It is liquid and amoeba-like, yet frail. This fragility, Maas warns, is both psychologically destructive and spiritually dangerous:

> If we have "gone to pieces" (literally), then we really don't know where the self ends and the other person begins — we don't have clear boundaries, and people without clear boundaries are easily exploited and abused. . . . If we let ourselves "go to pieces" then we will be constantly changing our opinions and values, depending upon whom we are with. . . . In short, *fragmentation leads to faithlessness.* We cannot be true to anyone or anything, because we lack integrity — or wholeness.[20]

The fragmented self cannot be true to itself or to others. It substitutes ephemeral passions for authentic love, since a constantly shifting self vitiates the need for anything (love included) to last very long. Without integrity — without a center that holds — adolescents not only become vulnerable *to* destructive outside forces; they often *become* destructive forces as well.

---

18. David Elkind, *All Grown Up and No Place to Go: Teenagers in Crisis* (Reading, Mass.: Addison-Wesley, 1984). See also Gergen, *The Saturated Self,* especially chapters six and seven. Kierkegaard noted that Christians are as vulnerable to this false understanding of self as anyone else. To Kierkegaard, the person without "being" is a person in despair, who "learns to copy others, how they manage their lives — and he now proceeds to live the same way. In Christendom he is also a Christian, goes to church every Sunday, listens to and understands the pastor, indeed they have a mutual understanding; he dies, the pastor ushers him into eternity for ten rix-dollars — but a self he was not, and a self he did not become." Søren Kierkegaard, *"The Sickness Unto Death": A Christian Psychological Exposition for Upbuilding and Awakening,* trans. Howard V. and Edna H. Hong (Princeton, N.J.: Princeton University Press, 1983), 52.

19. Maas, "Will the Real Me Please Stand Up?" 39.

20. Maas, "Will the Real Me Please Stand Up?" 39. Emphasis added.

Getting It Together:
The Unifying Power of Passion

Identifying with Christ inverts the normal developmental pattern of imitating a self-object. Normally, an adolescent takes in her representation of the "other" and eventually makes it her own. But imitating Christ does not make Jesus part of *her;* she becomes part of *him.* The Christ-event transforms adolescents into people who actually do "have it together" as they repent and identify with Jesus Christ instead of with the piecemeal fragments of consumer culture. Passion transcends lesser commitments of the self and binds them to a common higher order allegiance. Practices that imitate Christ align young people's disordered desires with Jesus' extravagant self-giving love, and through these disciplines the teenager finds herself able to love extravagantly, authentically, and unselfishly as well. The practice of passion transforms her utterly: it loosens her partial identifications with culture and frees her to identify with Christ instead. Her newfound self has constancy, not because it flows from the progressive stages of human development, but because of the constant presence of Christ who accompanies her every step of the way.

The church views human identity as God's gift, not as a Holy Grail to be pursued and possessed. Young people's conversion — more dramatically, perhaps, but no less surely than our own — depends on God's "re-membering" them: literally, on God putting them back together, forgiving, redeeming, and restoring the original integrity of their piecemeal, sin-fractured egos. In spiritual disciplines that imitate Christ, God imparts the grace that "detaches" adolescent passions from the therapeutic gods of consumer culture. In the imitation of Christ (a phrase I will nuance shortly), young people become the undivided persons God created them to be all along:

> There is a word for this wonderful state of unity or integration in the human person: *integrity.* God knew the potential split was there — that reason and passion, soul and body, could be an explosive combination — and so he gave the first humans the gift of integrity.... With integrity, we know who we are; we have a self that we can love and that we can love another with.... So integrity (or the integration of our minds and hearts, our thoughts and our feelings) is really the basis of human happiness.[21]

21. Maas, "Will the Real Me Please Stand Up?" 41.

The integrative power of Christ's Passion makes Christian identity — a self given, not earned — stand out in *bas relief* against the patchwork self. As Eugene Peterson has paraphrased it, "[Christ is] the source of life who puts us together in one piece, whose very breath and blood flow through us" (Col. 2:19, *The Message*).[22]

The biblical account of the life, death, and resurrection of Jesus Christ functions as an overarching narrative in which the passions of adolescence are subsumed in a larger, more encompassing story. Yet the Passion of Christ is more than a guiding narrative; it creates a community where the ongoing practices of passion invite young people to *participate* in this story as well as receive it. As adolescents imitate Christ, they *identify with* a Passion that transforms their own. Their developing egos are not destroyed, but a figure-ground shift takes place; as James E. Loder puts it, the psychological question of "Who am I?" becomes secondary to the theological question of "*Why* am I?"[23] Taking part in Christ's life and death on the cross, young people's fractured egos — *our* fractured egos — assume their rightful place at the foot of the cross, where God gathers each of us piece by piece into the arms of grace.

The Adolescent Advantage

In responding to Jesus' claim that choosing life first means losing it for his sake, youth possess a significant advantage: They have no hardened self to lose. The ideological openness of adolescents actually helps them identify with the suffering love of God. The ego is "under construction" during adolescence, but the created self, *homo religiosus* — the self that reflects the image of God — is a gift, fractured by sin but drawn toward redemption. During adolescence, the created self has not yet become encased in adult identifications; adolescents' very incompleteness provides an opportunity for divine reconstruction. In the unformed self, the *imago dei* remains faint but visible, if only in the ways youth "act out" human longings too powerful to be easily repressed.

22. The NRSV reads, "Do not let anyone disqualify you, insisting on self-abasement and worship of angels, dwelling on visions, puffed up without cause by a human way of thinking, and not holding fast to the head, from whom the whole body, nourished and held together by its ligaments and sinews, grows with a growth that is in God" (Col. 2:18-19).

23. Loder offers the description of ego-reconstruction in light of Christian transformation as a figure-ground shift; the ego is not destroyed. See James Loder, *Logic of the Spirit* (San Francisco: Jossey-Bass, 1998), 247-48.

In other words, *because* adolescent identity is so fragmented, youth's God-given passion seeps out unbidden between the cracks of newfound cultural identifications. *Because* they feel broken, young people seeking personal integration readily identify with the integrity of the Passion of Christ. *Because* the church, like many other institutions, increasingly recognizes its own fragmentation in the experience of young people, a renewed interest in both youth and Christian spirituality has emerged as we seek reformation. When Christian practices align adolescent passions with the magnetic force of divine love, adolescent identity is drawn together by the pull of God's self-giving passion. No wonder Scripture is awash in the witness of young people: who else would so blithely risk crucifixion?

Adolescents' Witness to the Church:
A Case for the Unifying Force of Passion

For Danish theologian Søren Kierkegaard, passion restores wholeness not only to fractured adolescents but to the fractured Christian community as well, for in the Passion of Christ humanity and God are made one in Jesus Christ.[24] For this reason, Kierkegaard believed, youth have a special witness to the church. Passion comes naturally to the young because they are so open to love, so willing to suffer for that which calls forth their fidelity. Passion, wrote Kierkegaard, constitutes "Christianity's two theses" — God's passion to love, and to be loved. Between God's decision to love us and our decision to love God lies a "*pathos*-filled transition."[25] The mark of true Christianity, therefore, is love suffering: love that does not suffer — love that is reasonable, that can be explained by reflection — is a sham. The truth of divine love lies in its unreasonableness: "God's pas-

24. "That in which all men are one is passion. Therefore everything religious is passion, hope, faith and love." Søren Kierkegaard, *Journals and Papers 1835-1855*, vol. 1, ed. and trans. Howard V. Hong and Edna H. Hong (Bloomington, Ind.: Indiana University Press, 1967), 400, #896 [IV C 96, n.d., 1842-43]. I am indebted to Mark Burrows, professor of church history at Andover Newton Theological Seminary, who many years ago pointed me to Kierkegaard's journals and their commentary on passion.

25. Kierkegaard, *The Last Years: Journals 1853-1855*, ed. and trans. Ronald Gregor Smith (New York: Harper & Row, 1965), 237 [XI A 98]. The complete entry reads: God's passion to love and be loved is "as though he himself were bound in this passion, in the power of this passion, so that he cannot cease to love, almost as though it were a weakness: whereas in fact it is his strength, his almighty love."

sion is to be found in the absurd; where this sign is to be seen, there God is present."[26]

Kierkegaard believed that passion provides the condition for transformation in the church just as it does for adolescents, a transformation that Kierkegaard compared to falling in love. He insisted that a passionate conviction transforms us every bit as much as falling in love does. When a young person is in love, Kierkegaard declared, the lover

> suddenly undergoes an emotional "transformation into another kind" in *pathos,* asks to kiss the beloved and for whatever erotic love can hit upon. It is the same with having a conviction. The person who really has ... a conviction properly undergoes a "transformation into another kind." ... As a lover begs to kiss the beloved, so he *feels the need to suffer for his conviction,* and it satisfies the *pathos* in him to suffer for his conviction.[27]

Kierkegaard derided modernity for undermining *pathos* with a kind of reason that ridiculed suffering for one's convictions. This "commonsensicality" made "unconditioned passion" nigh impossible, therefore making authentic transformation exceedingly rare.[28] If the church is to serve as a vehicle for God's transformation, then we must guard against relinquishing passion at all costs — and who better to enlist in this cause, he asked, than young people, whom Kierkegaard regarded as specially gifted for "the *pathos*-filled life"?[29] While acknowledging youth's susceptibility to distorted passions, Kierkegaard considered their calling to the "*pathos*-filled life" so important to the church that adults must help them navigate and redirect their passions rather than risk losing their witness.

26. Kierkegaard, *The Last Years,* 107 [XI A 268]. Jürgen Moltmann extends this concept to be a mark of the church. See Jürgen Moltmann, *The Church in the Power of the Spirit* (Minneapolis: Fortress, 1993), 68.

27. Kierkegaard, *Journals and Papers,* vol. 1, 375-76, #822 [X A 222, n.d. 1851]. Emphasis added.

28. "The first requirement [of a true Christian] is a man who in one way or another is desiring, seeking, possessing, etc. wholeheartedly ... with absolute passion. ... But how rare is such a person!" Kierkegaard, *Journals and Papers,* vol. 1, 193, #487 [IX A 297, n.d. 1848]. Kierkegaard realized that common usage of the word "passion" would equate it with impulse, appetite, or spontaneous enthusiasm, and he did not wish to be misunderstood. "Let no one misinterpret all my talk about pathos and passion," he warned, "to mean that I intend to sanction every uncircumcised immediacy, every unshaven passion" (427).

29. Kierkegaard, *Journals and Papers,* vol. 3, ed. and trans. Howard V. Hong and Edna H. Hong (Bloomington, Ind.: Indiana University Press, 1967), 427, #3127 [V A 44, n.d. 1844].

But Kierkegaard also recognized the subversiveness of his proposal. For despite the fact that churches often give lip service to youthful energy, the acculturated church actually requires youth to *surrender* passion for the sake of socialization into adult institutions — starting with the church itself. As we have seen, becoming an adult necessarily entails appropriating society's prevailing views of passion. But in an era predicated on common sense, that appropriation also means a loss: a forgetting, even a denigration of, young people's unique gift to humanity, the *pathos*-filled life.

So Kierkegaard proposed a solution: wise adults gifted in "mind and spirit" must make room for the *pathos* in which youth excel. Without such adults, youth cannot break through "commonsensicality" to fall in love with Jesus (or anyone else). For all their inferiority in terms of intellectual, emotional, and psychological maturity, Kierkegaard maintained that youth have superior powers of *pathos,* and they need adults to unleash the power and potential of this *pathos* for the church:

> Any young girl can truly fall in love. . . . But imagine an age which has sunk to such depths of commonsensicality that all the brilliant minds etc. applied their talents to making love ludicrous — then no young girl is able to cut through. *There must first of all be an older person who can crush this commonsensicality and create pathos* — and then, hail to thee, O youth, whoever you are — then there is a place for youth's in a sense far inferior powers. And yet in one sense the relation is such . . . that the young person stands higher than the older one.[30]

A church that makes room for the *pathos* of God and adolescents offers the conditions for young people to do what they do best: fall in love. In the *pathos*-filled transition, youth lay the foundation for the church's unity as well as for their own. Only a passionate church can so engage passionate young people — and we cannot aspire to be a passionate church if relinquishing passion is a tacit requirement for membership. Even with acute passion, no young person can "cut through" the norms of common sense without adults who can legitimize his convictions and invite him to lay them before God.

30. Kierkegaard, *Journals and Papers,* vol. 4, ed. and trans. Howard V. Hong and Edna H. Hong (Bloomington, Ind.: Indiana University Press, 1967), 241-42, #6521 [X A 157, n.d. 1849]. Emphasis added.

The False Modesty of Mainstream Protestantism

Despite our participation in a society given to excess, American mainstream Protestants have learned to appreciate the detached safety, not of *apatheia* — which properly understood is anything but safe — but of "commonsensicality," Kierkegaard's phrase for the straightjacket of modern objectivity. Most mainline Protestants are put off by passion — both ours and God's. Like lovers who kiss too much in public, religious passion embarrasses us. It is excessive, unseemly, over the top. It means losing control, being overtaken, becoming unleashed. It points to a God beyond our control who loves with abandon and who calls us to do the same. We would much prefer a God who is more "appropriate" — who respects our boundaries, who loves the same people we love, who does not humiliate us with "P.D.A." (public displays of affection, officially banned in many high schools and unofficially in much Protestant liturgy). Though we long for passion in the privacy of our movie seats (and we willingly pay for what passes as vicarious passion), by the time we reach adulthood most North American mainline Protestants have been conditioned to view passion as impolitic even for God.

And so, created for passion though we may be, we condition ourselves to settle for less. Witness this conversation between Faye Dunaway and Marlon Brando, who play a married couple nearing retirement in the movie mentioned in the opening of this chapter, *Don Juan de Marco:*

> HUSBAND: "What happened to all the passion of our youth? What happened to all that celestial fire that used to light our way?"
> WIFE: "Oh, listen, honey. All that fire — those fires were a lot of trouble. They flare up, and then they die. You know — a good, steady, warm glow. That does the trick."
> HUSBAND: "I'm telling you, that's bullshit. No fire, no heat; no heat, no passion — that's the equation."

A good, steady, warm glow may be the love we settle for, but it is not the love we seek — nor is it the love demonstrated by God in Jesus Christ. The God of Jesus Christ *does* love excessively, extravagantly, "outside the lines." Scandal though it may be, the God of Jesus Christ *does* choose passivity, vulnerability, and weakness as God's means of transformation — combustible tinder for holy fire. Christian tradition still struggles for a language that adequately conveys the force of God's love without compromising God's creative, transformative power. There are many kinds of love in God, but the love that defines our being — the kind of love that allows

Christ to supersede the ego by embracing young people in the *missio dei* —
that love is passion, embodied in the life, death, and resurrection of Jesus
Christ.

The Bottom Line

A passionless church will never address passionate youth. It is highly questionable whether a passionless church addresses anybody, or if it even is
the church in the first place. Christianity requires passion, and youth know
it. Passion, both human and divine, challenges the language of modern rationalism, and ushers in a way of life that subverts the basic assumptions of
an anesthetic culture with therapeutic goals. If the governing feature of
Christian passion is self-giving love, the governing law of therapeutic consumerism is self-fulfillment. The church is as guilty as adolescents of confusing the two.

The question of Christian identity is not whether a teenager identifies with adults, even Christian ones, and thereby achieves ego strength or
becomes socialized into the church. Underlying a teenager's Christian
identity is his decision to imitate Christ, the only adequate source of mimesis. When the passions of adolescence meet the Passion of Christ, a figure-
ground shift takes place: the developing ego moves back in order to make
space in the foreground for the passion of God. In the language of conversion, the young person relinquishes the partially constructed social self in
favor of her true identity as God's beloved.[31] But something else happens
as well. As teenagers take part in Christ's life, death, and resurrection, they
re-member God's passion for the church. In these practices of self-giving
love, God loosens the church's hold on sinful identifications as well, and
realigns our desires according to the true north of Jesus Christ.

The identity of the church is as much at risk as the identity of young
people; without passion, neither can truly be who God intends them to be.
At the same time, young people's openness to passion makes them important witnesses to the church in this regard, transforming youth into bearers
of suffering love, passionate because Christ's self-giving overcomes them,
undoes them, and remakes them — and us. This divine reconstruction
changes the world. It is also, as we shall see in Section Two, what makes
youth and the church such an explosive combination.

31. The Eastern church describes this as "divinization" and the apostolic Fathers as
"becoming little Christs." The Protestant tradition generally understands this as sanctification, or holiness — life in God made possible only by God's gift of grace.

DIMENSIONS OF PASSION

A View from the Bridge

Divine Passion is revealed as God's:	Addresses adolescent desire for:	Meets developmental need for:	Authenticated by:
Fidelity	Steadfastness	Acceptance	"being there"
Transcendence	Ecstasy	Feeling part of greatness	"being moved"
Communion	Intimacy	Camaraderie	"being known"

Chapter Three

LONGING FOR FIDELITY

If It stays, It Must Be True

The closest God comes to defining [God's] self is in the terms of being there.

William McNamara, *Mystical Passion*[1]

We'll be there.

Slogan of the American Red Cross

And remember, I am with you always, to the end of the age.

Jesus (Matthew 28:20, NRSV)

Few lines of Scripture sound more reassuring — or less likely — to young people than Jesus' promise at the end of the Gospel of Matthew. Contemporary culture offers little assurance that anything will be with them always; more than 16 percent of Americans (about forty-three million people) move each year, and between 1970 and 2000 the number of children living in single-parent families jumped from 13 percent to 31 percent.[2] The

---

1. William McNamara, *Mystical Passion: The Art of Christian Loving* (Rockport, Mass.: Element Books, 1991), 29. McNamara is citing Martin Buber's translation of I AM — "I shall be there as I shall be there." Martin Buber, *Moses: The Revelation and the Covenant* (Atlantic Highlands, N.J.: Humanities Press International, 1988), 51-52.

2. Jason Schachter, "Current Population Reports: Geographical Mobility," Washing-

Sloan Foundation reports that the average American teenager spends about three and a half hours alone every day, more time than with friends or family.[3] Teenagers in an affluent New Jersey congregation I know recently asked their pastor — not their parents — to sign the emergency release forms sent home from school last fall. "If we need something," they told her, "we know you'll be there."

The truth is, despite the gospel's claim that Jesus will be with us always, young people usually assume — correctly — that the church will not be. It is not for a lack of good intentions. Eugene Rivers, the pastor who organized "the Boston miracle" in which a handful of clergy reclaimed a Boston neighborhood tyrannized by drug dealers, describes how he and his colleagues were "evangelized" by crack cocaine dealers who "reached out to the Christians," inviting them into crack houses and introducing them to drug dealers, guns, and the drug game. One young heroin dealer told Rivers, "I'm going to explain to you Christians, who are such good preachers, why you are losing an entire generation. Listen, this is really all about being there."

"What do you mean?" Rivers demanded.

The heroin dealer coolly replied: "When Johnny goes to school in the morning, I'm there, you're not. When Johnny comes home from school in the afternoon, I'm there, you're not. When Johnny goes out for a loaf of bread for grandma for dinner, I'm there, you're not. I win, you lose."[4]

Churches that know how to "be there" for young people make the headlines, not the rule. I was stunned (and impressed) to discover a congregation that presents a key to the church building to every teenager at confirmation (as a pastor, I had trouble even getting a key to the church kitchen). After the 1998 school shootings in Jonesboro, Arkansas, a Baptist

---

ton, D.C.: U.S. Department of Commerce (U.S. Census Bureau, May 2001); Jason Fields, "U.S. Adults Postponing Marriage, Census Bureau Reports," Washington, D.C.: U.S. Department of Commerce (U.S. Census Bureau, June 29, 2001), 6-7.

3. Cited by Barbara Schneider and David Stevenson, *The Ambitious Generation: America's Teenagers, Motivated but Directionless* (New Haven: Yale University Press, 1999), 191-94.

4. Eugene F. Rivers III founded and co-directs the National Ten Point Leadership Foundation, and is pastor of Azusa Christian Community Church in Boston, Massachusetts. The National Ten Point Leadership Foundation's primary mission is to help provide African American churches with the strategic vision, programmatic structure, and financial resources necessary to save inner-city youth. This story is printed in Eugene Rivers, "New Wineskins, New Models and Visions for a New Century," in *An Unexpected Prophet: What the 21st Century Church Can Learn from Youth Ministry — The 1999 Princeton Lectures on Youth, Church and Culture* (Princeton, N.J.: Princeton Theological Seminary, 2000), 87.

youth pastor surrounded the younger brother of one of the gunmen with a group of supportive teenagers; perhaps the most notable aspect of the story was that the press found it notable.[5] A. P. Shaw United Methodist Church in southeast Washington, D.C., is widely respected for launching young people into ministry. But Shaw Church's commitment to teenagers was hard-won. Etched in the congregation's memory is a brutal murder on the church's front steps. One Sunday evening during worship, a young man fleeing gang assassins ran to the church's locked doors, trying literally to gain sanctuary. He collapsed on the front steps from gunshot wounds. Following his death, the congregation voted that "the church doors will always remain open so that young people can come into the church. If they are being chased by dealers and gangsters, there is no better place for them to run than to God's house."[6] Today, despite the neighborhood's high crime rate, Shaw Church keeps its front doors open.

Fidelity: The Power of Being There

In his analysis of Generation X faith, Tom Beaudoin asserts that the most significant question of young adults born between the 1960s and the 1980s is: *"Will you be there for me?"* Beaudoin traces this question to a pervasive sense of abandonment among Generation Xers, and certainly Florence Henderson and Bill Cosby did their share of virtual parenting for North America's first "latchkey" generation. In contrast, notes Beaudoin, Gen X's parents (the Baby Boomers) asked a different question as teenagers: *"Will my life have meaning?"* In 1967, for instance, the most popular value chosen by 83 percent of college freshmen was "developing a meaningful philosophy of life." By 1987, only 39 percent cited "developing a meaningful philosophy of life" as their most important goal, the lowest percentage in two decades.[7]

Beaudoin's insight should be taken to heart for developmental as well as social-scientific reasons. Baby Boomers (people who were teenagers in the 1950s and 1960s, when Erikson developed his theory of identity forma-

5. Mary Cagney, "What a Jonesboro Youth Group Learned," *Christianity Today* available at http://www.christianitytoday.com/ct/8t9/8t9035.html; accessed 7 December 2001.

6. Thanks to Joyce Harris of Shaw Memorial United Methodist Church for the details of this story.

7. W. Dunn, *The Baby Bust: A Generation Comes of Age* (Ithaca, N.Y.: American Demographics Books, 1993). Cited in Tom Beaudoin, *Virtual Faith: The Irreverent Spiritual Quest of Generation X* (San Francisco: Jossey-Bass, 1998), 140.

tion) focused on choosing a life "ideology," an integrative system of meaning that helped them make sense of the world.[8] Not surprisingly, Erikson — writing as Boomers were being swept into broad ideological movements of the 1960s — focused much of his work on ideology's significance for the transition into adulthood. Erikson's concept of adolescence required a "moratorium," a socially approved "time out" in which adult commitments are temporarily suspended so that the young person can consolidate identity and test nascent ideologies to find one worthy of commitment. *"Will my life have meaning?"* is a question of ideology, and Erikson viewed commitment to an ideology "the necessary condition for further individual maturation" beyond adolescence.[9]

The problem with choosing an ideology during adolescence is that it implies a readiness to be faithful to it. In the early stages of identity crisis, notes Erikson, the adolescent must learn to trust himself and others, so he "looks most fervently for [people] and ideas to have *faith* in." At the same time, he "fears a foolish, all too trusting commitment and will, paradoxically, express his need for faith in loud and cynical mistrust."[10] Erikson called the ability to be faithful the virtue of *fidelity* — "the cornerstone" of adolescence, the strength of being utterly true to oneself and others amid competing and contradictory value systems.[11]

Fidelity, then, is the opposable thumb of human development; it gives us the capacity to cling. With fidelity we can believe in, and remain true to, a person or an idea. Erikson viewed fidelity as the strength of a "disciplined devotion," and called it the "vital strength which [youth] needs to have an opportunity to develop, to employ, to evoke — *and to die for*."[12] Because fidelity enables us to be "for" another person, it can only be developed in the shadow of someone who is "for" us. We are not taught fidelity; we "suffer" it, experience it passively, participate in it as a believing partner, give ourselves over to it. In short, fidelity cannot be achieved; it can only be received from those who practice it on our behalf.

---

8. See Erikson, *Identity, Youth, and Crisis* (New York: W. W. Norton, 1968), 125. Erikson acknowledged the term's political baggage, but consciously retained it for its psychological import, which divests the term of political weight.

9. Erikson, *Identity, Youth, and Crisis,* 125, 189.

10. Erikson, *Identity, Youth, and Crisis,* 128-29.

11. "The mental and emotional ability to receive and give fidelity marks the conclusion of adolescence." Erikson, *Identity, Youth, and Crisis,* 265.

12. Erikson viewed fidelity as the center of youth's "most passionate and most erratic" striving (Erikson, *Identity, Youth, and Crisis,* 233). "We love because He first loved us" (1 John 4:19) serves as the biblical equivalent to Erikson's concept of fidelity.

Passion seeks fidelity. Without passion, fidelity fails, and our identity as *homo religiosus* — Erikson's term for the innate religiosity of human beings — collapses. The essence of fidelity (from the Latin *fidei,* or faith) is the ability to be faithful. It is not too much, then, to claim that acquiring the capacity for faith is a central task of postmodern adolescence. Without the ability to be faithful — that is, without fidelity, the strength that impels the search for something "to die for" — young people cannot live as *homo religiosus.* Unlike their Baby Boomer parents, who could assume a modicum of faithfulness from the adults who raised them, many contemporary young people simply have not experienced enough fidelity on their behalf to acquire it for themselves. Consequently, postmodern adolescents are preoccupied with fidelity: *"Will you be there for me?"* Before adolescents can take seriously the gospel's claim that Jesus will "be there" always, a community of affirming others must "be there" for them, demonstrating steadfast love on their behalf.

Where Have All the Grown-Ups Gone?

"Will you be there for me?" is the cry of an era, not just of a generation. As the first self-consciously postmodern generation in America, Generation Xers may have been the first to suspect fidelity's fading imprint, but they are hardly the last. Fifty years ago, adults were recognizable enough to contradict. Even during the 1960s, the sometimes dangerous and often maddening "rebellion" of adolescents helped differentiate them from adults, and therefore helped consolidate their emerging selfhood "over against" the preceding generation. (And in so doing, nonconformist Boomers neatly conformed to patterns of socialization that have been in place for centuries.)

Erikson believed that fidelity is inspired by "confirming ideologies and affirming companions." Such "affirming companions" commonly present themselves in the form of "adult guarantors," noted Erikson — representatives of the adult world who embody worthy ideologies, and who respond to the adolescent's plea to be recognized as more than he seems to be, with unique potentials needed by the world.[13] But while Erikson as-

---

13. Erik H. Erikson, *Insight and Responsibility* (New York: W. W. Norton, 1964), 125. These adults "become representatives of an elite in the eyes of the young quite independently of whether or not they are thus viewed in the eyes of the family, the public, or the police." The alternating ability of teenagers to be devoted conformists one day and deviants the next

sumed the presence of faithful adults as commonplace, this assumption would be quite optimistic today. Tagged "the Autonomous Generation" by the *New York Times* in 1998,[14] today's adolescents have few adults or institutions who are prepared to "be there" for them till the end of the age, or till the end of high school for that matter.[15] In her widely acclaimed profile of suburban youth in the mid-1990s, Patricia Hersch found that contemporary adolescents do not pull away from adults any more than they ever have. The distinctive feature of childhood in the late twentieth century, Hersch discovered, was the way *adults* pulled away from *youth*, despite young people's expressed desire for a significant adult presence in their lives. As a result, Hersch saw adolescents functioning as "a tribe apart," a default society in which young people attempt, usually in vain, to raise each other.[16]

In short, Erikson's theory of identity formation relied on an ingredient no longer widely available to North American young people: grownups. What fuels the "autonomous generation" is the sheer invisibility of adults who once served as explicit and even willing reminders to youth and adults alike that adolescence is temporary. As late consumer capitalism, an economy predicated on creating demand for goods we do not actually need, gripped the North American economy, advertisers searching for new markets began pitching adult toys and child make-up. Full participation in consumer society required money, not maturity, and teenagers proved to be willing and competent consumers. Meanwhile, the few adults available to youth often failed to function as adults. In May 1998 — four months before President Bill Clinton acknowledged "an inappropriate relationship" with a twenty-two-year-old intern — a Bennington College senior told *Rolling Stone:* "Adults no longer behave like adults. We have no models; they're talking about sex and therapy and substance abuse, just like us."[17]

is not to be wondered at, said Erikson, since every young person is training to be an adult able to react to a diversity of conditions. In Erikson's view, "Healthy individualism and devoted deviancy contain an indignation in the service of a wholeness that is to be restored, without which psychosocial evolution would be doomed." See Erikson, *Insight and Responsibility,* 248.

14. Anne Powers, "Who Are These People, Anyway?" *The New York Times,* Wednesday, April 29, 1998.

15. Boomer parents, by contrast, experienced such constant adult presence that Congress legally limited it in 1974's American Privacy Act. Every change in the American Privacy Act in the past thirty years has been in the direction of giving parents more access to information about their children, even while they are in college.

16. Patricia Hersch, *A Tribe Apart: A Journey into the Heart of American Adolescence* (New York: Ballantine Publishing Group, 1998), 10-30.

17. Edward Hoagland, "The American Dream 1998," *Rolling Stone,* May 28, 1998, 96.

Learning from Elephants

So what? Has the time come to abandon the distinction between adolescence and adulthood, which is getting blurrier every day? A number of contemporary authors have pondered "the end of adolescence," wondering aloud if adolescence has not outlived its usefulness in a postmodern world where protected developmental space seems out of reach.[18] When fourteen-year-olds can sabotage stock prices and nineteen-year-olds can threaten the entire music industry — and when countless youth are cast into adult roles *de facto* by poverty, pregnancy, crime, or other external factors that force a precocious adulthood — adolescence quickly looks irrelevant. Journalist Thomas Hine points out that the word "teenager" was created in the 1940s for the needs of a postwar economy, making the American teenager "a New Deal project, like the Hoover Dam":

> At most, we can say that the teenager is a social invention, one that took shape during the first half of the twentieth century in response to a society very different from our own. . . . Being a teenager is less and less what Erik Erikson proposed — a moratorium in which to find your identity. Teenagers are losing their license for irresponsibility while, at the same time, they continue to be denied a role in their society, other than that of style setters and consumers. . . . The teenager is a recent idea that may not deserve to be an eternal one.[19]

Maybe, suggest Hine and others, the time has come to expect young people to be adults, not adolescents — a view that seems to be supported by studies documenting earlier puberty in girls, and changing cultural expectations that put economic and social power in the hands of teenagers.[20]

But before we jump too quickly, a parable. Between 1992 and 1997, South African game wardens noticed an overabundance of elephants, and

18. See Thomas Hine, *The Rise and Fall of the American Teenager* (New York: Avon Books, 1999). This thesis is not new; it was first proposed in 1959 by Edgar Z. Friedenberg, *The Vanishing Adolescent* (New York: Dell, 1959).

19. Hine, *Rise and Fall*, 4, 8-9. Hine reminds us that standard references cite a 1941 article in *Popular Science* with the first published use of the word "teenager." The term became widely used during World War II and showed up in a book title in 1945, subsequently leaking into the language of advertising and marketing.

20. For early onset of puberty see Diana Zuckerman, "When Little Girls Become Women: Early Onset of Puberty in Girls," *The Ribbon* 6, no. 1 (Winter 2001), available at http://www.center4policy.org/children11.html#Kaplowitz99; accessed on 7 December 2001. Also see Michael D. Lemonick, "Teens Before Their Time," *Time,* October 30, 2000.

decided to cull the elephant population by killing some of the older bulls. Park rangers relocated seventeen young male elephants, orphaned in the herd cullings, to Pilanesberg National Park — where the young elephants promptly went wild. Rangers concluded that the young relocated bulls were prematurely entering "musth" — elephant puberty, accompanied by elephantine testosterone surges — and the alarming by-product of their escalated testosterone levels was an unpredictable and deadly level of aggression. Inexplicably, these young elephants directed their aggression against white rhinoceroses, with whom elephants usually peacefully cohabitate. After a number of brutal attacks killed more than forty of the park's rhinos, scientists began to investigate.

Although scientists (wisely, I think) declined to generalize their findings to other species, their conclusions have a hauntingly human ring. In a normal herd, young bulls entering musth attack older bulls — a form of sparring in which the older male usually soundly defeats his young rival, at least until the younger elephant reaches full strength and maturity. But defeat at the tusks of a mature adult teaches the young elephant something important. If he is to survive in the herd, he must learn to de-escalate his aggression during musth. When very young bulls were removed from the herd and transported to another park, they had no rivals against whom they could test their mettle. No stronger adult elephants were available, and the rhinos, unfortunately, proved to be poor sparring partners since attacking them usually killed them.

These young elephants, therefore, proceeded through musth without the experience of defeat — and as a result, their physical and sexual maturation proceeded faster than normal, and without the usual modifications. In the absence of adult bulls, these "teenage" elephants prematurely played the role of the dominant male/adult. Apart from the herd, a relocated bull had no reason to modify his aggression, and his testosterone surges went unchecked — escalating into brutal attacks on the nearest species.[21] Within the herd, however, experience with mature bulls led to patterns of interaction in which testosterone surges were ultimately used on *behalf* of the herd, for protection and reproduction, through modifications reinforced under the herd's protection.

21. Rob Slotow et al., "Older Bull Elephants Control Young Males," *Nature* 408 (November 23, 2000): 425-26; Michael D. Lemonick, "Young, Single and Out of Control," *Time,* October 13, 1997.

What Moratorium?

The idea is not to equate elephant aggression with adolescent passion; take it as a story, not an analogy. But it is a story with a moral, too. The 1997 Longitudinal Study of Adolescent Health emphasized the presence of adults who are actively engaged in supervising and setting goals for teenagers' lives as the most powerful factor determining their well-being.[22] The temporary protection afforded by an intergenerational "herd" provides a useful image for the "moratorium" posited by Erikson — a socially sanctioned "time out" from adult commitments in which playfulness, experimentation, rebellion, and exploratory commitments are both tolerated and expected by society.

Today, the moratorium Erikson considered crucial for adolescence has all but vanished. Adolescent psychologists like David Elkind blame the stress created by the absence of "protected space" for adolescent development for increases in self-destructive behavior — something like the unchecked testosterone surges that led elephants to attack rhinos in the absence of adult bulls.[23] With no moratorium, contemporary young people are thrust prematurely into adult roles, sometimes by circumstance, sometimes by choice, and sometimes by the consequences of choice; in all cases, the result is enormous pressure on the inexperienced and malleable adolescent self.

The argument against adolescence (as opposed to "teenagers") is difficult to substantiate, but we should examine it closely — for if adolescence is the result of the human life cycle's adaptation to our cultural "herd," then we can be sure that more adaptation is on the way. Just as the modern period gave rise to adolescence itself, changing life patterns forced by globalization and postmodernity have altered normative patterns of identity formation. These changing expectations shape the nature of adolescence, and press the church to "be there" for young people in new and more visible ways.

22. Michael D. Resnick et al., "Protecting Adolescents from Harm: Findings from the National Longitudinal Study on Adolescent Health," *Journal of the American Medical Association* 278 (September 10, 1997): 823-33.

23. See David Elkind, *All Grown Up and No Place to Go* (Reading, Mass.: Addison-Wesley, 1984).

Tracking Changes in Identity Formation

Before the Enlightenment, and certainly before the postwar creation of the "American teenager," identity meant social role: options were few, choices were clear (where they existed at all), and consequently, identity was certain, making the social construction of adolescence unnecessary. Children gained their identities and their adulthood simultaneously; the self became established at whatever point youth assumed an economic role that contributed to the community, usually by marriage, entering a trade, or assuming responsibility for property upon the death of a parent.[24]

But the Enlightenment's celebration of the individual gave rise to a new self-determinism. "Modern consciousness entails a movement from fate to choice," writes sociologist Peter Berger. Open, differentiated, reflective, individuated, and ultimately "homeless," according to Berger, modern people became afflicted with a "permanent identity crisis":

> Institutions cease to be the "home" of the self; instead they become oppressive realities that distort and estrange the self. Roles no longer actualize the self, but serve as a "veil of *maya*" hiding the self not only from others but from the individual's own consciousness. Only in the interstitial areas left vacant, as it were, by institutions . . . can the individual hope to discover or define himself.[25]

Adolescence, of course, constitutes one of those "interstitial areas" — i.e., "leftover" psychic space unclaimed by most modern institutions — which is why youth are so preoccupied with self-definition. Because youth is "unclaimed" by the roles of these institutions, claims Berger, adolescence is simultaneously where young people endure "the most acute experiences of self-estrangement and . . . the most intensive quest for reliable identities."[26]

To a large extent, the modern project drove a wedge between personal identity and social institutions. No longer could individuals primarily identify themselves with vocations, churches, schools, or even families with any certainty.[27] In a society with stable, coherent institutions, answers could be given with great confidence. But with postmodernity's endless supply of personal choice — a development that accentuated the modern project more than overturned it — these "objective" external truths

24. See Kett, *Rites of Passage* (New York: Basic Books, 1977), especially 14-36.
25. Peter Berger, *The Homeless Mind* (New York: Random House, 1973), 93-94.
26. Berger, *The Homeless Mind,* 93-94.
27. Berger, *The Homeless Mind,* 19.

eroded. Young people were confronted with a seemingly endless array of possibilities, an apparently infinite repertoire of ideologies to choose from, leaving them to look inward in search of certainty.[28] In the absence of valued communities with a shared moral consensus, young people relied on their own subjectivity to cull through belief systems. And not only youth, of course. Turning to an increasingly complex inner world, rather than to a community of confirming others, isolates adults as often as adolescents in the human quest for answers and sustenance.

Locating Adolescence: In the Herd or Beyond?

Within this matrix of subjectivity, Erikson posited identity formation as the central task of adolescence — a task once claimed by the church, now overtaken by modern psychology. Predictably, Protestants turned to social science instead of to theology to understand their task with young people, delving deeply into modern "stage theories" like those developed by Erikson and his admirers.

As a result, mainline Protestant youth ministry in the late twentieth century tended to define its task in relationship to Erikson's theory of identity formation, either in sympathy with or in reaction to twentieth-century developmental psychology. Some churches believed the adolescent "identity crisis" was best addressed by keeping young people "in the herd." Youth ministry in these churches sought to preserve adolescence as Erikson conceived it — as the last stage of childhood, a transition into adulthood in which identity must be mastered. These churches fostered conditions conducive to young people's ego stability: a safe moratorium, a shared community ideology, adult guarantors who could demonstrate fidelity on behalf of others.[29] At the same time, other churches attempted to "relocate" young people in adulthood, on the assumption that adolescence itself infantilized youth.[30] These ministries sought to minimize adolescence and shorten the so-called moratorium, giving young people adult (or pseudo-adult) responsibilities on the assumption that youth would then

28. Berger, *The Homeless Mind*, 21.

29. See Kenda Creasy Dean, "Practical Theology and Adolescence in America," *International Journal of Practical Theology* 2 (Berlin and New York: Walter de Gruyter, 1998): 143-45.

30. Ronald Koteskey, "Adolescence as a Cultural Invention," *Handbook of Youth Ministry*, ed. Donald Ratcliff and James A. Davies (Birmingham, Ala.: Religious Education Press, 1991), 42-69.

rise to the occasion and become adults. They urged young people to test their mettle in the adult world, and they sought adolescents' participation as full members of the Christian community in and beyond the local congregation.[31]

Much can be said in favor of both of these approaches. Yet neither of them pursues identity as a *Christian* objective, as something theology has a stake in forming. Christians value fidelity precisely because it underscores the inherent *relationality* of human identity, which is revealed only in relationship to God and others; true identity is ours by redemption, not by development.[32] For instance, when youth ministry treats adolescence as late childhood, the goal of ministry tends to become an established ego, not a contrite heart before God. Yet Christian identity requires a *differentiated* ego, not an autonomous one, the humility to recognize and value the other *as* other. Christian theology challenges Erikson's concept of identity "achievement" by proclaiming true humanity as God's gift, obscured by sin but restored by Christ. This differentiated ego is the result of conviction, not ego achievement, making Christian identity possible for persons at any stage in the life cycle, and not just adolescents.

At the other end of the scale are churches that conflate adolescence with young adulthood, short-circuiting important aspects of Christian formation that are accomplished only by long mentoring in a safe faith community.[33] Placing young people in adult roles may "adultify" them, but it does not make them adults (Christian or otherwise). The danger of visiting "adult" roles prematurely on ill-prepared adolescents are well-publi-

31. Dean, "Practical Theology and Adolescence in America," 146-49.

32. In this regard, the Christian critique of Erikson echoes that of feminist psychology, which has shown that women tend to form identity in the context of intimacy, rather than apart from it. A particularly thoughtful collection of essays on girls' development in light of the shortcomings of Erikson's stage theory is found in Judith V. Jordan et al., *Women's Growth in Connection* (New York: Guilford Press, 1991). The degree to which girls require intimacy or separation in identity formation is debated, and even feminist developmental research acknowledges that the orientation toward relationality in adolescent development does not break down neatly along gender lines. In addition to Jordan, see Cynthia S. W. Crysdale, "Gilligan and the Ethics of Care: An Update," *Religious Studies Review* 20 (January 1994); Richard K. Fenn and Donald Capps, *The Endangered Self* (Princeton, N.J.: Center for Religion, Self, and Society, 1992).

33. David Elkind discusses the phenomenon of adultified youth in *All Grown Up and No Place to Go,* 208-9. James Marcia furthers Erikson's work on identity formation by suggesting foreclosed, diffuse, and/or negative identities in the absence of positive identity formation. See James Marcia, "Ego Identity Development," *Handbook of Adolescent Psychology,* ed. J. Adelson (New York: John Wiley, 1980).

cized, and suggest that neither the church nor society in general can afford to completely foreclose on an adolescent moratorium. Using teenagers as willing mouthpieces for adult agendas, romantically assuming that young voices are always prophetic ones, pressing young people into ministries for which they are neither psychologically nor vocationally prepared all thrust young people into roles that require them to "act" adult rather than equip them to "become" adult. The passionate voices of adolescents *are* prophetic; but like all forms of witness, they require the interpretive lens of the Christian community to distinguish God's voice from the cacophony of others. We do not deny youth their prophetic role in the community by admitting that, sometimes — perhaps even often — adolescent passion is uninformed, poorly articulated, or hopelessly biased (which makes youth more like the rest of us than we thought).

The Plural Self

The root of the problem, of course, is that Erikson's concept of identity — which he never intended as a once-and-for-all hard encasement[34] — nonetheless took shape in an era when Western society was a far more coherent place. As a result, a number of efforts have been made to re-think Erikson's understanding of identity in light of more recent social forces. One recurring image in this discussion is the "plural self," the growing awareness that no single identity defines us, that who we are varies according to our shifting contexts, and that the need to "keep up" with the complexity of postmodern culture requires different identities at different points throughout the life cycle. Unlike its adolescent cousin, the "patchwork self" — a makeshift identity held together on the outside by psychological duct tape rather than by internal integration — the plural self is the result of chameleon adaptations to the multiple roles demanded by postmodern culture. The plural self seeks infinite flexibility, not integration, and thereby sacrifices "integrity" for a widened repertoire of potential selves, and the agility to shift between them. There is little doubt that plural selves are a fact of contemporary life, useful for navigating the multiple roles required by postmodern culture.[35] The bigger question is

34. "Identity is never 'established' as an 'achievement' in the form of a personality armor, or of anything static and unchangeable" (Erikson, *Identity, Youth and Crisis,* 24). Some postmodern approaches to identity formation misread Erikson on this score.

35. For examples of this new way of constructing identity, see Kenneth Gergen, *The Saturated Self: Dilemmas of Identity in Contemporary Life* (New York: Basic Books, 1991), 7.

whether or not the plural self contributes to young people's Christian identity. Should youth ministry champion the plural self or subvert it?

If, as Christianity teaches, God is responsible for our identity, the plural self is quite acceptable, says practical theologian Friedrich Schweitzer. In fact, observes Schweitzer, the plural self actually frees adolescents from some of the ideological trappings of Erikson's modern notion of identity formation.[36] Strictly speaking, the Christian view of self is not unitary anyway; Christian identity is irreducibly relational, involving the persons of the Trinity as well as the individual and the individual's community identifications. If only God can justify our human incompleteness, the plural self helps us relinquish our drive for perfection, making "partialness" — rather than wholeness — the norm for human identity. Pluralism, notes Schweitzer, is an inescapable fact of postmodern life; better to recognize its potential gifts than to waste energy on futile resistance. He therefore advocates a "principled" pluralism in young people, in which some ideologies take precedence over others — meaning, apparently, that youth must learn to recognize that some convictions are more "to die for" than others.

Yet the plural self poses risks for adolescents that are not easily dismissed. For one thing, it does not easily distinguish between "selves" and "social roles." While adolescents must develop role-taking "fluency," their God-given identity as *homo religiosus* transcends social roles, and offers a platform from which to critique cultural scripts that tend to reduce adolescents to our expectations for them.[37] The most significant question raised by the plural self, however, is whether it can engender fidelity, giving adolescents a secure foundation that allows them to explore and invest in an ideology of ultimate worth — an ideology embodied by adult guarantors whose loyalty and affirmation young people seek. The virtue of "being true" to something or someone does not belong to any one moment in his-

---

36. Among practical theologians, Friedrich Schweitzer has probed these issues most deeply in light of adolescence and the postmodern life cycle. Though Schweitzer is more optimistic about the plural self than I am, he offers a way to think about postmodern adolescence in a way that pushes the conversation about identity towards a thoughtful theology. Schweitzer believes that the plural self exhibited by adolescents may offer a number of advantages in the development of Christian identity, and he outlined this position in "Adolescence and the Postmodern Lifecycle" (Stone Lectures, Princeton Theological Seminary, March 2000). Taken from recorded lecture.

37. For an elaboration on adolescence and social roles and cultural scripts, see Don Richter, Doug Magnuson, and Michael Baizerman, "Reconceiving Youth Ministry," *Religious Education* 93, no. 3 (Summer 1998): 340-57.

tory or philosophical school; fidelity is a timeless requirement of faith, basic to the Hebrew/Christian understanding of God, and basic to adolescence itself. Schweitzer hints at the necessity of fidelity in his enigmatic argument for a "principled pluralism"; but whether the plural self can remain faithful to, or even discern, a central principle in the midst of the multiple voices of pluralism is quite unclear. Although Christian tradition supports the plural self's contextuality, brokenness, and even a normative partialness, it does not support its relativism: when everything matters, nothing matters most.

Fidelity gathers strength from focus; it is no accident that Erikson's original term for unsuccessful identity formation was identity "diffusion."[38] Youth tend to solve the problems of pluralism by relativizing truth to "whatever," compartmentalizing the self by carving life space into discrete cubicles. Integrity, however, requires integration, not relativity or compartmentalization. Even plural selves require enough traction to create an affinity between roles, a "stickiness" that allows the partial self to cling to a governing center. To have integrity, the plural self requires a theologically compelling center to which the self's plurality can cling, a core that remains faithful and true, and consequently bequeaths fidelity to the adolescent. Even the plural self requires a central voice that calls into question its fundamental plurality. If postmodernity signals the end of the "master narrative," it does not eliminate the human longing for a "master passion," a focal point for fidelity — an ultimate commitment that gives every fragment of self its *raison d'etre.*

The Unity of Divine Momentum:
A Perichoretic View of the Self

What is missing in the discussion of the plural self is a referent in the plurality of God, whose "being there" for us was disclosed on the cross. As Jürgen Moltmann has demonstrated, without a theology of passion our understanding of God's Triune nature (and consequently our understanding of human nature) remains seriously distorted.[39] Moltmann views

---

38. Erik Erikson, *Identity and the Life Cycle* (New York: Norton, 1980), 131-58.

39. Moltmann's position on the passion of God is laid out most completely in *The Crucified God* (Minneapolis: Fortress, 1993) and nuanced in the summary volume of his trinitarian thought *The Trinity and the Kingdom* (Minneapolis: Fortress, 1993). For this reason I focus primarily on his thinking in these two volumes. Moltmann's social doctrine of the Trinity assumes the primacy of God's relational nature, relying on the classical view of "person" as an

Christ's Passion as evidence that God invites our participation in the Trinity not by analogy, but by real incorporation into the life of God.[40] Theologian Sarah Coakley adds, "If human loves are indeed made with the imprint of the divine upon them . . . then they too, at their best, will bear the trinitarian mark."[41] Adolescents, therefore, participate in the Passion of Christ wherever they take up their crosses:

> The fellowship of Christ is experienced in common resistance to idolatry and inhumanity, in common suffering over oppression and persecution. It is in this *participation in the passion of Christ and in the passion of the people that the "life" of Christ and his liberty becomes visible in the church.*[42]

Christian identity depends upon identifying with the crucified God — which means identifying also with those with whom Jesus identified in his death.[43] In other words, young people take part in God's "being there" for

individual constituted by relationship. Thanks in part to Moltmann's indebtedness to a Western view of personhood, this view has been charged with tritheism; understanding the person as individual means that relationships are something God *has* rather than are something God *is,* a point of view disputed by the Eastern church. Moltmann acknowledges that he "took sides" in erring on the side of the Trinity's "threeness," and notes that a more ontological view of God's relationality (asserting that "God *is* love") — which serves as the foundation of a theology of passion — would have made it more difficult to charge his social doctrine of the Trinity with tritheism (Moltmann, *Crucified God,* 227). Thomas Torrence underscores the relationship between the Trinity and passion, arguing that even Calvin drew upon Gregory of Nazianzus for his images of the persons of the Trinity (Thomas F. Torrance, *Trinitarian Perspectives: Toward Doctrinal Agreement* [Edinburgh: T&T Clark, 1994], 39). The human impulse toward the other can only be understood analogously to God's own impulse toward the other — both *ad intra* (in the inner life of God) and *ad extra* (in the ways God reaches out to creation). God's passion is merely one divine attribute among many if love does not ontologically as well as functionally describe the Godhead.

40. Moltmann, *The Trinity and the Kingdom,* 172.

41. Sarah Coakley, "Living into the Mystery of the Holy Trinity," *Anglican Theological Review* 80 (Spring 1998): 223-33.

42. Jürgen Moltmann, *The Church in the Power of the Spirit* (Minneapolis: Fortress Press, 1993), 97. Emphasis added.

43. See Richard J. Bauckham, *Moltmann: Messianic Theology in the Making* (Basingstoke, Hants, U.K.: Marshall Morgan and Scott, 1987), 109. For Moltmann, God's identity is constituted by God's relationships within the Godhead as well as in the way God reaches out to the world. In fact, God's inner relationality is revealed by God's external relationship to humanity. Jesus' death must not be understood as the "death of God" but as "death *in* God" (Moltmann, *Crucified God,* 207). The crucifixion is the defining event not only for God's relationship with humans, but also for the relationship between the three persons of the Trinity who cannot stand apart from their relationship with creation: "In the trinitarian

them whenever they are "there" for others, making Christ's fidelity visible in the practices of suffering love.[44]

If divine passion reveals God's fidelity, it necessarily reveals the source of ours as well. In the passion of the cross, God the Father chose "being there" for us over "being there" for God's own self in the Son — but even then, God's fidelity remained uncompromised, for the Holy Spirit freely chose to "be there" with both Christ and creation, even in death.[45] Adolescents who imitate Jesus Christ obtain the virtue of fidelity not by overcoming fragmentation or substituting social roles for an integrated identity, but by casting their lot with the One whose fidelity never fails. In the Father, Son, and Holy Spirit, we have a divine blueprint for a self that coheres amidst differentiation.[46] The *perichoresis* (literally, the "dancing around") of the Trinity creates a unifying momentum that holds the differentiated persons of God together as one — distinct while in utter unity, passionately related to each other while ecstatically reaching out to humankind. When identity is viewed through a perichoretic lens, the adolescent's "plural selves" cohere around the cross. The adolescent developing a perichoretic self is relational and dynamic, differentiated around a unifying center, open to others while maintaining integrity, flexible but fixed around the fidelity of Jesus Christ.

---

event of the cross God is in himself what he is for us" (Bauckham, *Moltmann: Messianic Theology*, 98).

44. One of the questions in the contemporary discussion of the Trinity is what divine plurality implies for human identity, which will be addressed from the perspective of adolescents in the next section. For Moltmann, the Incarnation decisively addresses human fragmentation. The primary purpose of the life and death of Christ is neither to save our souls nor to show solidarity with human suffering, but — by the saving work of the Son — to make creation perfect and therefore multiply the bliss of God. Moltmann, *Trinity and the Kingdom*, 115-16.

45. Moltmann argues that the Father chooses to abandon the Son at the point of death on the cross in order to become God-forsaken, so that God identifies with our God-forsakenness. Even this does not breach God's fidelity, however; in abandoning Jesus to death, the Father chooses fidelity to humanity over fidelity to self. The Father chooses to "not be there" for the Son in order to "be there" for creation. Even so, the Holy Spirit remains faithful bringing humanity to God through Jesus' God-forsakenness — making the Holy Spirit "for" the Godhead and creation simultaneously. Christian tradition has treated the Holy Spirit as the "Advocate" for this reason.

46. Human language for the three persons of the Godhead is necessarily metaphorical, partial, and imperfect. I retain the use of the word "Father," not because it is male, but because its usual substitute "Creator" lacks the relational connotation that is critical for understanding divine passion. For adolescents, the value of relationality supercedes the value of gender neutrality. At the same time, I have avoided pronouns when referring to the Godhead as a whole, so as not to assign gender to the Godhead.

The Myth of "Being There":
Practicing Fidelity without Killing the Youth Pastor

When we talk about the importance of "relational ministry" in Christian youth work, what we really mean is that young people need the ability to give and receive fidelity, and they learn this in the fidelity of God that is glimpsed in human relationships of reliable love. To a greater or lesser extent, every person engaged in youth ministry knows the compelling witness involved in "being there" for young people. Youth ministry abounds with sagas of important adults who have won youth — who have won *us* — by extraordinary shows of fidelity. I am thinking of the priest who moved to Hell's Kitchen to be closer to the troubled youth he hoped to serve; the new pastor in Austin, Texas, who keeps a standing appointment on Thursday afternoons to play Ultimate Frisbee with teenagers from the high school; the Baptist youth worker in Pretoria who asked a local skater gang to teach him to roller blade and still maintains their trust; the Ohio Sunday school teacher who, after twenty-five years, still sends birthday cards to the sullen teenagers who stonewalled her every Sunday morning for a decade. (Yes, I was one of them.)

On the other hand, one of the most intimidating aspects of youth ministry is the relentless need to "be there" for teenagers who demand our presence if we say we love them. Adolescents do not just drink from our wells; they suck us dry. Young people are so thirsty for God that they absorb every ounce of prayer, love, and energy we have to offer, thinking that our fidelity can suffice for God's. The view that youth ministry is a place where pastoral leaders "do time" until they qualify for "real" ministry is alive and well, thanks to the self-defeating practice of throwing clergy, seminarians, and unsuspecting volunteers with little experience and less support into positions where adolescents, searching for fidelity, demand more than we have to give.

The truth is that none of us can "be there" adequately for young people. Youth ministry is rife with examples of leaders (and resentful offspring) who have sacrificed "being there" for their own children in order to make themselves available for the children of others — as if it were possible to do so enough for any young person. For many youth ministers, "being there" is killing us; unlike the Triune God, we cannot realistically make ourselves available for everyone, adequately, all the time. Research now suggests that youth pastors in the U.S. are staying longer in their positions than we once assumed;[47] yet people in youth ministry are also notorious

47. See Merton Strommen, Karen Jones, and Dave Rahn, *Youth Ministry That Trans-*

for burning out faster than those in other forms of ministry. Dry and depleted, we leave youth ministry sadly, hoping to find someone who will "be there" for us.

What's wrong with this picture? Simply this: we have forgotten that the practices of suffering love that define the Christian life ultimately convey God's fidelity, not ours. The mainline Protestant church has come to think of fidelity as an individual responsibility — as "our" responsibility. *It is not.* It is never "our" fidelity young people seek; our "being there" for adolescents serves as an icon, a smudged window through which they may catch a glimpse of the utter fidelity of God. In fact, fidelity *is never* only an individual responsibility; even the fidelity of God issues in three persons, who demonstrate God's steadfastness in ways unique to the Creator, the Son, and the Holy Spirit.

Fidelity in Youth Ministry:
Beyond the Designated Hitter

Because the adult guarantor plays such a critical role in fostering Christian identity, it is easy to assign the task of "being there" to a few "designated hitters" in the congregation, an assignment doomed to disappoint everyone involved. Despite our best intentions, none of us can incarnate Jesus' promise to young people to be with them always, which is the reason youth ministry is the *church's* ministry, not just that of specialists who can "relate" to young people. The mandate to "be there" for young people belongs to the Christian *community,* not to any individual or group of individuals. In each of the examples of Christian "being there" described at the beginning of this chapter — the congregation that keeps its front doors unlocked, the church that gives keys at confirmation, the coalition of Boston pastors who helped oust drug dealers — fidelity was practiced not only by a few determined leaders but by *congregations,* who revealed their passion for young people in practices and policies that risked on their behalf.

When churches engage in practices of suffering love, they convey Christ's assurance that he will "be there" with them always, making God's fidelity visible in the Christian community. Yet important as it is, fidelity alone is not enough. Passion yearns for something more; the capacity for "being true" must be filled with a content, an ideology in which teenagers

---

forms: A Comprehensive Analysis of the Hopes, Frustrations, and Effectiveness of Today's Youth Workers (Grand Rapids: Youth Specialties/Zondervan, 2001).

can invest their utter, undying devotion. Faith seeks a worthy object — a big enough god, a broad enough reach, a high enough calling — that can provide a springboard for self-transcendence. So now we must ask: even with fidelity in place, can the mainline Protestant church offer young people a god substantive enough to be worth being true *to?*

Chapter Four

LONGING FOR TRANSCENDENCE

If It Feels Good, It Must Be God

*There is this feeling that I had Friday night . . . that I don't
know if I will ever be able to describe except to say that it is
warm. . . . The feeling I had happened when Sam told Patrick
to find a station on the radio. . . . And finally he found this
really amazing song about this boy, and we all got quiet. . . .
After the song finished, I said something. "I feel infinite." And
Sam and Patrick looked at me like I said the greatest thing
they ever heard. Because the song was that great and because
we all really paid attention to it. Five minutes were truly
spent, and we felt young in a good way.*

Charlie, age 14, The Perks of Being a Wallflower[1]

*Passion is the break-through virtue. . . . The Incarnation, the
life of Christ, was the passion of God breaking through decisively.*

William McNamara[2]

---

1. Stephen Chbosky, *The Perks of Being a Wallflower* (New York: MTV/Pocket Books,
1999), 32-33.

2. William McNamara, *Mystical Passion: The Art of Christian Loving* (Rockport,
Mass.: Element Books, 1991), 11.

I just go where the life is, you know? Where I feel the Holy Spirit. If it's in the back of a Roman Catholic cathedral, in the quietness and the incense, which suggest the mystery of God, of God's presence, or in the bright lights of a revival tent, I just go where I find life.

Bono[3]

It could have been any moving worship service organized by a group of Divinity School seniors:

> The hymn done and the bell rung, the liturgy was open to the group. . . . Indeed it was an amazing grace, that grace that passes all understanding. I was moved; I was in communion with everyone else in the room. It was as if, at that moment, all barriers had come down, all suffering had ended, all pain had been relieved, all joys had been known. I forgave the offenses I had suffered and was forgiven for my sins. . . . I was healed. I was strengthened. I was redeemed.

But then the liturgist (who described herself as a shy Episcopalian) for the so-called "Harvard Agape" reflected on its peculiar power:

> As the sacrament slowly wore off, we quieted down a bit. . . . We all took turns sharing something powerful with the group. . . . How easy it is to feel safe in such a setting. MDMA helps tremendously, of course.[4]

The "sacrament" that "wore off" was methylenedioxymethamphetamine — MDMA, or "Ecstasy," a German drug that predates Kaiser Wil-

---

3. Cited in Cathleen Falsani, "Bono's American Prayer," *Christianity Today* (March 2003), http://www.christianitytoday.com/ct/2003/003/2.38, accessed Sept. 26, 2003.

4. "The Harvard Agape" is not, as far as I can tell, acknowledged by official circles within Harvard Divinity School, but is widely quoted in Internet accounts that describe religious uses of Ecstasy. See, for example, "The Harvard Agape: A Harvard Divinity School Graduating Senior Led a Parting Ritual Using Ecstasy in January 1995," available on the website for the Center for Spiritual Practices, www.csp.org/nicholas/A54.html; accessed on 7 December 2002; also Nicholas Saunders, "The Agony and Ecstasy of God's Path," *The Guardian* (July 29, 1995), available at www.ecstasy.org/info/god.html; accessed 7 December 2001; also "Monks Using MDMA as an Aid to Meditation," available at www.newciv.org/GIB/BI/BI-277.HTML; accessed 7 December 2002. For an account of attitudes toward psychoactive drug use in religious ritual, see Nicholas Saunders et al., *In Search of the Ultimate High* (New York: Random House, 2000).

helm but that resurfaced in the 1990s as the club drug of choice for American adolescents.[5] Never mind that the Harvard seminarians mistook artificial stimulants for the Holy Spirit (not unlike centuries of peyote-smoking shamans and inebriated priests). And put aside the fact that most of the world's major religions shun mind-altering substances that manipulate ecstatic experience in God's name. And forget for a moment that, in the United States, most of these substances are illegal anyway.[6] The fact remains that increasing numbers of American adolescents describe the "Ecstasy high" in spiritual terms, touting the drug's "virtues" as self-abandonment, empathy, and a sense of being moved beyond the self's boundaries toward union with others.[7] A Benedictine monk told researchers he believed Ecstasy made prayer easier; he used it to obtain "a very deep comprehension of divine passion," and to open up "a direct link between myself and God."[8] Perhaps the more

---

5. Outlawed in 1985, Ecstasy is commonly associated with "raves," techno-music/dance events accessorized with pacifiers, glow-sticks, and Vicks VapoRub (to open up the nasal passages), where deejays serve as shamans to conjure up a shared experience, or "empathy." Rave regulars cite a common creed: "PLUR" (Peace, Love, Unity and Respect), generated by an intangible pulse (the "vibe") controlled by a deejay, and assisted in no small part by the Ecstasy that flows freely at rave parties. As one young woman told *Time,* "[Ecstasy] makes shirtless, disgusting men, a club with broken bathrooms, a deejay that plays crap and vomiting into a trash can the best night of your life." MDMA has no medical benefit and is not addictive, but it does boost seratonin levels — the body's mood regulator — and a number of deaths have been linked to its use. Some describe Ecstasy as "no different from crack [or] heroin," while others advocate its use for such varied pursuits as treating schizophrenia and contacting dead relatives. Meanwhile, Ecstasy.org publishes gushy testimonies praising MDMA (much of it in awful poetry: "We sing, we laugh, we share/and most of all, we care"). See John Cloud, "The Lure of Ecstasy," *Time,* June 5, 2000, 66.

6. Anthropologists have long observed ritual connections between the life-altering nature of faith and the mind-altering qualities of certain drugs (e.g., peyote, LSD, hallucinogenic mushrooms, etc.), despite the fact that all the world's major religions forbid drug use. Christians, for instance, use wine for communion to connote fire and transformation, key elements of Christian pneumatology, which non-fermented substitutes lack.

7. Compared to other forms of adolescent drug use, Ecstasy use is on the rise. Eight percent of U.S. high school seniors say they have tried ecstasy at least once, up 5.8 percent since 1997 (John Cloud, "The Lure of Ecstasy," *Time,* June 5, 2000, 62-68). Other forms of drug use are declining among 12-17 year olds (9 percent reported illicit drug use in 1999, down from 11.4 percent in 1997), and are increasing among 18-25 year olds (U.S. Department of Health and Human Services, *Youth Today,* October 2000, 8).

8. Saunders, "Monks Using MDMA as an Aid to Meditation"; Thomas Roberts and Paul Jo Hruby, "Religion and Psychoactive Sacraments: An Entheogen Chrestomathy," in Jerome Beck et al., *Exploring Ecstasy: A Description of MDMA Users* (San Francisco: Institute for Scientific Analysis, 1989), available at www.csp.org/chrestomathy/exploring_ecstasy.html; accessed 7 December 2002.

revealing statement came from a rabbi in the same study: "Traditional religions have lost the ability to provide followers with mystical experiences. Instead, young people are far more likely to have such experiences while on LSD and Ecstasy."[9]

The Adolescent Need to Get High(er)

American young people routinely associate the numinous with the language of being "high" — an experience of being temporarily transported beyond our usual boundaries to a new plane of existence. While most young people do not seek a drug-induced euphoria, all adolescents long for a "high" because, points out educator Sharon Daloz Parks, for the first time, they are cognitively capable of it.[10] With the onset of formal operations, adolescents can think reflectively, express themselves extravagantly, and experience both wonder and dread in new, expansive ways. So the adolescent sets out to find a dream, a drug, an experience large enough to fill the existential cavern — Pascal called it a "god-shaped void" — that she suddenly senses yawning within her.

Yet ecstasy — from the Greek *ekstasis,* "outside of time" — can be misleading, even in its natural forms. Adolescents, new to the cognitive skills that allow them to explore emotional terrain, are notorious for making bad judgments on the basis of good feelings. In many ways, affect is the common thread wending its way through the life cycle; children, youth, and adults experience emotions in similar ways. Yet during adolescence, when the onset of formal operational thought bequeaths the capacity to ponder one's inner life, the need for sensation becomes subjected to the young person's newly acquired reflective capacities. As a result, youth become fixated on feelings, evaluating every experience according to its emotional topography: heights and depths, ecstasy and angst, heaven and hell. In short, during adolescence we develop *interiority.* As Parks puts it, "The soul grows larger to allow more space for becoming."[11]

9. Saunders, "Monks Using MDMA as an Aid to Meditation." The rabbi acknowledged that replacing devotion with drugs might be "cheating, but it gets you to the same place."

10. Sharon Daloz Parks, "Faithful Becoming in a Complex World: New Powers, Perils, and Possibilities," *1998 Princeton Lectures on Youth, Church and Culture* (Princeton, N.J.: Princeton Theological Seminary, 1999), 45.

11. Parks, "Faithful Becoming in a Complex World." This quote is from the oral presentation of this lecture (April 1998).

By the late nineteenth century, "establishment" Protestants — still reeling from revivalism's emotional excesses — had become suspicious of emotional terrain in religious expression. As mainline Protestants increasingly aligned themselves with the American middle class, they sought more distance from the demonstrative piety of many marginalized communities where worship offered cathartic release from daily hardship. For most of the twentieth century, except for occasional charismatic "renewal" movements, most Protestants remained content to observe the *mysterium tremendum* from afar. Little has changed; in 1994, according to Barna surveys, more than one-third (34 percent) of churchgoing adults said they had "never" experienced God's presence in worship.[12] In 1962, when cognitive psychologists David and Sally Elkind asked young adolescents where they were most likely to experience God, most of them said, "In a church or synagogue."[13] By 1999, however, only one in seven adolescents believed that participating in a church, synagogue, or other religious group was necessary to being "religious."[14]

The Sensation-alization of Passion

Feelings matter to adolescents. Social scientists record the "sensation-seeking" tendencies of adolescents; the higher a young person's place on the sensation-seeking scale (SSS), the more she is considered to be "at risk."[15] Like the two-year-old who discovers both herself and her world by tasting everything from fingers to fuzz balls, the adolescent probes the larger world now available to her by feeling it first. To be numb is to be dead; so adolescents seek the pulsating sensations of personal experience. The sheer decibel level of adolescence — not to mention the appeal of the gross, the horrific, and the sentimental to youth who otherwise seem to show little emotional range — all find their origins in the adolescent's need to experience herself.

12. George Barna, *Virtual America* (New York: Regal, 1994), 58-59. Another 24 percent say they "rarely" or "sometimes" experience God's presence there, while 27 percent say they "always" experience God's presence in worship.

13. David Elkind and Sally Elkind, "Varieties of Religious Experience in Young Adolescents," *Scientific Study of Religion* 2 (1962): 102-12.

14. George H. Gallup, Jr., *The Spiritual Life of Young Americans: Approaching the Year 2000* (Princeton, N.J.: George H. Gallup International Institute, 1999), 3.

15. For the original development of SSS, see Marvin Zuckerman, "Dimensions of Sensation Seeking," *Journal of Consulting and Clinical Psychology* 36 (February 1971): 45-52.

It has always been thus. Augustine recalled that, as a youth, "I loved to suffer, and sought out occasions for such suffering."[16] Youth still want to suffer in the Augustinian sense, to undergo *pathos,* to be completely affected, to be moved by overwhelming experience — so the louder, the weirder, the wilder, the sadder, the better, or so it seems. Tears are the measure of being passionately affected, and the knowledge that tears can be manipulated does nothing to mitigate their hold on us. We cry out of our desire for pleasure as well as from our desire to release deep pain, and as journalist Deirdre Dolan discovered when she interviewed New York teenagers who had seen the blockbuster *Titanic* ten or more times, teenagers unapologetically seek both.[17] One of the top-grossing films of the twentieth century, *Titanic*'s filmmakers deftly tapped into the adolescent desire for a love worthy of suffering and splashed it across the silver screen. One sixteen-year-old boy told Dolan, "The first time I saw it, I started crying when she jumped off the lifeboat, and the second time I started in the opening credits." Another girl who returned home in uncontrollable sobs reported, "My parents came home and they were like, 'What's wrong? This isn't right!'" Dolan concluded that these youth were clearly enjoying themselves.[18] Teenagers flocked to *Titanic* in true Augustinian style. They sought an occasion to "suffer" — to undergo an experience, to be *totally affected* — and they found that occasion as Jack and Rose laid bare (literally) what every young person desires: a love worthy of suffering.

Tears have always been associated with passion, divine and mortal. Despite our suspicion of crocodile tears, we usually take being "moved to tears" as evidence that we have been seized by something beyond us — maybe even God. Christian monasticism has often viewed tears as a gift from God, or a tribute to God. Thomas à Kempis counseled young monks to seek "the gift of tears"; Francis of Assisi's doctors blamed excess crying for his blindness in old age.[19] For the faithful, religious tears symbolize authenticity: in 1996, CNN reported a twelfth-century painting of Jesus

---

16. Augustine, *Confessions,* trans. Henry Chadwick (Oxford and New York: Oxford University Press, 1991), 37. The use of the word "suffer" recalls its archaic meaning: to undergo or be totally affected by feeling (hence the word "affect"). It is significant that Augustine mentions this desire to suffer in the context of his love for theatre, since movies provide a similar venue for contemporary adolescents.

17. Tom Lutz, *Crying: The Natural and Cultural History of Tears* (New York: W. W. Norton, 1999), 17ff.

18. Deirdre Dolan, "New York's Streetwise Adolescents Drowning in Their *Titanic* Tears," *New York Observer,* February 23, 1998, 1, 12.

19. Lutz, *Crying,* 47.

weeping in Bethlehem; a year earlier the Catholic Church had ordered DNA tests on an Italian statue that had reportedly wept blood.[20] But tears are not reserved for the arcane. When I was twelve, an itinerant gospel quartet in my small church crooned, "Tears are the language that God understands" — and sure enough, by the end of the concert, God was understanding lots of us, including a rail full of sobbing youth. Contrived as it was, it remains my first significant memory of "being moved" (literally, since there was an altar call) by something that *felt* inescapably holy. I felt both ridiculous and radical, as though I stood in a new place — which, of course, I did: American revivalism used altar calls to move people to the altar as a sign of newfound humility before God.

Feeling Our Religion:
The Emotional Topography of Adolescence

Passion deals unapologetically in affect; teenagers demand that religion "move" them. American adolescents (like many adults) go to church to feel moved, to feel changed, to feel God, to feel *something*, because personal experience represents postmodernity's one undisputed test of truth. Theologically, of course, this is wrong. Worship is for the benefit of God, not primarily for the benefit of teenagers. After all, hunger for visceral personal experience also causes adolescents to drive too fast, to have sex too early, to go to horror movies. The quintessential standard for excellence among adolescents is "Did it *move* me?" If the concert does, and church does not, the concert wins. In the stories that testify to Jesus' "compassion" (com + *passio*), the literal Greek means, "He was moved in his gut," or, less delicately, "His guts turned over inside him."[21] Postmodern young people recognize "moving" experiences — those marked by the heights of ecstasy or the depths of anguish, occasions when their "guts turn over" inside them — as truly authentic, the *sine qua non* of religion. As a result, adolescents tend to consider *any* moving personal experience, from roller coasters to orgasms, potentially "spiritual." Indeed, in both primitive times and in ours, people have often viewed moving experience to be what religion is

---

20. "Jesus Painting Said to Wink and Shed Tears in Bethlehem," *CNN Interactive World News* (November 29, 1996), available at http://www.cnn.com/WORLD/9611/29/weeping.jesus/index.html; accessed on 7 December 2002; see also Lutz, *Crying*, 59.

21. Simon Harak, *Virtuous Passions: The Formation of Christian Character* (New York: Paulist Press, 1993), 4.

for. The degree to which Jesus "moves" us when we practice faith, teenagers believe, is the degree to which Christianity is valid.

In part adolescents' attraction to ecstatic experience — experience that moves them "outside" their accustomed boundaries — can be traced to a modern emphasis on subjectivity. From the beginning, Protestant identity was subjectively gained, not from participation in religious ritual, but from a personal experience of God, a voice that has only been amplified by the postmodern accent on personal experience. Increasingly, we not only use our "feelings" to justify our artistic preferences ("I like it") but also, less reliably, to justify our behavior ("I felt like it") and our ethical choices ("It felt right").[22] As globalization dislocates young people from communities with shared value systems that once provided objective boundaries for the self, mobility and placelessness become standard. God, too, appears homeless, often operating outside traditional venues of religious institutions. Today God "happens" wherever God is "felt." As a result, notes sociologist Wade Clark Roof, contemporary young people tend to view life as a spiritual quest in which the destination is unimportant; what matters is the experience of the journey.[23]

Make That to Go: The Adolescent Need for Locomotion

Adolescent attraction to ecstasy is more than a byproduct of culture; ecstasy provides evidence of the human desire to shape identity around a source of ultimate meaning. The need to get beyond the boundaries of self — the wish, as Erikson put it, *"to break through to a provider of identity"*[24] — is part of adolescents' standard psychological circuitry. In a much overlooked portion of his work on identity formation, Erikson observed that the adolescent craving for "locomotion" causes young people to seek ways to be moved both physically and existentially.[25] Young people are constantly "on

22. Robert Coles, *Girl Scouts Survey on the Beliefs and Moral Values of America's Children* (New York: Louis Harris and Associates, 1989).

23. Wade Clark Roof, "Today's Spiritual Quests," *1997 Princeton Lectures on Youth, Church and Culture* (Princeton, N.J.: Princeton Theological Seminary, 1998), 93-102. Roof cites current models of automobiles as evidence of the pervasiveness of the "journey" metaphor in North American culture. Advertisers promote cars named Trek, Voyager, Explorer, Quest, Pathfinder; Nissan recently advertised under the slogan: "Life is a journey. Enjoy the ride."

24. Erik H. Erikson, *Insight and Responsibility* (New York: W. W. Norton, 1964), 66.

25. Erikson, *Identity, Youth and Crisis* (New York: W. W. Norton, 1968), 243.

the go"; they take drugs to "get high" or "take a trip"; they "lose themselves" in sports or dance or music; they are "swept off their feet" by romance and they "get a rush" from fast cars, extreme physical challenges, or lightning-paced action movies.[26] *Wanderlust* does not drive the adolescent desire for "locomotion" as much as the human need to break through the self's boundaries to be "transported" to a new place, from which they may glimpse a larger, more encompassing world that invites their participation.

Young people are moved by totalities that transcend their daily fragmentation and make them feel whole. If God is "whatever moves me," then any transporting experience — from orgasm to thrill seeking to dropping acid — feels "spiritual," at least temporarily. Rapt conversation, joining social movements, music, mystical experience, "making a difference," even worship all factor into the range of experiences youth broadly describe as "spiritual." The life-and-death language of adolescents — slang that is surprisingly resistant to generational change — speaks to their compulsion to live between ultimate limits:[27]

Surprise:	"It blew me away."
Dread:	"I would die if . . ."
Worry:	"My mom's going to kill me."
Admiration:	"She is drop dead gorgeous"; "He's to die for"; "It's killer."

Passion must *feel* like life and death — nothing less — or it is not passion.

26. Erikson cautioned against technology's tendency to delude us with "pseudo-locomotion," which he blamed for many "adolescent outbursts." "In connection with immature youth, it must be understood that both motor car and motion pictures offer to those so inclined passive locomotion with an intoxicating delusion of being intensely active. . . . While vastly inflating a sense of motor omnipotence, the need for active locomotion often remains unfulfilled." (Think what he might have had to say about video games.) Genuine transcendence points beyond the boundaries of self to a broader vision "beyond" in which youth are called to play an active part. Erikson, *Identity, Youth and Crisis*, 244.

27. Thomas J. Cottle calls this generationally consistent language pattern "scarification," or "self-inflicted wounds, suicidal but exhilarating, and somehow bringing one in closer touch with the others still in an extended moment of immaculate separation. And everything comes to be a dance of death: the mind as the womb and the flooding out or wretched trip as the miscarriage or abortion. The child's death is seen and felt before the child's birth. . . . Mental illness [the sense of 'going crazy'] and death [words that have to do with death] are the painful and presumably pleasurable ways this small but enlarging group of students deal with the problems of intimacy and the knowledge of others." See "The Connections of Adolescence," in *Twelve to Sixteen: Early Adolescence*, ed. J. Kagan and R. Coles, (New York: W. W. Norton, 1972), 333.

The chemical connection to the adolescent need for ecstasy has been explained as a need for self-transcendence that stimulates the neurological overflow leading to the feelings we associate with passion. In studies on gestalts — experiences in which our inner "mazeways," or ways of understanding, are transformed — researchers located the neurological activity associated with passion and ecstasy in the autonomic nervous system. Normally, the left side of the brain (the side that governs our ability to accomplish tasks and goals) and the right side of the brain (the side that governs maintenance functions like sleep and hunger) do a reciprocal, balanced "dance": when one system is stimulated, the other shuts off, and vice versa. However, continued, intensified stimulation of one system generates passion by strengthening that system so much that the opposite system cannot shut it down. In fact, stimulating the opposite system only activates the first system further. When both systems start firing at once, conditions are created for an ecstatic or even trance-like state that allows the brain to hold contradictory ideas together in a "dialectical identity" — including the paradoxes of faith like suffering and love, death and resurrection. This identity is "the culmination of the overflow of two systems, as if the imagination had finally managed to create a world that embraced the flow of passion."[28]

So as it turns out, the "spiritual high" sought by Christian teenagers is more than just a convenient analogy. Researchers at McLean Hospital in Boston discovered that when passion overflows the brain's mazeways, individuals experience five results, reminiscent of the "high" adolescents seek by taking Ecstasy or other psychotropic drugs: (1) a loss of the fear of death; (2) a sense of unity with others who have shared the experience; (3) a new sense of knowledge; (4) the return of the reciprocal, balanced "dance" between brain systems; and (5) self-transcendence. The sum of these sensations is an overwhelming sense of inner coherence that defies verbal expression. When such experiences overtake us — when they *completely affect* us — explanations evaporate. The only response is awe.[29]

---

28. The research of Barbara Lex and her colleagues is reported in James E. Loder and W. Jim Neidhardt, *The Knight's Move: The Relational Logic of the Spirit in Theology and Science* (Colorado Springs: Helmers and Howard, 1992), 270-73.

29. Loder and Niedhardt, *Knight's Move*, 273.

Intuitive Orthodoxy

The mystery of God addresses the adolescent's need for "locomotion" — the need to be moved ecstatically beyond the boundaries of the self to a posture of awe. Postmodern young people do not view mystery as a problem to be solved as much as a truth to be revealed in the course of human experience. Suffering love is a paradox, but this does not invalidate it for teenagers. On the contrary, for them passion is a sign of God's authenticity, a truth so valid that painstaking explanation would eviscerate it. While Christians in generations past appreciated the safe distance of mediated mystery, relying on the traditions of a community to convey God's presence, postmodern youth believe they can best apprehend divine mystery through events of *personal* significance — signs, symbols, and community actions related to the young person's own history. If God "happens," then God can only be grasped by experiencing what God *does* — especially, thinks the teenager, what God does to *me.*

In his analysis of Karl Barth's importance for the postmodern church, William Stacy Johnson argues that understanding God through what God *does* in human history is a profoundly orthodox point of view. The mystery of God became transparent in a personal event: the life and death of Jesus Christ; "God is as Jesus is; God acts as Jesus acts."[30] The Incarnation opens the door to a subjective and personal apprehension of God. Young people avow that knowing a person means more than knowing *about* that person; it means knowing the *truth* of a person. To know Jesus means to know him *personally,* to judge his authenticity based upon his interaction with them and their communities.

If, as Johnson puts it, the biblical story is not "a theological resting place," the truth of God's personal interaction does not stop with the biblical record. Johnson cites Barth here: "The truth demands complete openness. From the standpoint of the truth itself, thoroughgoing conservatives are as useless as thoroughgoing modernists."[31] Adolescents reject the postmodern assumption that there is no such thing as truth. The problem is not that there is no truth, but that there are so *many* truths to choose from. The test of postmodern faith is discerning which truth matters *most* — a judgment that

---

30. William Stacy Johnson, *The Mystery of God: Karl Barth and the Postmodern Foundations of Theology* (Louisville: Westminster/John Knox Press, 1997), 45.

31. Karl Barth, *Church Dogmatics* II/2, ed. G. W. Bromiley and T. F. Torrance (Edinburgh: T&T Clark, 1957), 648.

cannot be made simply by saying so. Rather, truth inevitably is discovered in the personal invitation "Come and see" (John 1:39, 46).[32]

In Search of an Awesome God:
Youth and the *Mysterium Tremendum*

While he was in seminary, Charles Atkins — now a pastor and hip-hop recording artist working with incarcerated teenagers — produced an MTV-style video of a song he wrote based on Ecclesiastes. The video referred to Ecclesiastes by its Hebrew name, Qoheleth. When I asked him why, Charles explained: "A lot of the kids in the neighborhood where I work are turning to Islam. In African-American culture, even kids who don't go to church have heard Christianity from their grandmothers' knees. It's old school. Islam feels exotic, mysterious, strange. If Christianity was going to register with these kids, I needed to 'make it strange.'"

Perhaps religion's distinct contribution to postmodern adolescent consciousness resides in its potential "strangeness." Nearly a century ago, in the intoxicating heyday of scientific rationalism, Rudolf Otto argued that "the holy" is a strange category peculiar to the sphere of religion. Otto believed that the "numinous" cannot be taught, only "evoked, awakened in the mind; as everything that comes 'of the spirit' must be awakened."[33] The holy, he avowed, is a mystery; and as a mystery, it must be *experienced* as present; it must be *felt*. "There must be felt a something 'numinous,'" he wrote, "something bearing the character of a 'numen' to which the mind turns spontaneously.... The numinous is thus felt as objective and outside the self."[34]

In other words, the holy — what Otto called the *mysterium tremendum* — is "strange" in that it cannot be unfolded or explicated, yet in an "overabounding," "exuberant," "mystical moment," it unites us ecstatically with a reality that lies "beyond." The *mysterium tremendum* emphasizes

---

32. Johnson, *The Mystery of God*, 189.

33. Rudolf Otto, *The Idea of the Holy*, trans. John W. Harvey (New York: Oxford University Press, 1958), 7.

34. Otto, *The Idea of the Holy*, 11. See Bernhard Lang, *Sacred Games: A History of Christian Worship* (New Haven: Yale University Press, 1997). Lang contrasts Otto's emphasis on a majestic, superior God that issues in "numinous" worship with "the friendly God [who] stands at the top of a great chain of benign beings," which Lang sees in ecstatic, charismatic worship and Catholic renewal movements that emphasize egalitarian relationships between clerics and laity and that, according to Andrew Greeley, tend to imagine God as "mother, lover, spouse and friend" (Lang, *Sacred Games*, 421-22).

God's awe and majesty — but this majesty must be grasped subjectively, even ecstatically, by human feelings evoked by the signs, symbols, and stories of "numinous" worship. For this reason, Otto believed the key to understanding the *mysterium tremendum* was Christ's agony, or passion. The agony of Gethsemane was more than the fear of death; it was "the awe of the creature before the *mysterium tremendum,* before the shuddering secret of the numen."[35]

Casper Doesn't Live Here Anymore

Youth ministry is often (justly) critiqued for espousing a simplistic "Jesus-the-friendly-ghost" theology that springs from the interpersonal needs of adolescents themselves, not the pages of Scripture. Yet while youth ministry may nurse "buddy theologies" uncritically, adolescents themselves respond to far more complex renderings of God. Young people do cling to a familiar Jesus, but not at the expense of God's mystery. If anything, their refusal to equate otherness with distance magnifies the Chalcedonian formula, "truly God and truly man." God is the divine mystery who ecstatically reaches toward them in passion, and the human mystery in whom joy and suffering, life and death cohere. The postmodern inclination to conceptualize truth in terms of paradox — "both/and" rather than "either/or" — embraces the three persons of the Trinity as *both* the source of ecstatic unity *and* the source of differentiated identity, as *both* a tremendous mystery *and* (as we will explore in more detail in Chapter Five) an intimate friend.

In short, the holy life never appeals to young people because our curriculum urges them to reach for God (in case you hadn't noticed); they are instead drawn to the holy life because God reaches for *them,* has become one *of* them, has entered the world *with* them in ways that become perceptible in the Christian community. To call the death of Jesus an ecstatic event, then, is not to reduce it to a feeling, but to proclaim that, in Christ, God is moving in the world: God has reached beyond God's own self to identify with that part of human existence that sits farthest from God — death. God's ecstatic reach bursts the Temple veil like a cosmic amniotic sac, announcing: "God is on the loose!"[36] God's passion has overflowed, never to

---

35. Otto, *The Idea of the Holy,* 84.

36. Thanks to my late colleague Don Juel for pointing me (passionately) in this exegetical direction. See Donald H. Juel, *A Master of Surprise: Mark Interpreted* (Mifflintown, Pa.: Sigler, 2002), 107-46.

be contained behind a curtain in church or cajoled by an altar call or cornered in a lesson plan. God tears the Temple veil, not because we can magically now come to God, but because the Holy Spirit has come to *us* — ready or not. This is no chummy deity, and youth know it. One of the anthems of Christian adolescents in the 1990s was Rich Mullins' "Awesome God," a song written in a minor key, rife with unapologetic anthropomorphism, but with no "buddy theology" in sight:

> When he rolls up his sleeves he ain't just putting on the ritz —
> Our God is an awesome God.
> There's thunder in his footsteps and lightning in his fists —
> Our God is an awesome God.
> Well, the Lord he wasn't joking when he kicked 'em out of Eden,
> It wasn't for no reason that he shed his blood.
> His return is very close and so you better be believing that
> Our God is an awesome God.
>
> Our God is an awesome God,
> [Who] reigns from heaven above
> With wisdom, power and love —
> Our God is an awesome God![37]

For adolescents, a personal experience of awesomeness is no oxymoron; in reaching beyond themselves toward God they discover that that God has already reached for them. By extending the divine reach to humanity in the life, death, and resurrection of Jesus Christ, God invites young people's own ecstatic reach in return. As they tentatively stretch toward Jesus and others, youth find themselves pulled beyond their comfort zones into the larger, awe-filled world.

The Way of Ecstasy: Shared Superabundance

Ecstatic expressions of divine love cannot be co-opted as "tools" for youth ministry. Manipulating adolescents to respond to encounters with divine ecstasy in prescribed ways — that is, shutting down on the possibility that they may, reasonably, run from it — smothers transcendence, refuses entry to the *mysterium tremendum*. The proper human response to God's startling movement towards us is awe. Ecstasy "provides a mystical experi-

---

37. The male language is original.

ence that draws us beyond the self, outside of time," into communion with others, notes theologian Catherine Mowry LaCugna, in her analysis of the economic Trinity.[38] In mystical Christianity, this "leaving of oneself" is called "the way of ecstasy," and constitutes the precondition for knowledge of God and union with God.[39] LaCugna finds the ecstasy of God best expressed in the Trinity, the location of God's *pathos,* and emphasizes God's suffering as a vulnerable lover who delights in and is willingly overcome by the beloved, overfull with creative, redeeming, "self-donating" love. Drawing on the Cappadocian use of *eros* for the love that is the soul's ecstasy, she describes God's "fecundity," which issues in a single ecstatic self-communication:

> God goes forth from God, God creates the world, God suffuses its history and dwells within it, redeeming the world from within. God makes an eternal gift to the world of God's very self. Through the outpouring of God into our hearts as love, we become by grace what God is already by nature, namely, self-donating love for the other.[40]

For LaCugna, God's self-giving love so leaps outward that it spills over boundaries, and therefore sweeps us, the beloved, into its bounty. "The centrifugal movement of divine love," she concludes, "does not terminate 'within' God but explodes outward."[41]

LaCugna does not employ the term "passion," but her sympathy with Eastern Orthodox trinitarian thought helps her capture the ecstasy of God's self-communication, implicit in the tradition of *pathos* as God's longing for creation that "explodes outward" in Jesus Christ.[42] Traces of this di-

---

38. LaCugna collapses immanent and economic Trinities into one, a position that differs from the one espoused here.

39. "The 'way of ecstasy' refers to the union of a human person with God," notes LaCugna. See Catherine Mowry LaCugna, *God for Us* (San Francisco: HarperSanFrancisco, 1993), 351.

40. LaCugna, *God for Us,* 353-54.

41. LaCugna, *God for Us,* 353-54. The absence of the term "passion" in LaCugna's work on the Trinity may partly be attributed to her tendency to overlook God's suffering in the event of the cross.

42. While Moltmann acknowledges a "double meaning" of Christian passion that includes both compassionate suffering with one another and passionate love for one another (Moltmann, *Trinity and the Kingdom* [Minneapolis: Fortress Press, 1993], 60), God's affection is not central to Moltmann's thinking, especially in Moltmann's early work. Moltmann seems to want to avoid portraying God's willing passivity in love. Yet by shortchanging divine exuberance, he risks portraying God's love as joyless, constraining God's ability to delight in the beloved, making the Father's love for the Son seem, for lack of a better phrase,

vine imprint are visible in human beings in many ways, observes LaCugna: in the dynamism of the mind toward truth and of the heart toward union; in the toward-the-other character of sexuality; in the life of selfless sacrifice and service; in creativity and fecundity; in the worship of God.[43] "Divine relationality becomes the paradigm for every type of relationality in creation," claims LaCugna. "And, every type of created relationality insinuates divine relationality."[44] In other words, God's ecstatic movement toward us is normative for adolescents' passionate desire to move, and to be moved, toward others.

Christianity's outward reach, therefore, provides the ecstatic thrust passion requires. Youth are quick to notice its absence in the church, quick to recognize the inwardness and awelessness of self-preservation. More and more, observes theologian Rosemary Haughton, Christians are discovering that they cannot discern in the methods of the modern church "the genuine passionate thrust of God's love toward humankind. The only kind of involvement that seems to have meaning is involvement with the ones who suffer."[45] Without passion, ministry has no thrust, no impulse to

---

discouragingly "neat." Moltmann does not intend to imprison God in a tidy rationality; he gropes for an image that will allow him to break free of the predictability with which he presents God's loving self-disclosure: "In the love which God is already lies the energy which leads God out of himself — and in that energy the longing, to use [Nikolai Berdyaev's] word. Love not only has the potentiality for this, but the actual tendency and intention as well" (*Trinity and the Kingdom*, 58). The fact that Moltmann is attracted to Berdyaev's term "longing" is a clue that Moltmann wants to acknowledge the affective dimensions of passion more fully. In his later work, Moltmann becomes increasingly explicit about God's deep-seated passion that begets God's passionate love: "Anyone who denies movement in the divine nature also denies the divine Trinity. And to deny this is really to deny the whole Christian faith. . . . This movement in God is made possible and determined by the fact that 'in the depth of that life emerges the divine mystery, the inner suffering thirst of the Godhead, its inner longing for its "Other," which for God is capable of being the object of the highest, most boundless love.' In his heart God has this passionate longing, not just for any, random 'Other' but for *his* Other — . . . and that is man, his 'image'" (Nicolai Berdyaev, *The Meaning of History* [London: ET Geoffrey Bles and Scribner's, 1939], 48; cited in *Trinity and the Kingdom*, 45). God could have been self-sufficient without creation, but chose not to be; therefore, God is not defined by God's relationship with humans, but by God's *desire* for those relationships, a yearning for community realized in God's own self as well as in God's love for creation. *Because* God is love, God desires a reciprocal relationship with creation, and this brings the Godhead both pain and joy. As a result, we can say that God's relationality reveals God's passion. As Moltmann puts it, "God suffers with us — God suffers from us — God suffers for us: it is this experience of God that reveals the triune God" (*The Trinity and the Kingdom*, 4).

43. LaCugna, *God for Us*, 352.
44. LaCugna, *God for Us*, 168.
45. Rosemary Haughton, *The Passionate God* (Ramsey, N.J.: Paulist Press, 1981), 305.

move beyond comfortable boundaries, no desire to share Jesus' self-giving love with those who suffer. Without ecstasy, the church lacks the voice of angels, as Peter Berger describes it, that calls us to rise above time and space, join hands, and fix our gaze on God.[46] In short, for the church to be sufficiently "radically Christian" requires an ecstatic movement — a leap of faith — beyond the self toward others, and ultimately toward God.

Weaving the "Canopy of Significance"

If fidelity is the strength of having something "to die for," ideology is the content of that fidelity, the substance of adolescent faith. Without an ideological commitment, Erikson warns, "youth suffers a *confusion of values* which can be specifically dangerous to some but which on a large scale is surely dangerous to the fabric of society."[47] Ideologies have compelling power, giving structure to the world and projecting a "vague inner evil" on society while promising to involve the youth in redeeming it.[48] Explicitly or implicitly, for better or for worse, ideologies function as divine authorities in our lives, which means that *which* ideology inspires our allegiance matters enormously. After many false starts, the adolescent soon discovers than not just any ideology will do; not all truths are equally trustworthy, not all causes are "to die for," not all gods offer a fidelity that invites our own. The practice of sorting out the sacred from the profane, the gods from the idols assumes critical importance during adolescence.[49] Drawing on H. Richard Niebuhr, Sharon Daloz Parks maintains that the true test of an adequate ideology is to ask, "What does your chosen god do in the face of being totally overcome — what does it do in the face of shipwreck?" Only a *transcendent* ideology is up to the task of integrating the self in the face of shipwreck — Paul's term (and Niebuhr's term) for the devastation that occurs when everything we believe in hits the rocks.[50] Not every ob-

---

46. Peter Berger, *A Rumor of Angels: Modern Society and the Rediscovery of the Supernatural* (Garden City, N.Y.: Doubleday, 1969), 78.

47. Erikson, *Identity, Youth and Crisis,* 188.

48. Erikson, *Identity, Youth and Crisis,* 189.

49. Without a way to navigate diverse claims on the self, Erikson warned, identity would collapse under "empty relativism" (Erikson, *Identity, Youth and Crisis,* 245). Similarly, H. Richard Niebuhr notes, "The necessity of believing in a god is given within the life of selves, but what gods are dependable, which of them can be counted on day after day and which are idols — products of erroneous imagination — cannot be known save for the experiences of inner history." Niebuhr, *The Meaning of Revelation* (New York: Collier Books, 1941), 58-59.

50. Cf. 1 Tim. 1:19.

ject can anchor the *pathos* of human existence. Consequently, it matters to what — or to whom — youth surrender themselves, and often it matters desperately.

The adolescent search for transcendence is both developmentally necessary and spiritually essential. The process of identifying with others in search of an ideology that "fits" allows adolescents to retain an openness to transcendence — a predisposition toward ecstasy — that can elude adults with more fixed ideological boundaries. When threatened, of course, adolescents (like adults) clamp down on their openness to others; since young people frequently feel threatened by the juggernaut of global culture, we sometimes experience them as ideologically airtight containers, zealously protecting whatever shred of identity they currently possess. Yet young people seek self-transcendence instinctively and incessantly. Without it, no ideology coheres and no identity can take root.

Parks calls the task of choosing an adequate ideology "weaving a *canopy of significance*" that embraces, orders, and relativizes all of our knowing and being. In the midst of swirling alternatives, every young person must somehow catch hold of what Parks calls a "worthy dream," and claim a trustworthy truth on which to set her heart.[51] This truth lies at the core of a worthy ideology, but the challenge is how to discern which of the information age's endless threads of meaning constitute sturdy fibers for a durable canopy. "One gives one's heart only to that which one 'sees' as adequate, trustworthy, and promising," Parks cautions.[52] Adequate ideologies tackle questions of shipwreck: What is worth living for? What is worth dying for? What shall I throw overboard? To what shall I cling? As Parks puts it, "Is there a pattern of meaning, a faith, that can survive the defeat of finite centers of power, value, and affection?"[53] An ideology devoted to a child, a single cause, or an aspiration is too small to function as God. If the child dies, if the popularity comes to an end, if an injury forecloses on the hoped-for ath-

---

51. Sharon Daloz Parks, *Big Questions, Worthy Dreams* (San Francisco: Jossey-Bass, 2000), 5.

52. Parks, *Big Questions, Worthy Dreams*, 24. Parks interprets this as part of the young adult quest, not part of the adolescent one. I find a more credible case to be made where adolescence extends through young adulthood, since the third decade of life normally involves the consolidation of identity, and since early versions of the search for fidelity and ideology may be discerned in early formal operational thought. Normally, fidelity and ideology cannot be fully addressed until the third decade, when we can more reliably depend on a particular "canopy of meaning," allowing ourselves to become guardians of other people's identities instead of our own. At this point we begin to make the transition into adulthood proper.

53. Parks, *Big Questions, Worthy Dreams*, 22.

letic career, do self, world, and God collapse? Does fidelity vanish? In short, does the substance of our faith allow us to experience pain without collapsing beneath its weight — and at the same time reach beyond devastation toward a transcendent source of hope and redemption?

If not, our god is too small. Weaving a canopy of significance amounts to a process of conversion, "setting our hearts" on what Niebuhr called a "radical monotheism": faith in the "One *beyond* the many." For postmodern youth who crave transcendence amidst a glut of truth claims, "radical monotheism" has fresh relevance, not because they have no other gods to choose from but because they have so many to choose from. Only a transcendent God rises above the rest, stays afloat in shipwreck, and carries us to shore.

Sagging Canopies:
Lowering the Bar of Transcendence

When social critic David Brooks compared Princeton University students in 2001 to their counterparts before World War I — an era when F. Scott Fitzgerald, John Foster Dulles, James Forrestal, and Adlai Stevenson were Princeton undergraduates, carving their names in tables of the Tap Room in the Nassau Inn — transcendence figured prominently into the university curriculum. So, of course, did classism, racism, sexism, and anti-Semitism, so Brooks's essay was not an argument for returning to the "good old days." But he noted a stark difference between their educational philosophy and ours: "The most striking contrast between that elite and this one is that its members were relatively unconcerned with academic achievement but went to enormous lengths to instill character. We, on the other hand, place enormous emphasis on achievement but are tongue-tied and hesitant when it comes to what makes for a virtuous life."[54]

In the early twentieth century, according to Brooks, students were "compelled by the knightly spirit." This was no accident: the university unapologetically sought to instill in them a sense of chivalry. Listen to university president John Hibben's commencement address to the Class of 1913:

> You, enlightened, self-sufficient, self-governed, endowed with gifts above your fellows . . . the world commands you to take your place and

54. David Brooks, "The Organization Kid," *Atlantic Monthly,* April 2001, 50.

to fight your fight in the name of honor and chivalry, against the powers of organized evil and of commercialized vice, against the poverty, disease, and death which follow fast in the wake of sin and ignorance, against all the innumerable forces which are working to destroy the image of God in man. . . . Such is your vocation; follow the voice that calls you in the name of God. . . . The time is short, the opportunity is great; therefore, crowd the hours with the best that is in you.[55]

Somehow, notes Brooks, students raised on such exhortations absorbed the sense that life is a noble mission, a perpetual war against sin, and "the choices we make have consequences not just in getting a job or a law-school admission but in some grand battle between lightness and dark."[56]

Today, however, "there's pretty much a self-conscious attempt *not* to instill character" as part of the university curriculum, says Jeffrey Herbst, professor of political science in Princeton's Woodrow Wilson School of Public and International Affairs. Brooks concluded that the "Class of 2001" reflected "the best of America. . . . They are responsible. They are generous. They are bright. But," he added,

they live in a country that has lost, in its frenetic seeking after happiness and success, the language of sin and character-building through combat with sin. Evil is seen as something that can be cured with better education, or therapy, or Prozac. Instead of virtue we talk about accomplishment.[57]

Maybe, Brooks wonders, the simple truth is that we no longer try to talk about character and virtue because we simply do not know what to say.[58]

Self-transcendence once figured prominently into the mission of higher education (the word "higher" not being accidental). Private schools like Harvard (motto: "For the glory of Christ" until 1843, when it was changed to "Veritas," or truth) as well as public schools like the University of California (motto: "Let there be light") unabashedly claimed a role in helping students wed their ideologies to a sense of higher purpose. At Princeton — where the seldom-translated motto on the university seal, *Vitam Mortuis Reddo* means "To Restore Life to the Dead" (and is portrayed over an open Bible) — young people still have difficulty hoisting

55. Cited in Brooks, "The Organization Kid," 53.
56. Brooks, "The Organization Kid," 52.
57. Brooks, "The Organization Kid," 54.
58. Brooks, "The Organization Kid," 53.

their canopies high enough to make raising the dead look more compelling than a Rhodes Scholarship or acceptance into medical school.

In contemporary culture's preoccupation with self-fulfillment, young people risk losing the sense that life is a noble mission on behalf of a greater good. Gone is the sense that they have a part to play in a cosmic battle between light and dark; that faith is about life and death; that *something is at stake* — and that society is duty-bound not only to acknowledge adolescent passion, but to cultivate it by stoking the fires of a grand sense of purpose. What might Brooks have found if he profiled the class of 2002 — the students graduating in the spring following terrorist attacks on New York City and Washington, D.C. — and compared them to the class of 1914, the year World War I erupted? Would students graduating today have the moral fortitude — indeed, the theological stomach — demanded of their forebears, who were called to confront evil and not just a bad day at the Dow?

Uncontained Passion:
A Worshipping View of the Self

Even with straight A's from Princeton, achievement cannot support a sagging canopy of significance. How, then, do we become part of God's ecstasy and help adolescents hoist their canopies upon Christ's Passion that reaches out toward God and others? LaCugna's answer is through praise — which is always directed toward the other, not the self, and which always creates communion between creature and creator:

> Praise is the creature's mode of *ecstasis,* its own self-transcendence, its disinclination to remain self-contained. The creature's doxology is evoked by God's *ecstasis,* God's glorification in the economy. Praise is the mode of return, "matching" God's movement of exodus. God creates out of glory, for glory. The return is part of the rhythm of life from God to God. In that communion of love is gathered all religious endeavor.[59]

Theologian David F. Ford demurely considers this human "disinclination to remain self-contained" to be evidence of "the worshipping self" — the self shaped by participating in God's "logic of superabundance" through

---

59. LaCugna, *God for Us,* 350.

the primary discourse of praise. "In praising," (Ford quotes Paul Ricoeur here) "one rejoices over the view of one object set above all the other objects of one's concern."[60] If a perichoretic view of the self enables adolescents to attain a differentiated unity, a worshipping view of the self allows young people to enjoy the focus of a "radical monotheism" — an orientation that unites the fragments of their existence around a god who matters most, who stands "beyond" all other gods, and who is therefore worthy of praise.

To worship God is to refuse to contain ourselves: worship enjoins us to the mystery of God and gives us an identity that is entwined with others.[61] Worship remakes us in practices like praise, sacrifice, and Eucharist that radically affirm us as valuable in God's eyes, and invite us to stretch beyond our comfort zones, reaching into the mystery of God and others.[62] As the Father ecstatically sends forth the Son and Holy Spirit into the world, worship provides adolescents a way of "return." In "returning" to God through praise, young people can attempt to match — however imperfectly — God's ecstatic movement toward them by reaching back toward God.

God's Boundary Issues

David Tracy reminds us that finding an "ultimate limit" to our human existence evokes the experience of religiousness, whether in the form of guilt, awareness of death, ecstatic love, or joy.[63] In the horrific aftermath of September 11, 2001, many Americans confronted shipwreck for the first time. On one level, God's ecstasy seemed impossibly far away from such gut-wrenching pain. On the other hand, as a nation, our guts turned over inside us; we did not remember the last time we were so moved. After September 11, young people — all people — were moved to *do* things: post flyers, donate blood, raise money, create shrines, cheer firefighters, visit neighbors,

---

60. Paul Ricoeur, *Figuring the Sacred* (Minneapolis: Fortress Press, 1995), 317, cited by David F. Ford, *Self and Salvation: Being Transformed* (Cambridge: Cambridge University Press, 1999), 98.

61. An identity based in worship cannot be understood apart from community of worship that testifies to God, retelling the past in light of new urgencies, reimagining the God of the past. See Ford, *Self and Salvation,* 99-100.

62. Ford, *Self and Salvation,* 100.

63. David Tracy, *Blessed Rage for Order: The New Pluralism in Theology* (New York: Seabury, 1978), 105.

worship God. People who wouldn't be caught dead at a tent revival flocked to makeshift altars during the week of the attacks, praying, lighting candles, receiving oil in spontaneous prayer services. To pray alone was to do something, but somehow to be physically *moved* when we worshipped together felt like we were doing more.

Days like September 11 underscore the mysterious authenticity of suffering that moves us to reach ecstatically "outside of time," beyond the boundaries of self towards others. The question at hand — for youth and for all of us — is whether our faith can withstand this kind of shipwreck. Is our God big enough? Is it true, as some have argued, that we live in an age of "shrinking transcendence" — that the resources of faith have been depleted by a secular age, and that all that remains for Christians is the moral pursuit of a good society?[64] Has our "canopy of significance" sagged so low that we cannot stand tall beneath it? Or can the God whose passion burst into human history walk through the valley of the shadow of death and rise above it, transcend it, and embrace it — and us — in a reality that is larger still?

Contemporary young people will not be "faked out" by a flannel-board Jesus and a flock of felt sheep. Even in a media culture that reduces awe to special effects, youth still seek the glory of the *mysterium tremendum,* a sense of the "numinous" that confirms their intuition that "the truth is out there" — and it's enormous. Young people look to the church for the high poles of passion that support a canopy of significance that will rise above the storm. But weaving this canopy requires durable fibers: practices that bear witness to the mystery of God, the proclamation of a God who is big enough, holy enough, awesome enough to reach out while at the same time, as Chapter Five suggests, being intimate enough to reach in.

64. See Ronald H. Cram, "The Future of Christian Religious Education in an Era of Shrinking Transcendence," *Religious Education* 96 (Spring 2001): 164-74. Cram critiques practice-based views of Christian education as being too insular, unlikely to "have a significant public voice" (p. 171). I disagree; an adequate understanding of Christian practice inevitably enacts the self-giving love of God in the public sphere, albeit in ways likely to be deemed dangerously countercultural.

Chapter Five

LONGING FOR COMMUNION

If It's Sex, It Must Be Love

*Every lived moment can be lived in the inconceivable close-
ness of God in the spirit: Interior intimo meo, said Augustine
— God is closer to me than I am to myself.*

Jürgen Moltmann[1]

*The primary and irreducible proposition about human be-
ings . . . is that "We all desire to be desired by the one we desire." . . . The only serious form of the religious question today
is: . . . "Am I a source of delight to the Source of my delight?"*

John McDargh[2]

*Communion with Jesus means becoming like him. With him
we are nailed on the cross, with him we are laid in the tomb,
with him we are raised up to accompany lost travelers on their
journey. Communion, becoming Christ, leads us to a new*

1. Jürgen Moltmann, *The Spirit of Life: A Universal Affirmation* (Minneapolis: Fortress, 2001), 35.
2. John McDargh, "Desire, Domination, and the Life and Death of the Soul," in Richard K. Fenn and Donald Capps, eds., *On Losing the Soul: Essays in the Social Psychology of Religion* (Albany: State University of New York Press, 1995), 226. Cited by Robert C. Dykstra,
"Wedding of the Waters: Pastoral Theological Reflections on the Self," *International Journal
of Practical Theology* 3 (Walter de Gruyter, 1999), 251.

> *realm of being. It ushers us into the Kingdom. There we be-*
> *long to Christ and Christ to us, and with Christ we belong to*
> *God.*
>
> Henri Nouwen[3]

On my very first lock-in as a youth leader, I pulled Paul and Janie out of the same sleeping bag. "But we were praying!" Janie blubbered. Right.

Maybe it was true. If desire represents the primary theological lens of adolescence, then the human desire for "otherness" is not simply or even primarily the foundation for sexual intercourse; it is the impetus for life with God, marking human beings among all creation as those God desires for companionship. Desire, therefore, serves as the foundation for Christian spirituality, and for the communion that stands at the heart of Christian life. Even the word "intercourse" — look it up — means "communion" or "connection." After all, Intercourse, Pennsylvania, an Amish town near my home, was not named for conjugal pleasure. It was named for two roads that intersect in the middle of town.[4]

Then there is sex.

Of the various dimensions of passion, the desire for communion — a yearning for union with the source of our delight — is by far the best publicized among adolescents. Communion (literally, *oneness with* another) is closely related to both fidelity and transcendence; faith, Sharon Daloz Parks reminds us, is an activity that reaches both "infinitely *beyond* and intimately *within* the particulars of existence."[5] Teenagers seldom distinguish their desire for God from their desire for one another. As a result, falling in love at fifteen feels like being on holy ground, and church camps spawn romances as well as conversions every time.

Yet within adolescents' acute desire to merge with others lies a

3. Henri Nouwen, *With Burning Hearts: A Meditation on the Eucharistic Life* (Maryknoll, N.Y.: Orbis, 1998), 74-75.

4. For an elaboration on these themes, see Kenda Creasy Dean, "Holding On to Our Kisses: The Hormonal Theology of Adolescence" and "The Sacrament of One Another: Practicing Fidelity through Holy Friendship," in *An Unexpected Prophet: What the 21st Century Church Can Learn from Youth Ministry — The 1999 Princeton Lectures on Youth, Church and Culture* (Princeton, N.J.: Princeton Theological Seminary, 2000), 1-32.

5. Sharon Daloz Parks, *Big Questions, Worthy Dreams* (San Francisco: Jossey-Bass, 2000), 25. Emphasis added.

deeper human hunger: *homo religiosus'* longing for communion with the God whose desire for intimacy is the reason for our own. Passion connotes *desire* (in Latin, "longing for the stars"), which is simultaneously a sexual and a spiritual phenomenon. Christian tradition recognizes God's desire for relationship as the impetus for divine revelation, reflected in the human impulse toward "otherness." Familiarity that does not risk suffering, that violates love's confidence, or that fails to delight is never intimate, whereas passion, which willingly exchanges one life for another, is profoundly so. *Intimus* (Latin for "inner" or "innermost") is the binding of one self to another, the communion that transforms "me" into "we."

Intimacy is primarily about attachment, not sex. As Robert Kegan notes, "Teens may want to have sexual experience, may feel the *need* for sexual experience, but, odd as it sounds, they have no real *need* for genital penetration *unless the culture builds a dazzling shrine to it*"[6] — which, of course, is exactly what we have done. The desire for intimacy is rooted in human attachment, the strong bond between an infant and the mother or mother figure that establishes the template for the child's future orientation toward others. Securely attached children are more sociable, self-reliant, curious, and involved than their peers; having experienced empathy themselves, they have a greater capacity to display it to others.[7] Attachment relations "trump" sexuality in our drive for human connection, which is why adolescents, despite their abiding interest in genitalia, ultimately desire relationships that bestow fidelity and self-transcendence as well as sex. Premature sexual behavior signals a *crisis* in intimacy, not its fulfillment, as young people longing for secure attachments are thrust into a sexualized public world that makes them feel anything but secure.

Passionate Intimacy:
To Know in the Biblical Sense

Intimacy carries with it the gift of "being known" in the true biblical sense of the word. The knowledge that one is deeply understood by another bequeaths to the developing self both the trust required for fidelity and the enlarged vision necessary for transcendence. If adolescents' search for fi-

6. Robert Kegan, *In Over Our Heads* (Cambridge: Harvard University Press, 1994), 67.

7. Research on bonding and attachment in families is summarized briefly in James Q. Wilson, *The Moral Sense* (New York: Free Press, 1993), 145-48.

delity stems from their need for reliable love and unconditional acceptance, and if their bid for transcendence enacts the human need for an ideology that gives the budding self significance and purpose, then young
people's desire for communion expresses their profound need to be
known and companioned by another. The intimacy of communion means
"being known" completely, in our innermost selves, by an utterly faithful,
inconceivably wonderful "other" whose fidelity is so true, whose transcendence is so grand, whose communion is so deep that it constitutes
revelation:

> O Lord, you have searched me and known me.
> You know when I sit down and when I rise up;
> You discern my thoughts from far away.
> You search out my path and my lying down,
> And are acquainted with all my ways.
> Even before a word is on my tongue, O Lord,
> You know it completely
> You hem me in, behind and before,
> And lay your hand upon me.
> Such knowledge is too wonderful for me;
> It is so high that I cannot attain it.
> Where can I go from your spirit?
> Or where can I flee from your presence?
> If I ascend to heaven, you are there;
> If I make my bed in Sheol, you are there. . . .
>
> For it was you who formed my inward parts,
> You knit me together in my mother's womb.
> I praise you, for I am fearfully and wonderfully made.
> Wonderful are your works; that I know very well.
>
> (Psalm 139:1-8, 13-14, NRSV)

In these ten brief verses, a form of the verb "to know" appears five times,
and synonyms appear three times. In celebrating God's intimate friendship, the psalmist sees no contradiction in conflating spiritual and sexual
imagery, shifting in verse thirteen to the life-giving nature of divine intimacy. The psalmist notes the presence of God even before birth, who gives
us bodies that are "wonderfully made." But the psalmist says more than
this, for he is overwhelmed by the *person(s)* of God and not just by God's
works and attributes. The source of God's unflagging fidelity and unfath-
omable transcendence is "You" who "have searched and known me," and

who is unfailingly "there" (v. 1, 8). In short, the psalmist describes "being known" by God as a source of boundless joy and deep satisfaction physically, cognitively, emotionally, spiritually — and, above all, personally.

Passion risks for the sake of "being known." Years ago, a crusty theatre professor warned our college directing class, "If you make two actors face each other with less than twelve inches between them, it had better be either a love scene or a fight scene." Intimacy can intimidate; if I am close enough to kiss you, I am close enough to kill you. "Being known" requires willing vulnerability, for revealing my innermost self to you gives you enormous power. When I lay myself "bare" before you, I strip myself of my defenses; I trust that you will love me and not level me. Intimacy with God is no less perilous.

Seeking an In-the-Body Experience

If transcendence draws young people beyond the confines of self, communion invites them to live radically *within* the boundaries of being human, starting with their own bodies. Communion always begins with bodies — the Eucharist takes place in the Body of Christ — and this embodiment gives Christian theology "traction" for young people, grounding it in the most real thing they know: physical embodiment. God's intimacy takes hold in human relationships through the Incarnation, or enfleshment, of God in Jesus Christ. We get spiritual, but God got carnal.[8]

Teenagers, therefore, respond to bodies — theirs and everyone else's — in both individual and corporate ways. They are preoccupied with their personal body images, but they also move through the world in "bodies": groups, cliques, packs, gangs, crowds that intensify their sense of spatial presence and physical prowess. Part of the adolescent fascination with physicality is culturally induced. Global media distorts body image in ways DNA cannot match, and promotes behaviors that compromise health as well as proportion. Fast food restaurants, for example, train salesclerks to ask teenage girls to "supersize" their orders, while at the same time inserting miniature Barbies in girls' "Happy Meals."[9] Acutely

---

8. The word "incarnation" comes from the Latin *carn,* meaning flesh or meat, the same root that gave us words like *carnivore, carnival,* and chili *con carne.*

9. If Barbie were real, she would stand 7'2" tall, have a bust-waist-hip measurement of 40-22-36, and sport a neck twice as long as other humans. The average North American woman, by contrast, stands 5'4" tall, wears a size 12, and measures 37-29-40. In 1950, the White Rock "mineral girl" weighed 140 pounds and was 5'4". Today, she is 110 pounds and

aware of the fact that they inhabit physical space, teenagers often use their bodies to enact their perceived relationships to their environment through starvation, engorgement, sex, cutting, piercing, and various other practices. Extreme sports, moshing at the concert, and working out at the gym all point to adolescents' intense desire to feel their bodies even as consumerism numbs their senses and as technology increasingly makes physicality a virtual experience. At the same time, adolescents often distance themselves from their bodies, especially in order to repress pain. Starving for acceptance in a system that fails to notice her true self, a teenager embodies her perceived invisibility through bulimia — a life that, literally, is wasted.[10] Abandoned by hoped-for intimacy, a young adult dramatizes unnoticed inner pain through cutting or extreme piercing, seeking congruence between the outer and inner self. Desperate to be recognized behind a fragile facade, an adolescent marks his slipping selfhood with tattoos. Like a name carved in the bark of an oak tree, the tattoos remind him and others that he was here.

Any theology that takes passion seriously requires embodiment, for sexuality is a rehearsal for communion with God.[11] "The bodily language of Christ's passion," writes theologian Mark A. McIntosh, "becomes the communicative medium in which divine meaning and human knowing are able to converse."[12] We experience the world first through our bodies. Before we can mentally grasp an object, we grasp it with our hands; before we mouth words, we mouth objects. Human intercourse requires material, not just conceptual, interaction; love has as its object a person, not an abstraction. Even passionate commitment to a cause often finds concrete expression in the life of a particular person whose face becomes the icon of an ideal: Martin Luther King, Gloria Steinem, Bill Gates. God, too, comes to us concretely, and communion with the Incarnate Christ — God-in-the-flesh — provides the objective of Christian faith.[13] Consequently, Chris-

---

5'10". Although cultural pressure disproportionately (and negatively) affects girls' satisfaction with their bodies, therapists have observed an increasing preoccupation with body image among boys as well, who seem to accept the equally unrealistic proportions of muscle-bound toy action figures as normative. See Mary Pipher, *Reviving Ophelia* (New York: Ballantine Books, 1995); also Walt Mueller, "What You See Is What I Am," *YouthCulture@today* (Center for Parent/Youth Understanding, Spring 2001), 1.

10. See Marya Hornbacher, *Wasted* (New York: HarperCollins, 1997).

11. See Ann and Barry Ulanov, *Primary Speech* (Louisville: John Knox Press), 14.

12. Mark A. McIntosh, *Mystical Theology* (Oxford: Blackwell, 1998), 79.

13. As Moltmann puts it, "The mission of Christ achieves its purpose when [humans] and creation are united with God" (*The Church in the Power of the Spirit,* trans. Margaret Kohl [New York: Harper & Row, 1977], 59).

tian passion is always an incarnational enterprise, replete with bodies where sexuality and spirituality are intimately connected.

Carnal Knowledge: The Core of Christian Faith

Think back — if you can stand it — to your first crush in junior high or high school. Remember what happened to you? Remember what you did? For me, angels sang when Kevin Anderson sat behind me in eighth grade algebra. I acted like a besotted idiot in his presence, but behind the scenes I remained super-alert to his voice, his look, his whereabouts. I wasn't sure whether I was in love or insane; I felt both nauseous and delirious. I suddenly needed the hall pass (a lot) so I could "accidentally" wander by his classes on my way to the restroom. I developed an immediate interest in basketball (rumored to be his favorite pastime), and in Marianne Main (rumored to be his former love). I spent the better part of a week once sleuthing around to find out the name of his dog. I typed voluminous letters to God during this period on my parents' aqua Smith-Corona, praying fervently that God would "let me get over him" — or maybe get with him — or, ideally, both.

I still feel ridiculous when I see this on paper. None of these were things I normally did, though some of them were actually beneficial (my letters to God made me a speedy typist). My heart was not the only thing smitten by Kevin Anderson; my behavior, my schedule, my rhythm, and my relationships were overcome as well. Bodies do not just *feel* passion; they *do* things as a result of passion. Infatuation is not real passion, of course; "puppy love" is primarily a matter of projecting the idealized self onto another, and then narcissistically falling in love with the self's projection — a far cry from suffering love given by or received from someone who is truly "other." Yet our first crush somehow constitutes a "dry run" for real passion, and often serves as our first taste of love's ability to inspire willing sacrifice.

Communion is not a state of mind; it is a state of being — and beings have bodies that respond physically, mentally, emotionally to what they love. Call it arousal; Christian faith is *supposed* to arouse us for intercourse with God. And human sexuality is "the most conspicuous way that human beings express themselves as persons who naturally seek communion."[14] It is not uncommon, says theologian Catherine Mowry LaCugna,

14. LaCugna, *God for Us* (San Francisco: HarperSanFrancisco, 1993), 156. LaCugna

"to liken the human person's deep yearning for God to sexual desire between two persons. There is a 'never to be satisfied' dimension to both
mystical and sexual acts."[15] Theologian Sarah Coakley goes further:
"There is a profound entanglement of our sexual desires and our desire
for God, and in any prayer of the sort in which we radically cede control to
the Spirit there is an instant reminder of the close analogue between this
ceding (to the Trinitarian God), and the *ekstasis* of human sexual passion."[16]

Yet the church is seldom eager to dust human passion for divine fin-
gerprints, preferring to spiritualize *eros* into a kind of wafty, celibate sentimentalism — a tendency with long historical precedent. In the early
church, the perceived danger of sinfully confusing human desire with divine desire led many theologians to pursue the *eros* of God only after renouncing their own fleshly expressions of sexuality.[17] Today's Protestants
have long since given up on celibacy, but the perceived danger of connecting spiritual and sexual desire lingers. Historian Urban T. Holmes is
blunt:

> A satisfying spirituality of sexuality, which is not tinged by a simplistic
> apatheia, is yet to be written. Perhaps it will emerge in the next genera-
> tion. Certainly the presence of genital arousal in spiritual experience is
> common and needs to acknowledged as a positive element — rather
> than repressed and made a subject of embarrassment.[18]

Holmes lays the blame for this oversight at the feet of northern European
males, whom he regards as "culturally retarded in regard to our sexual-

---

states: "Sexuality broadly defined is the capacity for relationship, for *ekstasis,* and for self-
transcendence. Sexuality lies at the heart of all creation and is an icon of who God is, the
God in whose image we were created male and female (Genesis 1). . . . Sexual desire and sexual need are a continual contradiction to the illusion that we can exist by ourselves, entirely
for ourselves. One of the greatest challenges to us is that our sexuality become catholic; sexual desire is specific and tends toward exclusivity; but exclusivity must transcend itself toward inclusivity — for example, openness to a new child or hospitality to the stranger"
(p. 407). LaCugna rightly notes that sexual customs can be iconic of the divine life, "true images of the very nature of the triune God" (p. 407).

15. LaCugna, *God for Us,* 351.

16. Sarah Coakley, "Living into the Mystery of the Holy Trinity," *Anglican Theological
Review* 80 (Spring 1998): 224.

17. Coakley, "Living into the Mystery."

18. Urban T. Holmes, *A History of Christian Spirituality: An Analytical Introduction*
(New York: Harper & Row, 1980), 150-51. I am indebted to Christian educator Korey Lowry
for pointing out this excerpt.

ity"[19] (a generalization I'm not prepared to support), and he turns the task of developing a spirituality of sexuality over to women and non-white men. Let me suggest another likely group of theologians of the body: adolescents, male and female alike — people whose bodies serve as sensitive compasses that point, invariably, in the direction of communion. After centuries of modern rationalism, youth ministry's legacy to the twenty-first-century church may well be the adolescent insistence that bodies matter to Christian faith, and that sexuality and spirituality meet in the desire for communion, first expressed in the passion of God.

Kissing and Cleaving: Falling in Love with Jesus

For those of us raised in a culture accustomed to separating sexual and spiritual intimacy, the association of intercourse with communion seems alien if not downright offensive. Yet long before the corset of modern rationalism squeezed passion out of our theological lexicon, the church recognized passion as a useful category of discourse for catechizing young people. In the early medieval church, many Christian teachers — for whom sexual ethics was hardly a fixed code — used *eros* as metaphor for divine passion, and employed erotic memory as a tool for understanding God's desire for communion with us. Such teachers as Augustine (354-430), John Cassian (360-435), and Gregory the Great (540-604) assumed that union with God was the purpose of human desire.[20] Even theologians who approached erotic descriptions of divine love cautiously (Origen advised against praying in a room where sexual intercourse has taken place, since people might confuse spiritual and sexual freedom) still used sexual images to describe God's desire for humanity.[21]

Throughout the Middle Ages, mystical writers capitalized on this trajectory of Christian thought, and routinely considered passion spiritual when directed to God. People like Bernard of Clairvaux (1090-1153), Catherine of Siena (1347-1380), and Teresa of Avila (1515-1582) believed that human experience provided an acceptable starting point for the quest for God, and that when a person seeks God, "the very nobility of his pur-

19. Holmes, *A History of Christian Spirituality,* 151.

20. Michael Casey, *A Thirst for God: Spiritual Desire in Bernard of Clairvaux's Sermons on the Song of Songs* (Kalamazoo: Cistercian Publications, 1988), 63-64.

21. Origen, *De Oratione* XXXI.4, The Classics of Western Spirituality, ed. Rowan A. Greer (New York: Paulist Press, 1979), 81-170.

pose has the effect of transforming his life, rendering it progressively more godly and open to the divine."[22]

As a result, sexual imagery was commonplace in medieval religious instruction. Gregory the Great's practice of using erotic imagery to instruct new priests on holiness became a standard mode of instruction for monastic students (who undoubtedly found catechesis more compelling than their contemporary counterparts). Bernard of Clairvaux encouraged young monks to recall sexual intimacy in order to understand prayer as being kissed with increasing intimacy by Christ. His allegorical commentary on the Song of Songs, intended for the tutelage of young monks, cast Jesus as the bridegroom — the object and source of passionate love — and the soul as the bride who loves him.[23] Fearlessly borrowing sexual images to teach conversion as a movement from "carnal" to "rational" and finally to "spiritual love," Bernard urged his students to "cleave" unto God, reminding them that God is also "overcome" with yearning for them. Citing God's *pathos* in Song of Songs 2:5 ("I am wounded by love"), Bernard proclaimed the atonement as the event in which "Love triumphs over God."[24] Women, too, described their relationships with Christ in erotic terms. Catherine of Siena and Teresa of Avila, both of whom supervised the formation of young nuns, addressed their teaching to "God's lovers."[25] They

22. Casey, *A Thirst for God,* 72.

23. By the end of the sixth century, Pope Gregory the Great (pope from 590-604) used so many erotic images to instruct priests that one historian dubbed him "the doctor of desire." See Michael Casey, *A Thirst for God,* 63-64; also Bernard of Clairvaux's "Sermons on the Song of Solomon" in *The Love of God and Spiritual Friendship,* abridged, edited, and introduced by James M. Houston (Portland, Ore.: Multnomah Press, 1983), especially pp. 169-75. Homiletician Anna Carter Florence's exegesis of the Song of Songs offers the intriguing thesis that these texts may have been intended for the religious instruction of young people in the Hebrew community. See "Elihu: Job's Unexpected Prophet," "To Dwell in the Gardens," "Wise in the World," and "Bread on the Water" (sermons on the Song of Songs, presented at the Princeton Forum on Youth Ministry, St. Simon's Island, Ga., January 11-14, 1999, available on audiotape from Media Services, Princeton Theological Seminary, Princeton, N.J.) For an exposition of the vocabulary of desire in Bernard's sermons on the Song of Songs, see Mark S. Burrows, "Foundations for an Erotic Christology: Bernard of Clairvaux on Jesus as 'Tender Lover,'" *Anglican Theological Review* 80 (Fall 1998): 477-94.

24. See Michael Casey, *A Thirst for God;* see also Bernard McGinn, *The Presence of God: A History of Western Christian Mysticism,* vol. 2, *The Growth of Mysticism* (New York: Crossroad, Herder, 1994), 203. Cited in Burrows, "Foundations for an Erotic Christology," 487.

25. See Teresa of Avila, *The Way of Perfection,* translated and edited by E. Allison Peers, from the critical edition of P. Silverio de Santa Teresa, C.D. (New York: Image Books, 1964), especially chapter six.

portrayed God as a smitten suitor — in Catherine's words, "nothing but a fire of love" who pulled creation from the divine self when God was "crazy" with love.[26]

The originators of these themes, of course, preceded Gregory, Catherine, Bernard, Teresa, and their counterparts. Their legacy is the *pathos* of Israel and the bridal theology of the New Testament.[27] Jesus desires our communion with him, and portrays God's reign as a wedding banquet

26. The prayer, in full, reads:

> Why then, Eternal Father, did you create this creature of yours?
> I am truly amazed at this,
> and indeed I see, as you show me, that you made us for one reason only:
> In your light you saw yourself compelled by the fire of your charity
> To give us being,
> In spite of the evil we would commit against you, Eternal Father.
> It was fire, then, that compelled you.
> O unutterable love,
> Even tho' you saw all the evils that your creatures would commit
>   against your infinite goodness,
> you acted as if you did not see
> and set your eye only on the beauty of your creature,
> with whom you had fallen in love
> like one drunk and crazy with love.
> And in love you drew us out of yourself,
> Giving us being
> In your own image and likeness.
> You, eternal Truth, have told me the truth:
> That love compelled you to create us.
> Even though you saw that we would offend you,
> Your charity would not let you set eyes on that sight — No.
> You took your eyes off the sin that was to be
> And fixed your gaze only in your creature's beauty.
> For if you had concentrated on the sin,
> You would have forgotten the love you had for creating [human]kind.
> Not that sin was hid from you,
> But you concentrated on the love
> Because you are nothing but a fire of love,
> Crazy over what you have made.
> But give me the grace, dearest love,
> that my body may give up its blood for the honor and glory of your name.
> Let me no longer be clothed in myself.

Catherine of Siena, *The Prayers of Catherine of Siena,* trans. Suzanne Noffke, O.P. (New York: Paulist Press, 1983), 112-13.

27. I am thankful to Susan Neder, who pointed out this connection to me.

in which Christ is the bridegroom and the church is the bride (Matt. 9:15). Significantly, Jesus' ministry begins at a wedding (John 2:1-11), and the end of history is described as a marriage feast (Rev. 19:7-9). The new covenant is a wedding covenant, and all of human history exists for the sole purpose of allowing the bride to make herself ready (Rev. 19:7).

Popular Culture's Body of Instruction

During the Enlightenment, the church — like many other social institutions that sought intellectual credibility — dismissed passion and became mute on sexuality, and on desire generally. Bridal theology was banished to the convent and monastery, while modern universities espoused more "rational" theologies that focused more on human reason than on the human body as the route to revelation. As a result, the basic connection between sexuality and spirituality in Christian theology was severed, allowing passion to atrophy into sexual intimacy, the most marketable form of passion in consumer capitalism. Unfettered by the need to remain faithful to a theological tradition — and it must be said, unchallenged by the church — popular media exploited the impression that desire is a human, not a divine, attribute. Pseudo-theologies of desire proliferated; in the contemporary West, for example, cultural philosopher Caroline Simon observes that we have "substituted romance for religion as a vehicle of self-transcendence. Popular songs chant the 'theology' of romance, worshiping the beloved with hymns of praise: 'You are my destiny,' 'I can't live without your love,' 'You are my everything.'"[28]

Little wonder. Without a way to probe passion from the perspective of Christian theology, teenagers are left to explore their God-given longing for communion with tools provided by the entertainment media, which inevitably reflect popular culture's limited theological imagination. Today's media-drenched popular culture tutors postmodern youth in a theology of passion derived not from the teachings of the church, but from the doctrines of the marketplace, where sensual spirituality sells. Popular culture's reliance on image, rhythm, and melody concretizes young people's tacit desire for communion, and often provides the only language they know to describe their longing for intimacy. Music is particularly powerful in this regard; music and dancing, observes adolescent psychiatrist Lynn Ponton, "allow teens to experiment with their bodies, to feel things they have never felt before. . . . A range of spiritual, sexual, and other feelings

---

28. Caroline J. Simon, *The Disciplined Heart* (Grand Rapids: Eerdmans, 1997), 6.

can be experienced at the same time." She quotes a young client named Ricky who gradually became aware that the good feelings he had while dancing at a concert were the same feelings he had in the presence of girls. "It's like the music is in your body," Ricky said. "It," of course, referred to his budding sexual awareness, expressed in the most powerful communion language Ricky knew — the language of the rock concert.[29]

Unlike the contemporary church — but very much like teenagers — contemporary media culture has no qualms about conflating sexuality and spirituality. From MGM to MTV, the entertainment industry portrays sex as love and love as spiritual. To be sure, the hope is to sell movies and CDs, not theology. Media culture weds sexuality and spirituality because the union makes money. Yet it sells for one reason: teenagers view the connection between body and soul, sex and spirit, as authentic enough to exact a price — a dangerously high price at that. Young people yearning for intercourse tend to stake their lives on whatever passion is most available. One in four sexually active youth told the National Longitudinal Study of Adolescent Health that they had sex within the first month of a relationship, with most relationships lasting one to three months.[30] Although teen sexual activity declined between 1988 and 1995, mostly among white males, one in ten teenage girls is infected with chlamydia; gonorrhea, which is decreasing among adults, is rising among teens.[31] Despite a 20 percent drop in the teen birthrate between 1991 and 1999, one in five sexually active girls ages fifteen to nineteen gets pregnant each year, according to the Henry K. Kaiser Family Foundation, and 10 percent of girls and boys report losing their virginity before age thirteen.[32] HIV rates are falling in the U.S. — but not among adolescents. The Centers for Disease Control estimate that half of those infected with HIV in the U.S. are now twenty-four years old or younger.[33] Worldwide, five young people are infected with the AIDS virus every minute.[34]

29. Lynn E. Ponton, *The Sex Lives of Teenagers: Revealing the Secret World of Adolescent Boys and Girls* (New York: Dutton, 2000), 90.

30. www.childtrends.org/PDF/FirstTimeRB.pdf.

31. Verna Noel Jones, "Sexually Transmitted Diseases a Ticking Time Bomb for Teens: Ignoring the Symptoms of STDs Puts Them at Risk for Infertility, Sterility, or Worse," *The Chicago Tribune,* July 25, 1999.

32. Anna Mulrine, "Risky Business," *U.S. News and World Report* (May 27, 2002), 2. available at www.usnews.com/usnews/issue/020527/misc/27teensex.htm; accessed on 7 December 2002.

33. Statistic cited in Ponton, *Sex Lives of Teenagers,* 214. It is easier for girls to become infected from boys than vice versa.

34. K. Kiragu, "Youth and HIV/AIDS: Can We Avoid Catastrophe?" *Population Reports,* Series L, No. 12 (Baltimore: Johns Hopkins University Bloomberg School of Public

What youth seek in all this sexual activity is the attachment conveyed by *intercourse:* physical, visceral, spiritual communion and the security, sensation, release, and even relief that accompanies it. Postmodern youth may be dying because of their dates, but what they are dying *for* is someone who will be there for them, someone who can draw them beyond themselves into the mystery of "we," someone who is "one" with them and therefore holds out the gift of "being known." And if the only route to this intimacy seems to be sex, then sex it will be.

Bats and Intimacy

Intimacy represents the deeply spiritual search for another who knows what it is like to be "me." The dilemma, of course, is that no one else can know what it is like being "me" except me; James Loder demonstrates the point by recalling Thomas Nagel's essay, "What Is It Like to Be a Bat?" in which Nagel concluded that, while he might understand what it would be like to be a bat, he can never understand how the bat understands being a bat.[35] In a similar way, Loder distinguishes authentic intimacy from both sexual and interpersonal intimacy:

> The great sex charade is the popular celebration in the media and in our society and culture at large of sexuality as the major indicator of intimacy between persons. . . . Culturally co-opted sexuality is a charade . . . to satisfy something that is far more profound, namely, the longing for an intimacy that ultimately ties us into the life of God.[36]

For Loder, sexuality is at best a derivative form of closeness that "needs to be redefined across the board according to the spiritual relationality of persons, community, and the Trinity."[37] This does not mean that sexuality cannot contribute to intimacy. On the contrary, God created human sexuality as a means to profoundly spiritual union. Sexual intimacy is in one sense the

---

Health, Population Information Program, Fall 2001), 7. Officials point out that since girls often have sex with much older males, it should be assumed that many of these cases are the result of incest and rape, not of consensual sexual activity among teenagers.

35. Thomas Nagel, "What Is It Like to Be a Bat?" *Philosophical Review* (1974); reprinted in Thomas Nagel, *Mortal Questions* (Cambridge: Cambridge University Press, 1979). Referred to by James E. Loder, "The Great Sex Charade and the Loss of Intimacy," *Word and World* 21 (Winter 2001), 81-87.

36. Loder, "The Great Sex Charade," 82, 86.

37. Loder, "The Great Sex Charade," 86.

closest we ever come to embodying the *imago dei:* it makes us co-creators of life, as we open ourselves to God's life-giving grace that flows through another person.

At the same time, there is no doubt that culture co-opts us into thinking that physical sexuality suffices for communion. No human being short of Jesus can "know" us as deeply as we know ourselves; no one but God (or another bat) knows how it feels to be a bat. Furthermore, it takes a bat to convince another bat that he really knows what being a bat is like — and this, of course, is the logic of the Incarnation. The Incarnation of Jesus Christ insinuates a three-dimensional view of intimacy. Intimacy involves you and me, but also takes place within the embrace of Jesus Christ whose suffering love redefines the intimacy between us. In other words, authentic intimacy requires the presence of a transcendent Other who sheds light on us from beyond ourselves, illuminating human relationships in a new way. In the light of this transcendent Other, you and I are both exposed for who we truly are — which is devastating. But in this light, we also discover that we are not primarily joined to one another, but to Christ — a discovery that is liberating and redeeming. Only in reaching toward Christ do we truly become closer to one another (see figure 1, p. 131).[38]

What this means is that the true self — the human self — reflects the relationality that is God.[39] The paradigm for human communion is the in-

38. This view of the self echoes the theological anthropology of H. Richard Niebuhr, who believed that the self cannot exist apart from relationships. "We are our relations and cannot be selves save as we are members of each other," Niebuhr wrote. To become a human self is different from becoming an individual; an individual needs merely to be born, but a human requires communion with an adequate God whose radical affirmation offers a self-confirming relationship in which I am known for who I truly am, a beloved child of God. "To be a self is to have a god," Niebuhr asserted. "To have a god is to have history; that is, events connected in a meaningful pattern; to have one god is to have one history" (Niebuhr, *The Meaning of Revelation* [New York: W. W. Norton, 1949], 52, 59). Niebuhr conceded that humans are fickle in their choice of gods, sometimes living for Jesus' God, sometimes for country, and sometimes for school or job or children. Yet without this faith in God, we might exist, but not as humans — not as "selves." Only as God reconstructs us into people who recognize that we share a past with the rest of human history do we experience a profound sense of unity: communion with God and communion with others in the communion of Christ.

39. Niebuhr, *The Meaning of Revelation,* 86. Revelation is only realized in us through faith, which is "a personal act of commitment, of confidence and trust, not a belief about the nature of things." Niebuhr always held the "decision of self" in balance with the revelation available through the community of faith, "all those who occupy the same standpoint and look in the same direction toward the same reality to which we look as individuals. Assurance that we are not mistaken in our ultimate convictions is not to be gained without social

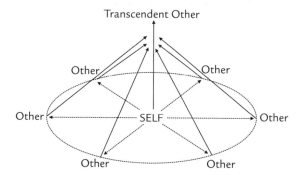

Figure 1. H. Richard Niebuhr's Three-Dimensional Structure of Faith[40]

timacy of the Trinity, the Passion within the Godhead. Created in God's image, young people are "wired" for life lived in the presence of the transcendent Other who illuminates all other facets of their existence. Passion, that deep-seated desire for a relationship that confers identity and meaning, impels young people toward the tri-relationality necessary for the formation of the self. This "three-dimensional relationality" defines them; in fact, it is what enables them to become human.

The Etherization of Passion:
If It's Spiritual, It Must Be Good

Meanwhile, back at the church, we often cordon off sexuality into one well-supervised junior high retreat, if that. Make no mistake: this is crucial ministry, even if only for the tiny fraction of young people we see in such sterile settings, even if communion is seldom acknowledged as the weekend's objective. The sexual and spiritual images offered by the media generally lack any referent beyond themselves, leaving adolescents to imbue them with content of their own making — a dubious proposition at best. In the absence of an alternative view of passion offered by the church, adoles-

---

corroboration, but it is not gained either from consultation with those who, occupying a different point of view, look in a different direction and toward other realities than we do in our history and faith. Assurance grows out of immediate perception plus social corroboration and out of neither one of these alone" (Niebuhr, *The Meaning of Revelation,* 103).

40. This is my own visual construction of Niebuhr's theological anthropology, explained in *The Meaning of Revelation.* Niebuhr does not use the language of "three-dimensional structures of faith."

cents have little choice but to invent their "theology" of passion from the resources at hand, which usually amounts to a cut-and-paste combination of family values, hormonal urges, social norms, and the Jedi-like belief that faith equals feeling: "If I trust my feelings, they will lead me to God."

The church's *de facto* decision to let popular culture define passion as sexual intimacy has disastrous theological consequences. On the one hand, separating body and spirit tends to reduce sexuality to "parts and plumbing" — the usual content of church-sponsored sexuality retreats — as the human desire for otherness becomes associated with biology rather than with our identity in God. An ethical conundrum invariably follows: When sexuality is primarily a matter of biological function, affirming sexuality (which Christian doctrine requires) means celebrating body parts, while at the same time telling teenagers not to use them. Teenagers are quick to see the inconsistency. While almost all older Americans who endorse religious belief condemn premarital sex (even among self-described liberals, 63 percent consider premarital sex immoral), only one in four young people ages eighteen to twenty-nine think that premarital sex is wrong.[41]

At the same time, the church's reluctance to connect body and spirit reinforces the disembodied view of Christian spirituality mentioned earlier. "If you despise the body, you despise Christ," wrote Origen — this from a man who is thought to have castrated himself — but contemporary Christians are equally inconsistent. When Christian spirituality loses its referent *in* the Incarnation of Jesus, its content becomes amorphous, uncoupled from the material world. By the late twentieth century, much of Christian spirituality had taken on a vague "God-ish-ness" that allowed it to be co-opted by any number of theologies and methods, and largely sapped it of substance and vigor. Such gnosticism is hardly new to Christianity, but it is deadly to passionate faith. "Whatever is spiritual and 'not of the flesh' is [considered] higher than what is bodily and sensuous," observes Moltmann. "The one is inward, the other external, the one profound, the other superficial, the one reflective, the other thoughtless. Soul-searching takes the place of practical *conversion*. But that means that this kind of spirituality introduces an antithesis which splits life into two, and quenches its vitality."[42]

41. George Gallup and Michael Lindsay, *Surveying the Religious Landscape* (Harrisburg, Pa.: Morehouse, 1999), 101.

42. Moltmann, *The Spirit of Life*, 84.

Communion and Identity Formation

Adolescents absorb this life-draining dualism, inadvertently shrinking intimacy to physical contact while banishing spirituality to the netherworld of good feelings. But "being known" is only partially represented by sexual intimacy. One of the consequences of the media's ubiquitous assumption that communion requires sexual intercourse is to obscure the fairly obvious fact that intimacy has a range (see figure 2, on p. 133). Sex often takes place without intimacy; sex that occurs in the absence of "being known" is rape — violent, dehumanizing, and unholy. Yet not only does media culture portray sexual intimacy as the preeminent route to communion; it presents only one form of sexual intimacy — vaginal intercourse — as truly sexual. A number of studies indicate, for example, that young people are turning to sexual behaviors that were once considered taboo in order to maintain their "technical virginity." Youth "are getting the message that abstinence is the goal," says journalist Anna Mulrine — and they are placing a premium on it. Vaginal intercourse declined among American high school students between 1991 and 1999; but in its place, Mulrine notes, is a letter-of-the-law, not spirit-of-the-law, approach to abstinence.[43] For example, a North Carolina State University study found that half of teens do not consider oral sex *sex,* and 24 percent consider anal sex abstinent behavior.[44] A fifteen-year-old told *USA Today,* "The mentality is that oral sex is as far as you can go without maintaining any level of emotional attachment."[45]

Without an understanding of intimacy's range — and the various forms of relationships that satisfy the human hunger for communion — intimate relationships frequently become more of a source of concern than comfort. Patricia Hersch observes, "Kids today are growing up without any understanding of the incremental steps of getting to know each other. . . . They have no way of knowing how to explore their first inklings of wanting to be with each other."[46] A Cornell University study of 8,000 adolescents reported that, while steady romantic attachments can improve adult health and well-being, romantic relationships tend to cause stress

43. Mulrine, "Risky Business," 4.

44. Reported in Mulrine, "Risky Business," 4. Sexually transmitted diseases can be contracted through oral sex or anal sex.

45. Marissa Robillard, cited by Karen S. Peterson, "For Many Teens, Oral Sex Doesn't Count," *USA Today* (November 16, 2000), 6.

46. Interview with Patricia Hersch, cited in Peterson, "For Many Teens, Oral Sex Doesn't Count," 3.

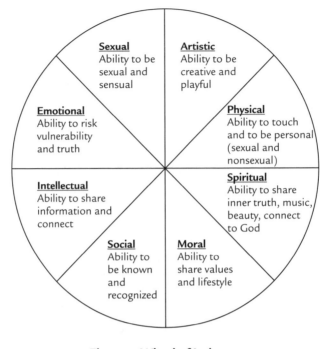

Figure 2. Wheel of Intimacy
Roland Martinson[47]

and depression in adolescents. At the University of Tennessee, a study of 1,300 high school students found that boys and girls experience a "loss of self" in romantic relationships, which leads to depression and isolation, especially in girls.[48]

The reason is clear: what adolescents seek, and what they need, is intimacy, not simply romance; communion, not just fellowship groups; intercourse, not merely sex. To be sure, some romance is intimate and some fellowship groups practice communion, but the ratio is wildly skewed in the other direction. While teenagers routinely equate emotional and physical closeness with intimacy, true intimacy requires a sense of self in order to "be known" in a relationship instead of devoured.[49] Here we are back to our old

47. Roland Martinson, unpublished handout, used with permission. Personal correspondence 12/8/02. Thanks to Paul Brookens for pointing this out to me.

48. Studies cited by Amy Dickinson, "Puppy Love's Bite," *Time,* April 16, 2001, 82.

49. This, admittedly, reflects a Western concept of identity formation, and since identity is a psychosocial construction, it always reflects the assumptions of an adolescent's host

conundrum: adolescents in the process of forming identity have not yet formed a reliable sense of self, which is precisely why youth experience a "loss of self" when dating. When I do not know where I begin and end, I easily become consumed by the other — who may be as boundary-less as I am.

The intimacy of divine communion, however, not only recognizes a God-given identity; it *bequeaths* it. While girls and boys take different paths to psychological maturity,[50] Christian communion has a leavening effect on human development. The church presupposes the God-given self as being formed in the image of God. Yet because this image is distorted by sin, we require communion with God in order to be restored. In Christian theology, identity is a function of intimacy with Christ, and intimacy with Christ is the true shape of human identity. In conversion, God offers identity and intimacy at once; as I join in Christ's communion, I come to know myself as one who belongs to Jesus and who is called to identify with others in his name.

Communion reveals God's desire to know young people in the *koinonia,* the fellowship of believers who break bread together and encircle youth with the Body of Christ. In this net of relationships, young people come to know themselves as being "in Christ." The boundaries of his Body become their boundaries; they become defined by his life, death, and resurrection. The liturgy of the Great Thanksgiving names them explicitly as participants in — not just onlookers to — communion, inviting God to "bless these gifts that we, receiving them, may be partakers in the Body and Blood of Jesus" and to "make us one body, one Spirit in Christ."[51] Commu-

---

culture. Thus, young people in the United States cannot escape the influence of Western philosophy on the development of the individual, despite the ways "individualism" and privatization distort Christian views of communion. However, theorists in other cultures have adapted Erikson in ways that allow for "fusion" as part of healthy identity formation. In this sense "fusion" does not represent a loss of self by absorption by a more powerful other; rather, it indicates a sense of oneness with creation itself, a sense that one is part of the cosmos. This view of identity formation, in fact, posits an even closer link between identity and communion than Western understandings of the individual allow. See Sudhir Kakar, ed., *Identity and Adulthood* (Delhi: Oxford University Press, 1979), chapter one, and *The Inner World: A Psycho-analytic Study of Childhood and Society in India,* 2nd ed. (Delhi: Oxford University Press, 1991), chapters one and two. I wish to thank Ajit Prasadam for introducing me to these conceptualizations of Erikson in Hindi culture.

50. Many feminist psychologists believe women invert Erikson's stages of "identity vs. identity diffusion" and "intimacy vs. isolation." See Carol Gilligan, *In a Different Voice: Psychological Theory and Women's Development* (Cambridge: Harvard University Press, 1993); Judith Jordan et al., *Women's Growth in Connection: Writings from the Stone Center* (New York: Guilford Press), 1991.

51. This language is taken from the Anglican communion services in the Book of Common Prayer, but similar phrasing is used in communion liturgies across denominations.

nion is never a spectator sport. It is a means of divine self-communication, in which God bestows sanctifying grace that makes imitating Christ possible.

Passion and *Eros:*
The Inconceivable Closeness of God

Without three-dimensional communion, human passion quickly flattens out into sexual gratification — which is why young people immersed in a global media culture find it difficult to conceive intimacy apart from sexuality and readily grant both sacred status. Witness the following exchange between sixteen-year-old Rachel and her friend Kiwi from the PBS documentary "American High":

> Kiwi: What do you think about kissing, the actual word?
> Rachel: I think it's more intimate than a lot of things. . . . It's kind of sacred.
> Kiwi: Sacred?
> Rachel: It's just the closest you can get, I think, [to] each other, you know, face-to-face.[52]

If we are to believe much of American popular culture, true human fulfillment lies in orgasm, not in union with God. Because we live in a culture of self-fulfillment, teenagers naturally infer a syllogism that goes something like this:

> *Premise A:* Orgasm leads to human fulfillment.
> *Premise B:* Human fulfillment is right and good.
> *Premise C:* Therefore I need an orgasm.

Yet what young people truly seek is intimacy and intercourse, not just orgasm. Conversation not only serves as the primary venue through which humans create intercourse; it is by far the easiest route to communion for adolescents. Social scientists (if not teenagers) often regard conversation as a surrogate for genital sex. As Erikson observed, "The optimal male-female situation is talking, playing, and talking, intense emotional ex-

---

52. Film excerpt found at http://www.pbs.org/americanhigh/characters/character_kiwi.html#, on 8 September 2003.

changes and talking; when the relationship becomes dependent on the physical aspect, it is a dying or already dead relationship."[53]

On the other hand, if adolescents find it difficult to conceive of intimacy apart from sex, they *do* recognize the multifaceted dimensions of passion, the many ways they suffer for what they love. The once sharp distinctions between *agape, philia,* and *eros* — Greek terms often used to distinguish selfless love, friendship love, and romantic love — have been muted by scholarly scrutiny.[54] All love endures the fortunes of another; all love makes the lover vulnerable; all love suffers the weak-kneed hope of love returned.[55] Yahweh proclaims the divine self as *El Kana,* a God longing with pure holy desire after men and women, whom God loves; and God demands *ahabah,* the same word used in the Song of Songs to describe the sexually aroused love of the bride and groom. *Eros* assumes a posture of alert weakness before the beloved. Overwhelmed by desire, the lover passively awaits the beloved's consent to be loved. Passion in the Christian tradition is always a three-way proposition, involving you and me but also the suffering love of Christ, and because of this it runs deeper than human intimacies alone, redefining human relationships in light of the friendship of God.[56]

53. Erikson cited in James Loder, *The Logic of the Spirit* (San Francisco: Jossey Bass, 1998), 220.

54. See Anders Nygren, *Agape and Eros* (London: SPCK, 1932), and M. C. D'Arcy, *The Mind and the Heart of Love* (London: Faber and Faber), 1946, both of whom object to using *eros* motifs for love toward God. Most recent scholarship disputes the opposition of *agape* and *eros,* and in fact reveals considerable evidence that *eros* not only was used by biblical and patristic writers alike to refer to divine love, but that *eros* cannot be conceived simply as sexual love. Cf. Catherine Osborne, *Eros Unveiled: Plato and the God of Love* (Oxford: Clarendon), 1996; Caroline J. Simon, *The Disciplined Heart* (Grand Rapids: Eerdmans, 1997); Alexander C. Irwin, *Eros toward the World: Paul Tillich and the Theology of the Erotic* (Minneapolis: Fortress, 1991).

55. Theologian Paul Tillich, for instance, viewed all love as having an ontological unity in God. In Tillich's thinking, "religious passion experienced as ultimate concern stands in a positive *relationship* to other seemingly more mundane forms of desire and appetite." Irwin, *Eros toward the World,* 26.

56. Loder, "The Great Sex Charade," 84. For Loder, this spiritual intimacy is "truly explosive and the most neglected force in the life and death of our church communities," which Christ intends to bear the life of God into the world.

Practicing Communion:
Why Youth Fellowship Is Not Enough

Not long ago, an Episcopal priest from a nearby parish met me for coffee. The St. Andrews congregation and the surrounding community adored John, but that morning he looked anything but adorable. The youth director had resigned suddenly, and John suddenly found himself responsible for the combined junior/senior high youth group on Sunday nights. "I know *nothing* about youth ministry," he moaned. He had met with the teenagers a few times; but on the very first night he had scrapped his plans because, when he arrived at the church, he found them distraught over a classmate's death in a car accident that weekend. "I didn't know what to do!" John confessed. "We all just looked at each other. Finally, one of the kids asked: 'Father John, can we have communion?'" He paused, miserably.

"So what did you do?" I asked.

"Well, I thought, Hey, at least I can do that. So we all went to the chapel, we prayed, we talked a little, we shared the Eucharist. Then everybody went home."

"Wow. What happened the next week?"

"Well . . . we had communion again." He looked at me, sheepishly. "Okay, look. The truth is, that's all we've done. They come on Sunday nights, we have communion. I suggested some games once, but they wanted to have the Eucharist. So that's all we do. We pray and talk and have communion."

He looked at me like he thought I would have a better idea. I didn't. It didn't sound to me like these teenagers really *wanted* to go back to the game format of the weekly youth fellowship group. And I couldn't think of a more honest expression of being young and Episcopalian — people weaned on the sacrament — or a more transparent way to address the adolescent need for being deeply known by God and one another than those intimate, informal weekly communion services. At a critical moment, the youth of St. Andrews had turned to a wise adult who made room for their *pathos,* who demonstrated that God knows them in the Eucharist. And they kept coming back for more. A year later, when John took another pastorate, I learned that volunteers had added other youth activities to the roster — but on Sunday nights, the youth at St. Andrews still met in the chapel to pray, to talk, and to have communion.

"Do This": A Eucharistic View of Self

For all the popularity of fellowship groups in the church — and mainline Protestants spent most of the twentieth century promoting and propping up fellowship groups in the name of youth ministry[57] — human transformation comes in communion, not fellowship. The vast majority of youth activities undertaken in the name of "communion" are really (often explicitly) for the sake of "community," a very different objective. Most communities of Christian youth (like communities of Christian adults) are governed by what my colleague Richard R. Osmer likes to call "the covenant of niceness" — which is a long way from being governed by the covenant of truth. Communion, on the other hand, is union with God and neighbor through the body and blood of Jesus Christ. "A Christian community's ability — empowered by the cross of Christ — to be truthful, to confess, and to love enemies," notes theologian L. Gregory Jones, "distinguishes it from those illusory communities based on friendliness."[58] Communion is created by passion made visible in the practices of holy friendship, starting with the friendship of God in the "outward and visible sign" of the Eucharist. It requires repentance and forgiveness, hospitality and reconciliation, not group-building.

When young people are shaped not by friendliness but by a *habitus* of communion, they undertake certain practices in response to Jesus' command: "*Do this* in remembrance of me."[59] The "eucharistic self," says theologian David Ford, joyfully participates in the face-to-face intimacy of the *koinonia,* the prophetic drama of the Last Supper, and the "non-identical repetition" of Christ's self-giving love through a life of praise — all of which are undertaken out of friendship "informed by the death of Jesus":

> Greater love has no man than this, that a man lay down his life for his friends. You are my friends if you do what I command you. No longer do I call you servants, for the servant does not know what his master is

57. See Mary-Ruth Marshall, "Precedents and Accomplishments: An Analytical Study of the Presbyterian Youth Fellowship of the Presbyterian Church in the United States, 1954-1958" (Ph.D. dissertation, Presbyterian School of Christian Education, 1993); Charles Webb Courtoy, "A Historical Analysis of Three Eras of Mainline Protestant Youth Work in America as a Basis for Clues for Future Youth Work" (D.Min. thesis, Vanderbilt Divinity School, 1976).

58. L. Gregory Jones, *Embodying Forgiveness: A Theological Analysis* (Grand Rapids: Eerdmas, 1995), 22.

59. David F. Ford, *Self and Salvation: Being Transformed* (Cambridge: Cambridge University Press, 1999), 137-66.

doing; but I have called you friends, for all that I have heard from my Father I have made known to you. (John 15:13-14)[60]

To risk love is to risk death. If there is a formula for human happiness, this is it. For in risking death out of love — in risking passion — we find freedom and joy, the ecstasy of love returned that far exceeds love given.

Spiritual friendship, a relationship to God and others that is both the vehicle for and the fruit of a eucharistic identity, helps adolescents come to know themselves eucharistically — as people who are *blessed, placed, timed,* and *commanded*.[61] A teenager knows himself to be *blessed* when he experiences himself as flourishing within God's infinite love and joy. He recognizes his *place* — his situatedness — in a body and in communities where God's words and actions converge. He experiences himself as *timed,* living in an unworried moment so that history can afford to be punctuated with family meals, conversing, singing, and worship — acts that relativize death and redistribute time and energy from other enslaving investments. Finally, he knows he is *commanded* — by none other than Jesus — who calls upon him for "daring faithful improvisations of new life" in the face of an unrepressed sense of death and resurrection.[62] In short, the eucharistic self allows adolescents to know themselves as God knows them, and to be called on the basis of God's holy friendship with them — a friendship so intimate that life is exchanged for life so that God can be known.

Passion seeks holy friendship, not just pleasant company. The primary friendship to which adolescents are called is friendship with the Triune God who has befriended them — an intercourse as life-giving as sex, as life-changing as falling in love. Holy friends can rival lovers in intimacy and passion, as any glimpse at early monastic correspondence between spiritual friends confirms.[63] Holy friendships create a "space" in which

---

60. Ford, *Self and Salvation,* 160.

61. Ford, *Self and Salvation,* 160ff.

62. Ford, *Self and Salvation,* 160ff.

63. Evidence of such friendship abounds in monastic literature. Guibert, Benedictine abbot at Gembloux (in Belgium), who wrote to Hildegard of Bingen and a nun named Gertrude as well as many men, offers women the same status as his male friends. To a certain *magister* named Joseph, Guibert writes: "Drawn by [your] attractions I desire and yearn to see you, to embrace you, to speak to you, but I do not yet grasp you, I do not get hold of you as I desire. Uncertain and changeable between faith and affection, between hope and fear I do not know what to choose or to obtain. . . . What is even more serious, affection is afraid of being forever cheated" (cited in Brian Patrick McGuire, *Friendship and Community: The Monastic Experience 350-1250* [Kalamazoo: Cistercian Publications, 1988], 378). The Cistercian Adam writes to Agnes, a nun at Fontevrault: "In my own way, most beloved, I wholly cling to

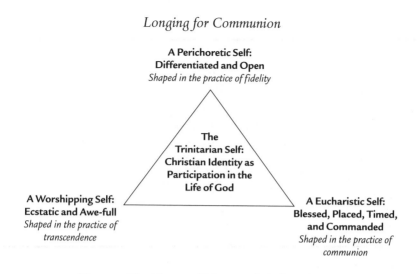

Figure 3. The Shape of Mature Christian Identity

eroticism leads to communion, and not merely to orgasm, as union with God brings us closer to union with one another.

The Shape of Mature Christian Identity

Inevitably, sin disrupts young people's attempts at fidelity, flattens their stabs at transcendence, and fractures their efforts at communion — and therefore impedes any chance that they might reflect God's image clearly. For that reason, adolescents' identity in Jesus Christ only becomes truly visible when youth recognize God's presence, purpose, and unity in the witness of the Christian community. As young people participate in communities that respond to Jesus' imperative *"Do this!"* they discover their own muted passions transformed into practices of vibrant self-giving love.

The Passion of Christ reveals God as a trustworthy, ecstatic, and intimate lover whose self-confirming presence shapes mature Christian identity, what we might summarize as a "Trinitarian self": a self explicitly given by God as an expression of the *imago dei,* even in the absence of develop-

---

you, and on your soul, mine depends. In this joining of individuals, the love of Christ has made itself our bond" (p. 391). Bernard of Clairvaux wrote to Peter the Venerable: "If I had perhaps grown cold toward you, as you reproach me for having done, there is no doubt that cherished by your love I shall soon grow warm again. . . . I must say I enjoy your fun" (p. 255). See Bernard McGinn, *The Presence of God: A History of Western Christian Mysticism,* vol. 2, *The Growth of Mysticism* (New York: Crossroad, Herder, 1994).

mental and social resources that have traditionally provided the raw materials for identity formation. Christian identity is a gift, not an achievement, which means that an adolescent with a Trinitarian self is liberated from a number of the constraints on identity formation imposed by post-modernity. Against society's endless demands for reinventing the self, Trinitarian selves are perichoretic: differentiated and open, they are dynamic and fluid without compromising their essential unity in God. In a context where pluralism and openness to the other are taken for granted, Trinitarian selves are worshipful: ecstatic and full of awe, they mirror God's own inner relationality and fearless pluralism, which makes them capable of reaching beyond their own boundaries without fearing their own disintegration. At a time when social differentiation and mobility challenge integration and belonging, Trinitarian selves perceive a different relationship to others, to space, and to time. Called to be "set apart" for mission "for such a time as this," they proceed with a sense of purpose and belonging as they bring Christ's self-giving love into the world.

The church cannot offer young people Christ's Passion; this is God's gift, already given. What the church *can* do is wrest from popular culture the dimensions of passion — the fidelity, transcendence, and communion of God — that popular culture has redefined in the church's absence. These are the footholds adolescents use to gain entry into the holy life. God's passion trumps adolescent ones; yet mature Christian identity depends upon the church's ability to practice the passion we preach. The final section of this book, therefore, makes the case for a curriculum of passion for youth ministry based upon the historic practices of the Christian community, and then explores three practices — exhortation, pilgrimage, and spiritual friendship — that illustrate how a passionate church might connect the adolescent search for fidelity, transcendence, and intimacy with the Passion of Jesus Christ.[64]

---

64. I have chosen these particular practices somewhat arbitrarily; all Christian practices point to God's passion, and all enact Christ's fidelity, transcendence, and communion to a degree. At the same time, exhortation, pilgrimage, and spiritual friendship provide useful points of entry for ministry with youth for several reasons: (a) They evoke self-giving love on a number of levels and address varying spiritual depths, providing a reasonably "balanced" entry into the imitation of Christ; (b) Their highly communal nature offers developmental as well as theological benefits for adolescents with acute interpersonal needs; (c) A large repertoire of Christian actions embody exhortation, pilgrimage, and spiritual friendship — only some of which are addressed here — giving young people some flexibility in expressing the passion of faith; (d) They have received little theological attention from youth ministry or practical theology, making their contemporary relevance easy to overlook.

PRACTICING PASSION

A View from the Bridge

Divine Passion is revealed as God's:	Visible in the church as:	Historic trajectory:	Forms practice may assume in youth ministry:	Leadership called forth:
Fidelity "being there"	A sacred solidarity (example: the practice of exhortation)	Didache	Christian conference Compassion	Coaches
Transcendence "being moved"	Holy momentum (example: the practice of pilgrimage)	Leitourgia	Play Praise and lament	Trail guides
Communion "being known"	The sacrament of one another (example: the practice of spiritual friendship)	Koinonia	Chastity Prayer	Mentors

Chapter Six

VESSELS OF GRACE

Christian Practices as Scaffolding for Faith

*After your heart has thus become firm in Christ, and love, not
fear of pain, has made you a foe of sin, then Christ's passion
must from that day on become a pattern for your entire life.
Henceforth you will have to see his passion differently. Until
now we regarded it as a sacrament which is active in us while
we are passive, but now we find that we too must be active. . . .
That is a proper contemplation of Christ's passion, and such
are its fruits.*

Martin Luther[1]

*Spiritual practices have always been recognized in religious
traditions as the core around which any life of faith must be
built.*

Robert Wuthnow[2]

*If youth are members of communities of radical practice,
youth ministry will flourish.*

Michael Warren[3]

1. Martin Luther, "A Meditation on Christ's Passion," *Devotional Writings* I, Luther's
Works, vol. 42, ed. Martin O. Dietrich, general ed. Helmut T. Lehmann (Philadelphia: Fortress, 1969).

2. Robert Wuthnow, *Growing Up Religious: Christians and Jews and Their Journeys of
Faith* (Boston: Beacon Press, 1999), 192.

3. Michael Warren, unpublished address given at United Methodist Forum Adults in
Youth Ministry, January 6, 1996.

Author Anne Lamott concedes that the reason she makes her young son Sam go to church now is because she can ("I outweigh him by nearly seventy-five pounds").[4] But she knows that she will have to do better than this. She hypothesizes that, "like alcoholism, born-again Christianity skips generations. There will come a point," she said in a recent interview, "when I can't reasonably force Sam to go to church, and then I think he'll stay away for a long time. I assume he won't be a Christian [when he grows up], though I think he'll always believe in God."[5]

Support for Lamott's hypothesis is mixed. On the one hand, religious training in the home is the best predictor of adult church attendance, suggesting that active Christianity does not "skip" generations — and furthermore, that it dare not skip generations. To hear sociologists tell it, Sam stands a better chance than most people of being a Christian when he grows up, which is to say that he might be among the 48 percent of American children from practicing Christian families who grow up to attend church on a weekly basis — not exactly compelling odds, but still worth cultivating.[6] Sociologist Robert Wuthnow offers more concrete evidence: "Family devotions as a child is the best predictor of adult [church] attendance, followed by seeing one's parents read the Bible at home, and after that, by parents having read the Bible to the child."[7] (By contrast, saying table grace or being sent to Sunday school has a relatively weak effect on adult church attendance.) Because Sam comes from a self-consciously Christian home, and participates in a faith community chock full of adults who notice and encourage him, Sam's emerging identity has already internalized a set of beliefs and practices that make him and his mother seem "Christian-ish" — which, Lamott admits, is generally easier for people to swallow than the truth, which is that she has bought into Jesus hook, line, and sinker, and she hopes Sam will too.[8]

On the other hand, conforming to a community's practices, even Christian ones, does not necessarily create Christians. Theologically

---

4. She recounts her full thoughts on "Why I Make Sam Go to Church" in Anne Lamott, *Traveling Mercies: Some Thoughts on Faith* (New York: Pantheon, 1999), 100.

5. Anne Lamott, "What Do You Know?," interview by Michael Feldman, National Public Radio, October 13, 2001.

6. Robert Wuthnow, "Religious Upbringing: Does It Matter, and If So, What Matters?" *Christ and the Adolescent: A Theological Approach to Youth Ministry — 1996 Princeton Lectures on Youth, Church and Culture* (Princeton, N.J.: Princeton Theological Seminary, 1997), 79.

7. Wuthnow, "Religious Upbringing," 79.

8. See Lamott, *Traveling Mercies*, 61.

speaking, Lamott is correct. Faith is the gift of the Holy Spirit, meted out by degrees or by debacle, and is not the product of religious practices. There is no telling God how or when or where the gift of faith is to be received. So Lamott is right: the dramatic conversion that rescued her from alcoholism and established her passionate relationship with Jesus could elude Sam and anyone else intentionally nurtured in the church. After all, this is partly *why* we bring our children to church — to spare them from *needing* Jesus to swoop in and save them from their own self-destruction. This is sheer fantasizing on our part, of course. Churchgoing young people are protected from self-destructive behavior only somewhat statistically and not at all existentially, for safety does not constitute salvation.

The Limits of Religious Socialization: Mules versus Horses

While religious socialization can create Christian-ish youth, by itself it cannot create Christian ones. Christian nurture offers a sense of group affiliation, but — as decades of confirmation graduates bountifully illustrate — this is not the same thing as a passionate commitment of faith.[9] Reflecting on his days as a youth in a prosperous southern California church in the 1970s, Wesley Theological Seminary president David McAllister-Wilson laments their rate of attrition. "We had sixty-some teenagers active in our youth group. Do you know how many of them still attend church as adults?" he asked me recently. "Five. Only five. Not that the others are in trouble," he added. "The youth group gave them a place to be healthy teenagers who grew up to be productive, interesting adults. We went to Disneyland and served at church barbecues and had our own band. It was the classic marriage of liberal Protestantism and American culture. And it created a mule: The offspring are healthy, but they can't reproduce."[10]

9. A large-scale sociological study noted that 48 percent of adults confirmed in the Presbyterian church during the 1950s and 1960s had left the church once they reached adulthood (Dean Hoge, Benton Johnson, and Donald Luidens, *Vanishing Boundaries: The Religion of Mainline Baby Boomers* [Louisville: Westminster/John Knox, 1994], 68); more than half of adolescents who attend church as children leave the church before they reach age seventeen. Wuthnow observes that while "growing up religious" often provides memories of people who serve as models of spiritual practices, a faith good for the long haul cannot rest on memories alone. We must rediscover these models, and sometimes transcend them, taking greater responsibility for our own spiritual development. See Wuthnow, *Growing Up Religious*, 167.

10. David McAllister-Wilson, personal conversation with author, October 5, 2001.

Despite tepid efforts during the 1960s to bring youth ministry under the umbrella of the larger mission of the church,[11] twentieth-century mainline Protestant youth ministry in America — by design — served primarily as a sanctified holding tank that protected young people from evil and educated them for a life of faith they were seldom asked to actually lead, at least not fully, until they became adults. Typically, churches viewed adolescents as objects of mission, not as agents of mission — recipients of, but not bearers of, divine grace in the Christian community. The result has been many more mules than horses. Congregations seldom invited young people into identity-shaping practices that undergirded the church's mission. Even in "active" youth programs, young people "gave devotions" but seldom preached, held fundraisers but seldom tithed, enjoyed fellowship but were seldom asked for a sacrificial commitment, took part in service projects but seldom developed meaningful relationships with those in need. In short, youth ministry lacked wonder-producing, faith-provoking, life-altering acts of witness that engaged young people in mission in their own right. Instead, youth ministry relied on adults' participation in the Passion of Christ on youth's behalf.

There have been, of course, exceptions. African-American churches, for instance, have often immersed young people in nurturing, familial relationships and leadership within the worshipping community. United by a shared experience of suffering, minority-culture Christians often identify with the gospel's passion narratives from the perspective of being "scape-

11. The most notable of these was Albert Van den Heuvel, *The New Creation and the New Generation: A Forum for Youth Workers* (New York: Friendship Press, 1965), who headed the department of Youth Work of the World Council of Churches at the time. See Ans Van der Bent, *From Generation to Generation: The Story of Youth in the World Council of Churches* (Geneva: World Council of Churches, 1986). In the United States, mainstream Protestant denominations — whose declining memberships forced cost-cutting measures — saw this move as theologically desirable and financially viable, and proceeded to annihilate denominational youth offices in the name of ecclesial "integration." In fact, chaos ensued; local congregations, wholly uncertain what integrating young people into the church's mission meant, could no longer turn to denominational offices for human, financial, or programmatic resources that would mediate the change in perspective. Most maintained age-segregated ministries, and after floundering for a decade, began to turn to entrepreneurs who provided independent training, personnel development, leadership programs, and even curriculum (giving rise to companies like Youth Specialties). Missing from most entrepreneurial responses, however, was a guiding theology capable of nuancing a market-driven "generic evangelicalism," leaving pragmatism to rule the day. Today, seminaries in the U.S. are showing increasing interest in filling this theological void, sometimes in partnership with their sponsoring denominations, whose youth departments never recovered from cuts in the 1960s, and who benefit from the resources provided by seminary partnerships.

goated" by the dominant culture. In these communities, taking part in practices that self-consciously identified with the suffering love of Jesus became important to the cultural fabric as well as to religious identity.[12] (Not surprisingly, Christian practices factor into the identities of Hispanic and African American youth more prominently than for their European American peers.)[13] Faith practices also are important to temporary Christian communities like camps and mission trips. These informal educational settings tend to rely on relational methodologies, and view youth as primary, though not permanent, partners in ministry. Many camps and mission events turn over the task of leadership to young people themselves, catapulting them directly into practices of worship, hospitality, and service usually reserved for adults "back home." Predictably, these young people commonly return from such events with significant faith decisions in hand.

Religious nurture does contribute to psychological development in important ways, offering among other things a sense of belonging to a community of caring peers and adults. Wuthnow's research indicates that young people who lack "a sense of belonging" in a faith community, even if they attend services regularly, seem to have difficulty understanding religion and integrating it into their life as adults.[14] Sociologists argue that interpersonal networks are the most important factor preceding conversion, and communities tend to be healthier overall when the majority of youth are involved in religious youth programs.[15] As a result, nurturing a sense of

12. In the U.S., at least, Hispanic communities tended to privilege the crucifix, Korean-American communities upheld the centrality of prayer, and African Americans brought the cadences of "call and response" worship to politics and popular music.

13. See Thomas J. Everson, "Spiritual Life Research Overview," *Pathways: Fostering Spiritual Growth among At-Risk Youth* (Boys Town, Neb.: Boys Town, USA, 1993), 5. In studies of high-risk teens, Hispanic youth report higher interest in church involvement, believe more strongly in God's unconditional love, and rate themselves higher on ability to pray "to get closer to God" and to apply the Bible to life than do either African American or Caucasian youth. African American young people score higher in all dimensions of spiritual life than Caucasian youth do. Although the economic privilege granted to European Americans in the U.S. makes corporate ideology prevalent even in small white churches, some rural congregations share certain kinship features as well, especially where farming requires the creation of temporary "extended families" for economic survival.

14. Wuthnow, *Growing Up Religious*, p. 192.

15. See Rodney Stark and Roger Finke, *Acts of Faith: Explaining the Human Side of Religion* (Berkeley: University of California Press, 2000); also, Dayle A. Blyth with Eugene Roehlkepartain, *Healthy Communities, Healthy Youth* (Minneapolis: Search Institute, 1992), 43: "Communities with a majority of youth attending religious services at least once a month are twice as likely to be among the healthiest versus the least healthy communities." While it

belonging in a Christian community is an article of faith for youth ministers, for socialization into a community of faith can lay a foundation for relationships that make God's love visible to young people.

The Necessary Lurch of Faith

Yet nurture alone cannot transform the passions of youth into the self-giving love of Christ. In fact, religious socialization can dull the blade of passion if its goal is to bring young people into productive church membership instead of into the passionate life of God. At some point, Christianity requires what Lamott calls a "lurch of faith" — a "decision of self," to use H. Richard Niebuhr's more delicate phrase — a choice that finally flings us into the arms of the One who seeks us. For Niebuhr, knowing *about* Jesus (knowing Jesus externally or objectively, apart from a relationship) and *knowing* Jesus (knowing Jesus internally or subjectively, as a participating "insider" in a relationship with him) are two different things, and in between them lies the chasm that separates God from humanity. There is only one way to cross it: Jump. Both feet must leave the ground — hope must replace certainty — and our being, our identity, must depend on being caught by grace. It is a paralyzing fear, for we know we cannot jump this far. So Christ established the church: a community to surround and testify that our inability to reach God will not stop God from reaching *us*. A transport exists; in Christ's Passion, Jesus has leapt into the void to meet us long before it occurs to us to reach for him.[16]

Of course, the so-called leap of faith is much too graceful to describe what happens to most of us in this process. We break down, get lost, and find our way again more times that we can count. When we need to refuel, the ancient practices of faith — rusty, dented, ordinary vessels of divine grace — are the best we have, proof that the church has been preparing for our lurching faith for centuries. Christian practices sustain these lurches, large and small, as we move toward God again and again with varying degrees of experience and efficiency.

The practices of the Christian community provide the human *framework* for faith, not its substance. At the same time, Jesus Christ, who

---

is tempting for churches to ascribe religiosity as the mitigating factor in youth's risky behavior, the likelihood of parental involvement and supportive structure of the community must also be taken into account.

16. H. Richard Niebuhr, *The Meaning of Revelation* (New York: W. W. Norton, 1949).

knows better than to trust our sense of direction in trying to reach him, indwells these human actions and comes to us through them — and consequently, comes to the world through us. In the church, the Spirit moves and breathes through communities that imitate Christ in these practices, supporting us as we wobble toward God. Of course, God does not *only* transform us in congregations. By "Christian community" I mean the visible church in all its forms, beginning with families and congregations but also — especially where youth are concerned — in parachurch groups, Christian camps, schools, missions, and informal faith communities like small groups, Bible studies, Internet gatherings, prayer networks, and the like.[17] We may encounter God in some off-road experience, but God's chosen location for transformation is the Christian community, and every practice of passion leads us there.

God's Grace in Human Practice

The term "practice" comes from a Greek root meaning "to do," or "to act." Practices knit us into the long history of Christian "doings" and strengthen us for the active mission God lays before us. But practices do not transform us; *grace* transforms us. Practices are God's multifaceted *means* of grace in the material world of human interaction, conduits of love that enliven our witness and that imbue us with the grace that makes holy passion possible. Practices are trail signs, left by generations of Christians who have gone before us, that point the way to the cross — reminders that in dying to self there is new life, assurance that in leaping into the chasm that separates us from God we will find God. They are as life-changing as Easter and as ordinary as Dixie cups by the sink in the middle of the night: small, useful (yet by themselves insignificant) containers God gives us so we may drink Living

17. In Protestant congregations, the most common form of ministry with young people (offered by nine out of ten Protestant congregations surveyed) is Sunday school, followed by camping (78 percent), confirmation (75 percent), and formal youth groups (74 percent). About half engage in some form of community service involving young people (47 percent) and only one in ten offer after school programs developed either locally or nationally (e.g., scouting, Logos, or Campfire groups). See Eugene C. Roehlkepartain and Peter C. Scales, *Youth Development in Congregations: An Exploration of the Potential and Barriers* (Minneapolis: Search Institute, 1995), 41-45. In the present study I have considered Sunday school a type of youth group, though it has distinct historical roots. Churches and curriculum vary in terms of how they distinguish Sunday school from youth groups generally, with substantial overlap in terms of both purpose and participants.

Water, and so we may carry it to others. These practices echo the life, death, and resurrection of Jesus Christ, and as a result they establish new patterns of relating to God and others on the basis of passion, defusing the socially constructed ego so that Christ may restore it to its proper place at the foot of the cross. Like a river whose currents cut a canyon over time, Christian practices carve what Dorothy Bass has called a "cruciform pattern" in the Christian community, a way of life that gives the church its distinctive identity as a community conformed to the passion of God.[18]

What unites practices, then, despite centuries of innovation, is their common referent in the suffering love of Christ — which is why, after two thousand years, we still recognize them. Praise celebrates God's suffering love in contemporary worship bands and in the Divine Liturgy. Justice imitates the self-giving love of God in intentional Christian communities and in youth groups collecting for UNICEF. Testimony points to the passion of God on the lips of a preacher or on the t-shirt of a teenager. In fact, practices' fidelity to the Passion of Christ is the only safeguard the church has against a time-bound, culture-bound, or style-bound Christianity. In every place and every time, we hear the gospel proclaimed in our own "language" through the practices of faith — the "tongues" of Christian tradition.

For this reason, Christian teaching has long commended these practices for establishing identity in young people, and for creating the conditions in which Christian transformation takes place.[19] Even today the practices of the Christian community bear a strong family resemblance to those shared by the first converts in Acts:

---

18. Dorothy Bass to Kenda Creasy Dean, March 31, 2002, personal correspondence.

19. The conversation linking social identity to community practices has reemerged recently with new force, spanning a number of disciplines. The seminal work of communitarian ethicist Alasdair MacIntyre (*After Virtue: A Study in Moral Theory* [Notre Dame: University of Notre Dame Press, 1981]) draws on Aristotelian ethics, and in many ways established the terms for the current discussion. Sociologists like Stark and Finke (*Acts of Faith*), Christian Smith ("Religious Practices of American Youth" [project in progress]), and Robert Wuthnow (*Growing Up Religious*), and theologians like Dorothy C. Bass (*Practicing Our Faith* [San Francisco: Jossey-Bass, 1998], and, with Miroslav Volf, *Practicing Theology: Beliefs and Practices in Christian Life* [Grand Rapids: Eerdmans, 2002]), Craig Dykstra (*Growing in the Life of Faith: Education and Christian Practices* [Louisville: Geneva Press, 1999]), James Fowler (*Becoming Adult, Becoming Christian: Adult Development and Christian Faith* [San Francisco: Jossey-Bass, 2000]), L. Gregory Jones (*Embodying Forgiveness: A Theological Analysis* [Grand Rapids: Eerdmans, 1995]), and Richard R. Osmer (*The Teaching Ministry of Congregations* [Louisville: Westminster/John Knox, forthcoming]) have been prominent voices in this discussion.

Those who welcomed [Peter's] message were baptized, and that day about three thousand persons were added. They devoted themselves to the apostles' teaching and fellowship, to the breaking of bread and the prayers. Awe came upon everyone, because many wonders and signs were being done by the apostles. All who believed were together and had all things in common; they would sell their possessions and goods and distribute the proceeds to all, as any had need. Day by day, as they spent much time together in the temple, they broke bread at home and ate their food with glad and generous hearts, praising God and having the goodwill of all the people. And day by day the Lord added to their number those who were being saved. (Acts 2:41-47, NRSV)

Two millennia later, we have refined — but we have yet to improve upon — the basic parameters of practices set forth by the earliest Christians (see figures 4 and 5).[20] *Leitourgia* (liturgy), *koinonia* (hospitality and fellowship), *kerygma* (proclamation), *didache* (teaching and discipleship), *diakonia* (compassion), *doxologia* (praise and worship), and *marturia* (witness) pro-

---

20. Christian practices share, with some modifications, the same external characteristics as practices in other communities, as described by MacIntyre. The most obvious of these is their *performative* nature: practices do things — and, the Christian asserts, through these practices God does things as well. MacIntyre describes practices as cooperative; I believe a more adequate term is *playful*: practices absorb us in the "back-and-forthness" of a cooperative relationship (though that relationship might be with a text or an object as well as a human being), with whom we observe certain rules and boundaries that tacitly point beyond the practice itself toward a larger reality. Like a game of basketball or a good conversation or a mesmerizing liturgy, a practice allows us to "lose" ourselves in play even while observing its governing structure, momentarily setting aside the ego so that we may partially identify with the larger reality to which it points. Playfulness serves the important function of reducing the ego in the reconstruction of self. In addition, practices are socially established — they arise over time from a community's history to sustain its ethos. Nobody votes to start a practice, and since practices have internal goods — benefits only available to those who participate in them, that come from doing the practice, not from the practice's results — no one votes to suspend them, either. The benefit of worship, for instance, comes from the act of worshipping, not from the quality of the sermon or the music. Even so, we recognize standards of excellence in practices that we pass on to our children. Since these standards are intrinsic to the practice itself, they tend to resist cultural accommodation — even though the external form of a practice may be extensively adapted to context. And because we deem them valuable, practices bear moral weight. Dykstra adds the significant observation that they bear epistemological weight as well; that is, they are conditions for certain kinds of knowledge we cannot grasp outside of the practice itself, and therefore they shape our identities and constitute our communities (Dykstra, "Reconceiving Practice," in *Shifting Boundaries: Contextual Approaches to the Structure of Theological Education,* ed. Barbara G. Wheeler and Edward Farley (Louisville: Westminster/John Knox Press, 1991), 42-46.

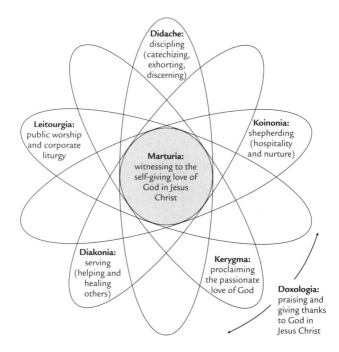

Figure 4. Constellation of Christian Practices (Classical View)

vide the historical framework for this discussion. In "real life," of course, every act of witness is braided thickly into the others — and more harm comes from over-categorizing than under-categorizing them. Christian life is a totality, and the acts of witness that compose it resist unraveling thread by thread. The distinctive feature of Christian practice is grace, and divine grace always defies classification (though this has not stopped contemporary scholars from adapting classical categories of Christian practices for the contemporary church and for youth ministry in particular).[21]

21. Among the first major efforts to put the language of practice in adolescent hands is the attentive work of Dorothy Bass and Don Richter, eds., *Way to Live* (Nashville: Upper Room, 2002). They paired scholars with teenagers to develop a sampling of Christian practices adapted for adolescents: joining the story (Bible study), welcoming, eating, and drinking in the spirit of Jesus, body caring, discovering your work, playing, taking time (sabbath-keeping), managing your stuff (living simply), caring for creation, choosing well (discerning), living truthfully, being friends, healing the hurt (forgiving), facing grief and loss, seeking justice, being creative, making music, prayer. Comparing it to Dykstra's list of practices gleaned from Christian tradition is instructive — if nothing else, for seeing the limits of categorization. (Originally, the youth list was based on Bass's earlier work, *Practicing Our Faith* [San

Figure 5. Constellation of Christian Practices (Contemporary View)[22]

We could, therefore, justly insist that every practice of Christian life is a form of witness and worship — a position to which I subscribe — since every practice of the Christian community bears witness *(marturia)* to Christ's life, death, and resurrection, and culminates in praise and thanksgiving *(doxologia)*. But definitions have limited use, for practices do not park neatly in their spaces. Some take up many parking spots (is prayer an act of compassion, a form of divine catechesis, or an act of praise?) while others are quite specifically located (baptism and the Eucharist always occur in the context of *doxologia, kerygma,* and *leitourgia*). While every practice incorporates us into the suffering love of Jesus, baptism and

---

Francisco: Jossey-Bass, 1997]). The adolescent practices include a number of practices related to creativity (being creative, making music, playing) and stewardship (body caring, caring for creation, eating and drinking) that Dykstra does not mention explicitly, though they could reasonably be imbedded in others (for example, "making music" is often a form of worship for young people, and Christians of every century would acknowledge "being creative" as a faithful practice constitutive of many others). No single list can offer a true picture of the way practices penetrate human communities at multiple levels.

22. Dykstra, "Reconceiving Practice," 42-43. I have slightly reworded for clarity.

communion are normative in this regard, incorporating us into Christ's Passion quite explicitly. For the most part, however, we can agree that practices in the Christian community

- are meaningful human actions that mark us as, and shape us into, people who follow Jesus;
- are imperfect in ways that require a certain amount of "improvisation" to address particular situations across generations and cultures; and
- comprise the constituent elements for a way of life that God acts in and through to infuse grace into the world.[23]

To say it another way: no matter what form a practice takes, all Christian practices contribute to the transformation of passion.

Now may be a good time to ask yourself: Does youth ministry as I know it do these things? Does ministry with adolescents where I go to church resemble the faith community in Acts, or does it seem more like a moral club or a service organization? Is my canvas for ministry with young people stretched across a frame of Christian practices, or is it tacked onto the beams of wholesome entertainment, content mastery, and

---

23. In *Ecclesial Reflection* (Philadelphia: Fortress, 1982), Edward Farley notes how the church has been sustained through the ages by Christian practices which he describes as proclamatory, sacramental, and caring activities. I am grateful to Don Richter for clarifying the contrast between Farley's concept of "ecclesial activities" and Alasdair MacIntyre's concept of "social practices" that characterize human communities generally. Richter sets up the differences this way: (1) Ecclesial activities have both a near and far horizon; they are directed toward a specific community and away from that community to environments near and distant (including the eschatological faith community). Social practices have a near horizon, yet have a far horizon only in projecting how present activity might shape the future — not discerning how the future shapes present practice. (2) Ecclesial activities reflect the structure of ecclesial process as a "celebrative remembering" of a normative, originating event (i.e., the Passion of Christ), and this remembering serves as the lens of interpretation for the present reality. Social practices may rehearse their origins but are not continually reconstituted by celebrating original events. The prevailing sense is that the "state of the art" is to be found in the present development of a practice. (3) Ecclesial activities serve a universalizing function in two ways: they relativize the cultural artifacts of their mediation while intending an openness that subverts sectarianism. They exist for the sake of the world and not only for the church. Social practices invite others into provincial cultural forms as the way to become co-participants; they have no "missionary impetus" requiring members of the practice community to share their group activity with the wider world. See Don Carl Richter, "Christian Nurture in Congregations: Ecclesial Practices as Social Means of Grace" (unpublished Ph.D. dissertation, Princeton Theological Seminary, 1992), 269-71.

good works — valuable activities, but bereft of power to bestow identity because their transformational connection to Christ's life, death, and resurrection has been lost? Immersing young people in practices of self-giving love in a self-fulfilling culture makes them subversive, dangerous, odd — much like the Christ they follow. How subversive, dangerous, or odd are the Christian youth I know? For that matter, how subversive, dangerous, or odd am I?

Christian practices do more than re-enact historic events to shape young people into members of religious communities. In every practice, Jesus enters the room though the doors be closed. The church reconstitutes the suffering love of Jesus Christ in human acts of self-giving love that imperfectly draw us into Christ's Passion through grace, making it present again and again. From the earliest days of the church, these practices have *heightened* the tension between the faithful and the secular order, clearing the highway so that Christ may enter. When young people are participants in — not just recipients of — Jesus' Passion, they are drawn into a "cruciform pattern" of suffering love that changes how they relate to God, to one another, and indeed to all creation.[24] In this way, youth ministry becomes a vehicle for the Holy Spirit's ongoing conversion — and by conversion I mean both adolescents' personal, lifelong journeys of faith, and the Holy Spirit's "conversion" of young people into vessels of grace for the sake of the world.

The Transformation of Identity

Most of us assume that our beliefs lead us to act in ways consistent with those beliefs. If that were true, I would drink far less Diet Coke and spend a lot more time at the gym. I would pray at dawn and be in bed after "West Wing," which I would have watched lovingly with my husband because the bills would be paid and the grading would be done and the children (after engrossing conversation about the day) would be nestled snug in their beds. I would anticipate tomorrow as an unfolding promise, not as the prisoner of my Palm Pilot. I would live like this because I believe all of these things matter for a holy life.

I don't need to tell you what life is *really* like at our house. Suffice it to say that I succumb easily to the myth that behavior follows understanding,

24. I am indebted to Dorothy Bass, who pointed out to me the importance of relational language in the discussion of Christian practices, and who suggested the language of a "cruciform pattern" to describe the shape of self-giving love in human relationships.

that what I believe issues in the way I act. In fact, my behavior invariably "leaks" my true theological priorities — which painfully and all too often contradict the ones I profess. Our Christian forebears knew full well that a change of behavior is at least as likely to produce a change of heart as vice versa, and thought enlightenment stemmed from doing "sacred acts." As theologian Margaret Miles puts it, "Practices both prepare the conditions under which religious experiences are likely to occur and, subsequent to such experiences, provide a lifestyle that integrates and perpetuates them."[25] Thus, the "Acts" of the Apostles is the early church's record of apostolic "praxis" that convinced people that Jesus is Lord, and that composed a convincing lifestyle for this witness.

What are the conditions in which such convincing religious transformation is likely to occur? And what kind of lifestyle integrates and perpetuates this transformation? Youth do not "will" themselves to identify with Christ any more than we do; God begins this process of identification, unleashing unasked-for grace by preveniently fanning wavering flames of curiosity until they take hold as nascent faith. Consequently, uncommitted youth who take part in Christian practices through, say, a mission trip to Appalachia or a moving Lenten liturgy are as likely to be as changed by their participation in these practices as stalwart believers, although *persistence* in a practice does alter our experience of it. As youth draw nearer to God's *pathos* in the practices of faith, they approach these acts of witness less and less as deeds that dramatize their beliefs, and more and more as means of grace that help them remain responsive before God.

If we were to explain this shift theologically, we would say that social formation represents a gain by helping youth identify with a community, but that Christian transformation requires a *loss,* a brokenness of ego, as young people identify with Jesus' death. As Miles explains, "Because the religious self is created from the very same energy that was formerly spent on the social self and its agenda, the self-importance of the socialized self must be reduced to nothing in order to achieve the new self-identification, . . . a self defined by its relation of trust and confidence in God."[26] The church uses unambiguous language in this regard. We must "crucify the self" and "die to sin" (Rom. 6:6-11) to be "united with Jesus in a death like

25. Margaret Miles, *Practicing Christianity: Critical Perspectives for an Embodied Spirituality* (New York: Crossroad, 1988), 90.

26. Miles, *Practicing Christianity,* 110. Although Miles fails to recognize the depth of transformation available in Christian practice, I found her work extremely helpful in giving a language to the transformation of the socialized self into a religious self, which she attributes to participation in Christian practices.

his" in order to "be united with him in a resurrection like his" (Rom. 6:5). Faith practices occasion "little deaths" of the fractured, socially constructed ego. In giving ourselves away in love, we continually "die" and "rise" along with Jesus, decreasing so that Christ may increase (John 3:30).

But here is the surprising news: Jesus does not obliterate the ego, he transforms it. In the hands of the One who made us, we are reconstructed by grace. As we participate in practices of self-giving love, the Holy Spirit tenders a *habitus* of passionate responsiveness to God that becomes so ingrained in us that it defines us as Christians. In this crucible of transformation, the illusory, incomplete, socially constructed self — the "false" self, as D. W. Winnicott called it[27] — is "crucified" and we are made new (Gal. 2:20) as the Christ in whose image we were made becomes visible in us through the practices of faith. In these practices, we are literally given "new birth" as we are incorporated into the life of God, and as Christ's identity becomes our own.

To put it simply, in the practices of the Christian community Christ recreates us by restoring our "true self" made in the image of God — the person God created to be in the first place. In this process, the ego becomes relativized to the cross. The Holy Spirit roots the flimsy adolescent ego in the safe soil of Christ's Passion, causing teenagers to experience themselves as "saved," quite literally, from whatever formerly threatened their fragile sense of being. Stanley Hauerwas and William Willimon are characteristically blunt: "Acquiring practices is another way to say *conversion*. Something is gained; something is lost as well. Rarely are practices acquired without some cost, without detoxification, without letting go of the practices of a former existence in order to embrace another."[28]

---

27. See D. W. Winnicott, "Ego Distortion in Terms of True and False Self," *The Maturational Processes and the Facilitating Environment* (London: Hogarth Press and the Institute for Psycho-Analysis, 1965) and *Playing and Reality* (London: Routledge, 1971), 68, 102. Winnicott considered the false self one who complies with a false personality that masks that which is original to the self. Thus, false selves compromise the creative impulse, though not altogether successfully: "There cannot be a complete destruction of a human individual's capacity for creative living. . . . Even in the most extreme case of compliance and the establishment of a false personality, hidden away somewhere there exists a secret life that is satisfactory because of its being creative or original to that human being. Its unsatisfactoriness must be measured in terms of its being hidden, its lack of enrichment through lived experience" (Winnicott, *Playing and Reality,* 68). We can attribute Winnicott's observation that "there cannot be a complete destruction of a human individual's capacity for creative living" to the faint echo of the *imago dei* that, though broken and defiled by sin, still resides in us.

28. Stanley Hauerwas and William Willimon, *Where Resident Aliens Live* (Nashville: Abingdon, 1996), 80.

For adolescents, those in whom the "social self" is only half formed at best, being "saved" is extremely good news. Mainline Protestants tend to cringe at this language, which comes loaded with generations of theological baggage. But the sense of rescue implied by the term "salvation" is not lost on teenagers, whose slippery selfhood imbues them with the constant sense that they are about to go under — the fear that they could be a nobody. Yet here, in the Passion of Jesus Christ, is a Somebody who loves them with utter fidelity, ecstasy, intimacy — the raw materials that make "nobodies" into "somebodies" and that transform *homo sapiens* into human beings. Consequently, trading in the incomplete social self for a new identity in a passionate God seems like a tremendous gain, and faith practices are a route to this transformation:

> The "self" cultivated by religious practices is not the socialized self, crusty with habits, imbedded in a society that shapes and conditions desire around available and approved objects and lifestyles. Rather, the self identified and strengthened in religious practice is the self in relationship to God. The goal of the practice of Christianity is to make this self strong enough to form the center around which the whole personality can be organized so that, as Gregory of Nyssa put it, the two aspects of the person, body and soul, can become one, and a "harmony of dissonant parts" can be achieved.[29]

Liberated from cramped cultural definitions of personal identity, the authentic identity God restores in young people as they practice faith gives the self newfound traction. This new self finds its center in the cross and its mortar in the practices of the Christian community that make the Passion of Christ visible in the world.[30]

29. Miles, *Practicing Christianity,* 32-33.

30. It should be clear that the loss of self implied by identifying with, and participating in, the life and death of Jesus Christ is not the same loss of self (and in fact counters the loss of self) experienced by those who are socialized into invisibility. On this score Miles stops too soon, equating the surrender of ego in Christian practice with "self-sacrificing attention to the needs of others . . . [that do] not provide a correction to gender conditioning that encourages and rewards women's self-abnegation and single-minded attention to the needs of men and children" (Miles, *Practicing Christianity,* 90). Miles' concern should not go unnoticed by youth ministers, especially since many girls seem to abnegate the self around age eleven in favor of preserving relationships, especially with boys (cf. Lyn Mikel Brown and Carol Gilligan, *Meeting at the Crossroads: Women's Psychology and Girls' Development* [Cambridge: Cambridge University Press, 1992]). Yet she is led to conclude, "The imitation of Christ's gentleness, compassion, and self-sacrificial love is damaging to women in societies that demand of women, and socialize them to, such attitudes and behavior" (Miles, *Practicing Christianity,*

A Curriculum of Passion: Finding Our Depth

What I am suggesting, then, is that the practices of the Christian community should comprise the core of Christian curriculum for young people. That may look tidy on paper, but in fact it requires a revolution in the way mainline Protestants have approached youth ministry for over a century. Yet for most of Christian history the practices of faith were the only "curriculum" the church knew, for young and old alike. A brief glance at the ascetic and mystical Christians of the early and medieval church illustrates the point, and the substance of their teaching can guide our own. For no one was more concerned with identifying with Jesus than these hardy disciples, and Living Water came to them in the same vessels it comes to adolescents: in the ordinary practices of the faith community.

The basis for ascetic and mystical theologians' teaching on discipleship can be described in terms of the *purgative, illuminative,* and *unitive* phases of spiritual awareness that characterized Christian formation in the early and medieval church.[31] Because Christian practices do not simply enact our belief in God — rather, they help *shape* our belief in God — practices instill theological insight as well as enact it, for in these acts of witness God "practices" grace in us. Charting youth ministry through these "levels" of spiritual practices gives our work with young people a rough correspondence to the classical stages of spiritual formation, but it also raises the bar for adolescent discipleship. The goal of Christian identity is sanctification, not individuation; holiness, not just conversion. And youth ministry grounded in the practices of faith stops at nothing less.

---

40). This conclusion is astounding in light of Miles' own research. The heart of Christian identity is the surrender of the culturally cultivated self in order to receive the new life intended for us by God. In baptism, after all, we not only die with Christ; we are raised with Christ. Her critique is all the more surprising in light of the fact that she cites the lives of Teresa of Avila, Julian of Norwich, and others — women who developed highly individuated selves and resisted much of the oppressive socialization of their time precisely by devoting themselves seriously to Christian practice. In Christian tradition, to lose one's life in Jesus Christ is to gain it; to surrender the ego is to receive it back, transformed. Authentic Christian practice counters Miles' concern by grounding the emerging self in the Passion of Christ — a Passion completed by resurrection, composed of love that is both passive and proactive. Only by failing to adjust Christian practices for the particularities of ministry would practices become "dangerous." In those cases, practices would also cease to be authentic.

31. Sarah Coakley, "Deepening Practices: Perspectives from Ascetical and Mystical Theology," in Miroslav Volf and Dorothy C. Bass, eds., *Practicing Theology* (Grand Rapids: Eerdmans, 2002).

Ascetic and mystical theology sought to deepen human identification with God through three stages of Christian practice: (1) *Purgative* practices that rid the self of attachments that impede our ability to receive God's grace, and are especially important for distinguishing the religious self from the social self in the early stages of faith; (2) *Illuminative* practices that seek Christ's presence in daily life, and that offer the grace necessary for intentional, day-to-day faithfulness in Christian community; and (3) *Unitive* practices that enjoy God's gracious "practice" of holiness *in us,* giving us new insights about God and forging us "by degrees into 'the image of his Son'" (Rom. 8:29).[32] The practices of earlier stages are never discarded; rather, they are taken in (and taken for granted by) the levels that follow — and, of course, the progression is always messier in real life than on paper.[33] Alluding to W. H. Vanstone (who once compared the church to a swimming pool: "All the noise comes from the shallow end"), Sarah Coakley contends that discomfort about religious practices tends to come from those who have not engaged in them long enough or seriously enough to get to the "deep end" of the pool.[34] Certainly youth have not; nor have many of their parents, youth leaders, or pastors.

Watch Me, Watch Me:
Youth Ministry in the Shallow End

So here is the crux of our problem: For most of the twentieth century, mainline Protestants have done youth ministry in the shallow end of the theological pool. No wonder we are exhausted. In the theological shallows, Christian practices seem self-propelled, not grace-propelled, and we tire quickly. The shallow end of theology has its purpose; here young people test the theological waters, take their first tentative strokes toward Jesus, and spend an enormous amount of energy just trying to figure out what

32. Coakley, "Deepening Practices," 79.

33. Coakley acknowledges the risk of spiritual elitism that comes from "grading" practices, but she maintains that Christian maturity cannot happen on a flat plane: "There is a subtle sliding scale here: one starts from practices one might be tempted to regard as entirely self-propelled; but they are joined over time by practices that involve deeper and more demanding levels of response to divine grace and that uncover by degrees the implications of our fundamental reliance on that grace as initiated in baptism." Coakley, "Deepening Practices," 80.

34. Coakley, "Deepening Practices," 81.

Christian life *is.* To be sure, even before we acquire theological depth, God infuses even small acts of witness with grace, but in the shallow end we continually attempt to reduplicate God's effort, which is a little like bringing a life jacket to the baby pool. In truth, neither young people nor the adults satisfied with serving God from the shallow end have any inkling how little we actually risk for faith. Our unfamiliarity with the depths of grace makes every act of passion feel like a high platform dive. And, given adolescents' lack of faith experience and our own lack of theological muscle tone, practicing passion in the shallow end *is* a high risk proposition for most of us. Consequently, we overlook opportunities to dive deeply into Christian tradition, and focus on clever antics designed to win young people's attention instead.

Like adults, young people quickly tire of watching grownups do somersaults to win their approval and affection. After all, we are the people who *lead* the church, and who profess an interest in nurturing the discipleship of our young; we are supposed to know how to navigate the deeper parts of the pool, and teach them to do the same. The point of ministry is never to "watch me," but to "join me" — patterning our lives more perfectly after the passion of God in the process. Ascetic and mystical theologians believed that imitating Christ is like eating an artichoke: you start on the outside and move to the center, one layer at a time. But the point is, no matter how long it takes, Christian life has a destination: identification with the Passion of Jesus Christ. The disciplined life of faith, therefore, starts with practices that assist youth and their communities in the *extrinsic* imitation of Christ, but they must go deeper than this; they must move to *intrinsic* identification with Christ, and finally to *union* with Christ.

Practices of faith are not intended for accumulation; they are intended for transportation, as inroads to the fidelity, ecstasy, and intimacy — the passion — of God. So what would happen if we *adults* in mainline Protestant youth ministry ventured more deeply into Christian practices to begin to fathom divine passion? And how might we invite adolescents, once we have found our depth, to come into the "deep end" with us?

Level One — Purgation:
Learning to Put Down the Ducky

At one point on the PBS children's series *Sesame Street,* Ernie — rubber ducky in hand — tells Mr. Hoots that he wants to learn to play the saxophone. In one of the show's most memorable numbers, Mr. Hoots (a jazz-loving owl) gives Ernie a lesson in purgation: "You gotta put down the ducky if you wanna play the saxophone."

The faith practices most of us learn in youth ministry are practices of purgation: acts that pry our fingers loose from our "duckies," our old attachments that impede our ability to fully receive God's grace. These spiritual disciplines imitate Christ extrinsically, seeking detachment — the "letting go" of sinful passions that misshape the self. Obviously, this is a lifetime pursuit. Yet beginning with baptism forward, the church emphasizes a course of life that distinguishes a Christian ethic from a secular one, because new believers (youth included) need precise instruction on actions that do, and do not, inculcate a virtuous life.

For this reason, the church has historically viewed purgative practices as a starting point in the life of faith, in many cases leaving very little to the imagination. Tertullian (c. 160–220) instructed female converts to watch how they walk: "It is your obligation to be different from [pagan women], as in all other things, so also in your gait, since you ought to be perfect as your heavenly Father is perfect."[35] Clement of Alexandria (153-220) instructed new converts by dispensing moral advice on everything from "behaviour in the baths" to earrings ("Take away, then, directly, the ornaments from women");[36] he called upon men to avoid effeminate conduct, argued against plucking out the beards of youth, and warned women to avoid "occupying themselves in curling at their locks . . . anointing their cheeks, painting their eyes, and dyeing their hair."[37] John Chrysostom (347-407) used his ninth baptismal instruction to forbid swearing and other "sins of speech" among the "newly-illumined."[38] In purgative practices, fidelity to one's convictions is acted out in literal, sometimes legalistic ways as the new believer imitates Christ "externally," seeking to distinguish herself as a follower of Jesus in a pagan culture.

---

35. Tertullian, "The Apparel of Women," 1:4, in *Tertullian: Disciplinary, Moral and Ascetical Works,* trans. Rudolph Arbesmann et al. (New York: Fathers of the Church, Inc., 1959), 130.

36. Clement of Alexandria, "The Instructor," ed. Alexander Roberts and James Donaldson, in *The Ante-Nicene Fathers: Translations of the Fathers Down to A.D. 325* (Grand Rapids: Eerdmans, 1986), vol. 3, chapter 6, 280. Chapter 5 is devoted to "behaviour in the baths" (279).

37. Clement of Alexandria, "The Instructor," 277, 273. The wearing of make-up earned special ire from Clement: "Thrice, I say, not once, do they deserve to perish, who use crocodiles' excrement, and anoint themselves with the froth of putrid humors, and stain their eyebrows with soot, and rub their cheeks with white lead" (273).

38. John Chrysostom, *Baptismal Instructions,* trans. Paul W. Harkins (Westminster, Md.: Newman Press and London: Longmans, Green and Co., 1963), 145-49.

Youth ministry has always instinctively swerved in this direction, perhaps motivated by equal parts faith and fear. Let's return to the W.W.J.D. movement for a moment. Although teenagers tended to treat "What Would Jesus Do?" bracelets as expressions of personal witness, parents and pastors (apparently naïve to the amount of questionable behavior going on between youth wearing their W.W.J.D. bracelets) remained steadfast in their conviction that these bracelets imparted an unambiguous moral standard — the example of Jesus himself — that believing teens would follow. In fact, one of the problems with purgative practices is that *only* believing teens follow them (and even then, there are few guarantees). Uncommitted youth generally fail to see the point of such arbitrary ethical standards and sometimes feel ostracized by youth who practice them, since one purpose of purgation is to hold the pagan world at bay.

Christian history weighs in decisively on the importance of unambiguous moral standards and clear catechetical instruction for beginning believers, who must daily distinguish between the socially constructed ego and the self constructed by grace. In the early stages of faith, Christian identity remains fragile, and requires a degree of protection — a shallow end where the young person can "touch" ground in practices that give her skills and buoyancy in deeper theological waters. Youth ministry in the shallow end of the pool focuses on boundaries and basics. Although every generation adapts spiritual practices for the particulars of its age (few of us would want to precisely replicate Clement's advice for twenty-first-century teenagers), practices of purgation nonetheless play an important role in youth ministry. Since every young person is a relatively new Christian, practices of purgation help young people learn to distinguish themselves from consumer culture, and therefore make a crucial contribution to the adolescent's quest for a sustainable self.

Level Two — Illumination:
Discovering the Daily Grace of Running Water

At the same time, many young people — especially those with deep roots in the church — often have less fragile Christian identities than we think. Imitating Christ requires *intrinsic,* as well as extrinsic, identification with Jesus, and as young people develop the cognitive and spiritual capacities that make intrinsic identification possible, they need the challenge of deeper parts of the theological pool. The purpose of purgative practices, after all, is not to *keep* young people in the shallow end, but to help them develop the strength and skills to swim *out* of it. Failing to invite these youth into deeper theological water only convinces them that, because they are too big for the baby pool, they have "outgrown" the church.

We don't have to look far for evidence of this misperception. When confirmation fails to lead to mission, it quickly mutates into a rite of passage *out* of the congregation. When church school curriculum avoids problematic biblical passages and hermeneutical critique (which young people usually offer anyway), adolescents with their newly acquired cognitive skills quickly conclude that Christian education (and maybe Christianity) is better left to those with lesser intellects. When youth groups take "What would Jesus do?" to mean "Who would Jesus date, what would Jesus wear, how would Jesus relate to his parents, and what college would Jesus go to?" their premise not only suffers from exceedingly slim documentation (the documentation we do have would not cheer most parents); it implies that Jesus is no longer with us, and fails to convey Christ's life as *sacrificial* — thereby missing the point of self-giving love altogether.

Practices of illumination invite young people into a deeper awareness of God by challenging them to pursue holiness in the company of others. It is one thing to resolve to live a life of self-giving love as an individual; it is quite another to do so in the context of a concrete community of faith. Benedict's famous *Rule* offers a prime example of illuminative practices, which are far less explicit (and punitive) than the purgative instructions to new converts. The *Rule* explicitly recognized a role for purgation in the outset of Christian life, and advocated it especially for children and youth.[39] But the *Rule*'s purpose was to guide life in the monastery — a form of community intended to train people for a lifetime of faithfulness *together*. "We must establish a school for the Lord's service," wrote Benedict in the *Rule*'s prologue. "In its organization, we have tried not to create anything grim or oppressive. In a given case we may have to arrange things a bit strictly to correct vice or preserve charity. When that happens, do not immediately take fright and flee the path of salvation, which can only be narrow at its outset. . . . We will participate in the passion of Christ through patience so as deserve to be companions in his kingdom."[40]

---

39. See Rule 30: "Every age and mentality should have an appropriate regimen. Therefore, as regards children or youths, or those who have little understanding of the gravity of excommunication, when such people misbehave, they should be deprived of food or pressured with sharp blows to correct them." Benedict of Nursia, *Benedict's Rule: A Translation and Commentary*, trans. Terrence G. Kardong (Collegeville, Minn.: Liturgical Press, 1996), 249-50.

40. Benedict of Nursia, *Benedict's Rule*, prologue, 3.

Benedict focused on *illuminative* practices that stress the subtle transformation available in ongoing, repeated acts of witness that shape the communal as well as the personal life of witness, like singing the psalms, harvesting the grain, welcoming the stranger. The *Rule* was followed, not to keep the world at bay, but to develop a lifetime *habitus* of self-giving love. This *habitus* washed over the community like running water, slowly smoothing sharp edges and creating flows that allowed people to live and work together. As a result, Benedict took seriously daily, bodily concerns like sleeping arrangements, attending to the body's proper use in worship, and adapting clothing and footwear to the local climate. Benedict trusted that daily attentiveness to the community's life together, enacted through disciplined repetition of these practices, would almost subliminally "re-modulate beliefs, . . . [causing] us to find Christ . . . in new and unexpected places."[41] Illuminative practices assume a clear identity forged by purgation but soften its boundaries, allowing the believer to internalize a *habitus* of self-giving love to the point that encountering the "other" is no longer threatening:

> Christ ceases to be merely an external model to be imitated, but is recognized in the poor, the stranger at the gate; creeds cease to be merely tools of judgment, but rather rules of life into which to enter and flourish; beliefs cease to be merely charters of orthodoxy dictating right practice, but rather practices start to infuse beliefs with richer meaning.[42]

For Benedict, the source of spiritual re-modulation was not prayer (about which Benedict says remarkably little) but the faithful repetition of daily practices that imitate Christ for the sake of others (about which Benedict said quite a lot).[43] Illuminative practices alter our grasp of God over time by enacting God's grasp of us, leaving nothing outside of God's embrace: bodies, work, play, praise, neighbor and stranger.

On the one hand, contemporary Christians — teenagers especially — are put off by repeated practices, thinking they contribute to a rote, automatic, and therefore inauthentic faith. As youth leaders, we cower before the tyranny of the new in an effort to interest young people who have invariably "been there, done that." Yet the contemporary cry for "community," sounded loudly by adolescents, inevitably draws them to precisely the kind of illuminative practices Benedict advocated. Communities de-

---

41. Coakley, "Deepening Practices," 86-87.
42. Coakley, "Deepening Practices," 85, 92.
43. Coakley, "Deepening Practices," 87.

pend on repetition, and religious ones are no exception; sociologists insist that repeated practices *deepen* commitment to faith and intensify the faithful's sense of authenticity.[44] Educators note that the single most important variable in learning is redundancy — and despite their protests to the contrary, young people surround themselves with it. CD technology allows youth to play their favorite songs again and again; school years are marked by liturgical rhythms (homecoming, winter break, wrestling season, prom, finals, summer vacation). In some cities, friends pour libations on the curb after a teenager's death or emblazon their fallen comrade's school picture on t-shirts and teddy bears; in suburban and rural areas, students enshrine classmates killed in automobile accidents by marking the site of the crash with white crosses, flowers, and other expressions of grief. Adolescents impose rituals where none exist (try changing "traditions" on the last night of camp) and seek concrete symbols as a way to return again and again to transcendent experiences. The t-shirt from a rock concert, the ring from a boyfriend, the story (retold for the hundredth time) about how Bob faked out the substitute teacher are all sacred artifacts — not because they have intrinsic value, but because they are breadcrumbs in the forest, providing a way to return to something that mattered. In ways that are both subtle and explicit, recognized and unrecognized, teenagers practice redundancy in an effort to capture the ineffable, to touch transcendence, and to receive comfort and insight.

When youth ministry draws its primary energy from special events, "cool" leaders, and high-voltage youth gatherings more than from the long tradition of practices through which youth identify with the life, death, and resurrection of Christ, we communicate a version of faith that has no analogy in the adult church — or in real life, for that matter. Let me be clear: I love special events, I am grateful for "cool" leaders, and I do my share of high-voltage activities that "hype" mission and ministry among young people. But by themselves, these activities lack the necessary fuel to get adolescents to the cross. They cannot shape Christian identity either by helping young people relinquish the social self or by helping them acquire a new self through imitating Christ. Christian identity requires redundancy as well as revelation, a daily rhythm of grace that may or may not be punctuated by "spiritual highs."

Worship and liturgy often function in this regard as the community

---

44. Wuthnow points out that people who "who engage most fervently in spiritual practices are most likely to admit that the spirit of God is more encompassing than any human practice could adequately address." Wuthnow, *Growing Up Religious,* 192.

regularly interrupts its labors — every few hours, if you are a Benedictine monk or nun — with the good news that God has entered the world yet again. If purgative practices underscore Christianity's distinctiveness, illuminative practices underscore its openness. These practices order work, play, worship, and relationships according to the cruciform pattern of self-giving love and draw young people to Christ almost imperceptibly. As Coakley points out, the passion narratives facilitate "a progressive, albeit slow, identification of the self with the 'handing over' of Christ to his death" — and to be sure, there can be long stretches without obvious progress.[45] Yet within the practices of illumination lies a paradox. Although they foster daily and uncelebrated "little deaths" to the developing ego, illuminative practices also yield a communal life that evokes genuine ecstasy for teenagers. Longing for belonging, adolescents willingly trade pizzazz for the deep satisfaction of authentic community, where self-giving love is the norm for relationships with one another as well as with God.

Level Three — Union: Contemplating Change

One of the most intriguing developments in mainline Protestant youth ministry in the 1990s was a renewed interest in contemplative prayer, much of it grounded in Ignatian spiritual exercises and supported by a number of research projects on Christian practices during this period.[46] It must also be said that most contemplative prayer in youth ministry (in the United States at least) bears little resemblance to the uncompromising, even reckless life of prayer advocated by ascetic and mystical theologians, which was understood to be the purification and culmination of every other practice of faith. In youth ministry, contemplative disciplines are frequently (and unapologetically) co-opted for temporal as well as eternal purposes. The fact that most of these practices require detailed instruction — the kind of catechesis normally reserved for the purgative phase — re-

45. Coakley, "Deepening Practices," 82.

46. This interest can be traced directly to the influence of the Lilly Endowment's support of the San Francisco Youth Spirituality Project, in which youth minister Mark Yaconelli played a public and persuasive role. Yaconelli's personal history made the project all the more compelling for youth ministers, who knew Yaconelli's spirituality project to be the "deconstruction" of the program-based vision of youth ministry marketed by Youth Specialties, Inc. — of which Yaconelli's father is the well-known and beloved founder. It is worth noting that the father has been converted by his son's practice-based vision for youth ministry; the deconstruction proceeds with his full cooperation and blessing.

veals our relative inexperience in emptying ourselves before God and our tendency to dismiss contemplative practices as quietist curiosities or as proof, finally, that Aunt Geraldine is a religious "nut." Yet because these practices empty us most completely of our own ambitions, they are the means by which we glimpse Christ most transparently and in which sanctifying grace is most lavishly offered.

Contemplative Christian practice is normally considered the fruit of mature faith, which Protestants tend to assign to mystics and grandparents, or to people with lots of time on their hands. Yet such practices have an important purpose for young people *in search of* Christian maturity, regardless of denominational tradition. The most significant outcome of so-called "contemplative practice" in youth ministry (so far) has been to infuse congregations with large doses of regular, intentional, intergenerational prayer, when not long ago they were wheezing along on the prayer-fumes of a few faithful members who seemed to do the praying for everyone. Not surprisingly, where youth and adults pray together and often, youth ministry typically receives a fresh bolt of energy. Of course, any congregation that asks for God's grace this directly *should* experience renewal, if not outright revival. Prayer changes churches as well as youth ministries, regardless of the perceived "spiritual maturity" of those who pray.

True union with God knows no tactical shortcuts. There is no other route to true communion save a lifetime of faithful practice, which contemplative practices simplify, purify, and bathe in prayer, leading ultimately to silent responsiveness, "an empty waiting on God that precedes union in its full sense."[47] Strictly speaking, therefore — and this is the crucial point — contemplative practices are God's practice *in* humans, creating a less impeded form of human receptivity to grace that is itself a divine gift. Contemplation does not make other practices unnecessary; it transforms them, revealing that they have never truly been "our" practices at all, but always signs that God is graciously working through us. In contemplative practices, God is the sole catechist. We satisfy our ultimate desire to participate in divine passion through contemplation in which God *incorporates* us into the Triune life where true communion resides.[48]

Obviously, this kind of Christian maturity cannot be attained in the span of one spaghetti supper, or in the span of an entire adolescence, for that matter. So what use is advocating these practices for youth ministry,

47. Coakley, "Deepening Practices," 92-93.
48. Coakley, "Deepening Practices," 93.

when we can hardly expect teenagers to have accumulated a lifetime of practices leading to God? Union with Christ requires the intimacy of *pathos* — the willed vulnerability of the soul's total passivity (Coakley prefers the term "responsiveness") before God. In practices of union, "contemplation is clearly now no *human* practice at all, but the direct infusion of divine grace. . . . The Trinity is no longer seen as an obscure . . . doctrine of God's nature, but rather a life which we enter into and, in unbreakable union with Christ, breathe the very Spirit of God."[49] Communion with God in Jesus Christ is never ethereal; God incorporates us into the state of divine union by material means, beginning with our own bodies, and co-opts creation as a conduit of divine grace.[50] Practices of union therefore prepare us for this communion with God, pointing to Christ's presence in the bread, the wine, the oil, the water, the word — all of which we absorb into our bodies, and reenact in the practices of passion.

Coakley views practices of union as the culmination of a faithful religious life, but there is another tradition that allows these practices to serve as "converting ordinances," as John Wesley called them: means of grace with sacramental significance. "When the passion of Christ becomes present to us through word and sacrament, faith is wakened in us — the Christian faith in God," writes Moltmann.[51] All practices are "means of grace" to a degree, providing connective tissue between God's mystery and embodied human life. So just because adolescents' participation, incorporation, and insight in sacramental practices is incomplete does not make

49. Coakley, "Deepening Practices," 90, 93.

50. The Incarnation is the archetypal evidence of this. Sixteenth-century Carmelites Teresa of Avila and John of the Cross taught that the long practice of contemplation actually knits the soul into the life of God, a union that takes place in the *body*. For Teresa, intimacy with God is found "in the extreme interior, in some place very deep within"; for John, communion begins in the lungs and nostrils, as the soul breathes the "very breath" of the Spirit moving between Father and Son. See Teresa of Avila, *The Interior Castle* 8:1, in vol. 2, *The Collected Works of St. Teresa of Avila,* trans. K. Kavanaugh and O. Rodriguez (Washington, D.C.: I.C.S. Publications, 1980), 430. John writes, "By His Divine breath-like Spiration, the Holy Spirit elevates the soul sublimely and informs her and makes her capable of breathing in the Son and the Son in the Father, which is the Holy Spirit Himself who in the Father and the Son breathes out to her in this transformation, in order to unite her to Himself . . . This kind of Spiration of the Holy Spirit . . . is so sublime, delicate, and deep a delight that a mortal tongue finds it indescribable . . . for the soul united and transformed in God breathes out in God to God the very Divine Spiration which God — she being transformed in Him — breathes out in Himself to her." Cited by Kieran Kavanaugh, O.C.D., and Otilio Rodriguez, O.C.D., *The Collected Works of St. John of the Cross* (Washington, D.C.: I.C.S. Publications, 1991), Spiritual Canticle, Stanza 39, No. 3, 558.

51. Moltmann, *Trinity and the Kingdom* (Minneapolis: Fortress Press, 1993), 21.

them unimportant. Union with God follows an awakened faith that engages in practices that incorporate adolescents into the resurrected Body of Christ. In the material forms like air and water, bread and wine, Christ allows himself to become part of teenagers' molecular makeup. Full mystical union with God eludes all but the rarest of teenagers — and, we should admit, all but the rarest of adults. But baptism and the Eucharist, and to a lesser extent all other Christian practices, provide adolescents with ritual forms of "willed passivity" — a *pathos* — that introduces them to the passion of God. While every practice draws young people into the passion of God, the explicit, consistent-through-the-centuries quality of baptism and the Eucharist is normative for Christian practices, and demonstrates the dying-to-self, rising-with-Christ pattern that awaits young people as they venture toward union with God.[52]

Practicing Passion in Spite of Ourselves

Episcopal priest and homiletician Barbara Brown Taylor recounts a day when, in college, she found her faith plunged unexpectedly into deeper water. During her sophomore year, two eager "missionaries" from a campus Christian organization greeted Taylor in her dorm room. Her nominally Christian upbringing had imparted a passing interest in religion, so she let them in — whereupon they invited her to get down on her knees and pray to accept Jesus Christ as Lord and Savior. Partly out of curiosity, but mostly to get rid of them, Taylor complied. The "missionaries" left, overjoyed at their conquest. But Taylor goes on:

> After they left, I went out for a walk and the world looked funny to me, different. People's faces looked different to me. I had never noticed so

52. Because the early church understood the entire life of faith as "sacramental," originally it felt no need to restrict the understanding of sacrament to those with dominical status. Augustine cites dozens of sacraments; significant strands of Christian tradition still understand the church itself as "sacramental." See James White, *Sacraments as God's Self-Giving: Sacramental Practice and Faith* (Nashville: Abingdon, 1983), 33. Theologian David Willis notes that all the ways the church lives out God's reconciliation — marriage, anointing the sick, ordination, etc. — are signs of the church's new life in Christ, though their "peculiar link" between sign and reality lacks explicit words of institution. Yet "they are ritual actions by which faith is strengthened and the corporate life of believers is ordered in ministry. . . . Every aspect of the community's corporate worship and mission has a sacramental quality." David Willis, "Sacraments as Visible Words," *Theology Today* 37 (January 1981): 456.

many details before. I stared at them like portraits in a gallery, and my own face burned for over an hour. Meanwhile, it was hard to walk. The ground was spongy under my feet. I felt weightless, and it was all I could do to keep myself from floating up and getting stuck in the trees. Was it a conversion? All I know is that something happened, something that got my attention and has kept it through all the years that have passed since then. I may have been fooling around, but Jesus was not. My heart may not have been in it, but Jesus' was. I asked him to come in, and he came in, although I no more have words for his presence in my life than I do for what keeps the stars in the sky or what makes the daffodils rise up out of their graves each spring. It just is. He just is.[53]

What Taylor experienced was a convolution of Christian practices — shotgun testimony, awkward prayer — methods of witness and worship that I hesitate to recommend. But they were Christian practices nonetheless, and in spite of their clumsiness, they served as vessels of divine grace, moments of divine-human encounter that could neither be predicted nor controlled, and that left those involved more full of grace than they were before.

All of this means that no practice of passion can be taken lightly, even the half-hearted or ill-conceived ones, for while Christian practices are echoes of the life, death, and resurrection of Christ — reverberations of Christ's Passion in which the Word of God, distorted though it may be, still is audible — Christ is really and truly in the echo. In every practice of passion, Christ is truly and efficaciously present. When the fourth-century Donatists, disgruntled by poorly qualified clergy, asked whether human ineptitude could disqualify a sacrament, the Council of Arles (314) replied with a resounding "no": even a clueless priest who administers a valid sacrament badly cannot impede God's gift of grace.[54] Most of us place our-

---

53. Barbara Brown Taylor, *The Preaching Life* (Cambridge, Mass.: Cowley Publications, 1993), 104-5.

54. The Donatist controversy reappears in many forms — even in youth ministry. John Wesley addressed the issue, saying, "The unworthiness of the Minister doth not hinder the efficacy of God's ordinance. The reason is plain, because the efficacy is derived, not from him that administers, but from Him that ordains it. He does not, will not suffer his grace to be intercepted, though the messenger will not receive it in himself." John Wesley, "On Attending the Church Service," cited in Colin Williams, *John Wesley's Theology Today* (Nashville: Abingdon, 1960), 145. Since all are unworthy, the more legitimate question, and one we may be sure youth will raise, is, Why do so many people who participate in Christian practices remain unaffected by them? The facile answer is that people are "doing it wrong," or the practice is "boring" or "irrelevant." These concerns should not be dismissed; part of

selves in grace's way unconscious of it, unaware of the persistent tug of the Spirit until catechism or cataclysm forces us to reexamine these sacred encounters. Christian practices form identity in Christ not because of what young people do in these practices, but because of what God does in them.

The question before us, then, is *How can mainline Protestant youth ministry move beyond the shallow end of the theological pool?* This much seems certain: youth will not leave the shallow end of the pool unless we do. We cannot give them what we do not have.

The Great Homesickness We Cannot Overcome

In October 2001, a small band of scientists — disguised in gray fabric costumes to conceal their human forms — took to the skies in ultralight aircraft to lead a flock of young whooping cranes on a 1,250 mile migratory route from Wisconsin to Florida. It was a one-way trip for the scientists, but they hoped it would establish a new migratory path for generations of cranes to come. Because the young birds had been reared in captivity as an endangered species, they lacked the benefit of whooping crane parents who could lead them safely south when the cold sets in. "The need to migrate is genetically pre-programmed into these birds," explained Joe Duff, the migration's lead pilot. "But the direction and the destination are taught by the parent, on a one-way trip."[55] The destinations and routes of whooping crane migrations evolve over thousands of years — but they exist only in the memories of the birds that use them.

In a similar way, the practices of faith establish a migratory route to the cross, but like whooping cranes, we only learn this route from those

---

the task of practical theology, in the congregation as well as the academy, is to develop rules of art by which these practices may be more "excellently" pursued. Fortunately, the fact that God employs Christian practices to impart divine grace and to bring Christ's Passion into the present means that they do not depend on our efficacy to transform us. The goods of practices inhere in the practices themselves, not in their outcomes. In Christian practices, the "goods" are the presence of Jesus Christ, guaranteed by the shared nature of practice ("Where two or three are gathered together, I am in their midst." Matthew 18:20). The question of efficacy is fundamentally a question that should be addressed to the *participant* in the practice, not the administrator — and it can only be asked from within the practice, not apart from it.

55. Joe Duff, interview with "Living on Earth," National Public Radio (October 12, 2001), available at www.loe.org/archives/011012.htm#feature10; accessed 7 December 2002. Information on the reintroduction project as a whole available at www.bringbackthecranes .org; accessed 7 December 2002.

who have traveled it before us. Human beings, too, are created to migrate toward the One who made us; as Rainer Maria Rilke has put it, "God is the great homesickness that we could never shake off."[56] But young people, like young birds, require wise adults who can show them the way and teach them the practices Jesus uses to draw their passions into his. Without the memories of those who have traveled before them, the migratory route is lost, and young people journey aimlessly, mired in self-fulfilling passions that obscure the steadfastness, ecstasy, and intimacy of God.

Rerouting youth ministry through the historic practices of the Christian community — those actions by which centuries of Christians have conformed to the Passion of Christ — establishes a sacred sense of direction in adolescents, transforming them into bearers of God's grace simply because love of this magnitude begs to be shared. But adolescents follow footprints better than blueprints, so what lies ahead are not prescriptions for ministry, but sets of footprints that point in the direction of a passionate church. Following where they lead, adolescents longing for something "to die for" discover traces of divine fidelity, ecstasy, and intimacy in the Christian community, where the passion of God still echoes in humble acts of witness that call us to the cross.

---

56. Rainer Maria Rilke, "I Love You, Gentlest of Ways," in *Rilke's Book of Hours: Love Poems to God,* trans. Anita Barrows and Joanna Macy (New York: Riverhead Books, 1996).

Chapter Seven

THE ART OF "BEING THERE"

Exhortation as a Practice of Fidelity

The ultimate purpose of a prophet is not to be inspired, but to inspire the people; not to be filled with a passion, but to impassion the people with understanding for God.

Abraham Heschel[1]

There's something about going all the way, without compromise or equivocation, that appeals to young people when commitments of all kinds, from employment to marriage, seem temporary and conditional.

Danny Duncan Collum[2]

First, therefore, see that ye love God; next, your neighbor — every child of man. From this fountain let every temper, every affection, every passion flow.

John Wesley[3]

---

1. Abraham Heschel, *The Prophets,* vol. 1 (New York: Harper & Row, 1962), 115.
2. Danny Duncan Collum, explaining the appeal of Orthodox monasteries as "hangouts" for punk rockers on the West Coast, in "From Punk to Monk," *Utne Reader,* July-August 1997, 17.
3. John Wesley, "Sermon 114: The Unity of the Divine Being," last paragraph; available at http://www.ccol.org/w/wesley/sermons/sermons-html/serm-114.html.

S haron Daloz Parks tells the best story about adolescent solidarity I
know. It involves her teenage friend Barbara, who at seventeen was invited to attend a national gathering of Lutheran young people.[4] Barbara,
who had been paralyzed from the waist down from a car accident a few
years earlier, didn't think much of the church; she considered it out of
touch with young people and events in the real world. Still, when Barbara
learned that another girl who also used a wheelchair would be attending
the event as well — and that they could be roommates — she decided to go.

On the last night of the event, the youth held a dance. Barbara and her
roommate debated whether or not to attend; after all, how much fun would
a dance be if you're in a wheelchair? At last they decided to go, making
their way to the edge of the dance floor where they could watch.

That's when a young man from Latin America startled Barbara by
asking her to dance. Flattered — and curious — she said yes. He wheeled
Barbara out to the middle of the gymnasium, grabbed a chair from around
the rim, and sat down facing her. Then the two of them began to dance together, sitting down.

Soon another boy asked Barbara's roommate to dance. He wheeled
her out to the middle of the dance floor, grabbed a chair for himself, sat
down, and they danced. Before long, the rest of the room had followed suit
— and soon the gym was flooded with 500 Lutheran teenagers, all dancing
sitting down.

Parks adds, "Barbara came home *very* high on the church."[5]

The Sacred Solidarity: Belonging Before We Believe

First we belong, and then we believe. "We love because [God] first loved
us," John's first letter informs us (1 John 4:19), and psychology concurs.
The interpersonal ego state precedes the ideological, or institutional, ego
state; before there is a self to share with another, the other is required to
bring the self into being.[6] We tend to adopt the beliefs and values of our

---

4. Not her real name.

5. A written version of this story appears in Sharon Daloz Parks, "Home and Pilgrimage: Deep Rhythms in the Adolescent Soul," *Growing Up Postmodern — Imitating Christ in
the Age of "Whatever" — 1998 Princeton Lectures on Youth, Church and Culture* (Princeton,
N.J.: Princeton Theological Seminary, 1999), 61. This account is taken from her oral lecture
by the same name delivered at Princeton Theological Seminary, April 1998.

6. Robert Kegan, *The Evolving Self: Problem and Process in Human Development*
(Cambridge, Mass.: Harvard University Press, 1982), 97.

"primary groups," whose approval we greatly desire, and who we hope will desire us. To "have" a group as a teenager — and to know a group "has" us — is to possess something profoundly sacred. Apart from other people who "like me" during adolescence enough to "be there" for me, there *is* no "me," making solidarity with those who like and accept me critical in constructing my identity.[7]

This "sacred solidarity" reinforces the fragile self by amplifying fidelity, the assurance that someone will "be there" for me. Fidelity connotes truth, trust, honor, steadfastness. When fidelity is absent, young people activate its mutant forms instead. For example, gang members are often expected to "be there" for one another unto death as well.[8] For teenagers, true love is bound to the promise that they are "to die for," whether that promise is enacted by the Crips or the Bloods or their parents.

A curriculum of passion depends first on practices of fidelity, acts of witness in which the church practices the art of "being there" instead of simply insisting that youth "be there" for us. "Being there" is a function of *didache,* the early church's term for shaping disciples — a task that historically involved moral as well as doctrinal instruction, since catechumens' admission to the church depended not only on their confession of the creed but also on the community's testimony that they *lived* by it.[9] As liturgical theologian Aidan Kavanaugh notes, "Catechesis is not about doctrinal or ecclesiastical data, but about conversion"[10] — and the standard to which the early church unapologetically held a new convert included a radical change of habit as well as a decisive change of heart.

Didache privileged formation over information, practical wisdom over empirical knowledge, the ability to make faithful judgments over the

---

7. Kegan, *The Evolving Self,* 96. Kegan maintains that it would be wrong to say that an ego is lacking in the interpersonal ego state, or that it is a weaker ego. "What there is," says Kegan, "is a qualitatively — not a quantitatively — different ego, a different way of making the self cohere" (p. 96).

8. See Evelyn L. Parker, "Hungry for Honor: Children in Violent Youth Gangs," *Interpretation* 55 (April 2001): 148-61. For the role of family in urban street culture, see Elijah Anderson, *Code of the Street: Decency, Violence, and the Moral Life of the Inner City* (New York: W. W. Norton, 1999), 37. Descriptions of fidelity in gangs can be found in William Finnegan, *Cold New World: Growing Up in a Harder Country* (New York: The Modern Library, 1999), 241; also Sanyika Shakur, a.k.a. Monster Kody Scott, *Monster: The Autobiography of an L.A. Gang Member* (New York: Atlantic Monthly Press, 1993), 14-15.

9. See William Harmless, *Augustine and the Catechumenate* (Collegeville, Minn.: Liturgical Press, 1995), 43ff.

10. Aidan Kavanaugh, "Initiation: Baptism and Confirmation," *Worship* 46 (1972): 262-76.

ability to process data. Ultimately, *didache* aimed for a posture of prayerful receptivity, an openness to the promptings of the Holy Spirit that was assumed by teacher and learner alike. Students cultivated this receptivity in community, often by literally walking alongside a teacher wise to God's ways until the practices, attitudes, and beliefs of the teacher and student were congruent.[11] As this role was partially taken over by lay sponsors in the early church, supplemented by formal exhortation by a bishop, *catechesis* (Greek for "teaching out loud") became the standard mode of instruction in the beliefs and practices of the Christian community. Although originally *catechesis* referred to a new believer's entire program of formation, the term meandered into the Protestant vocabulary through the Reformers who penned question-and-answer "catechisms" to instruct young people on the basics of faith.

The Reformers never intended their catechetical method to define Christian formation; taking their cues from classical education, they employed the canon of memory to help students internalize sacred texts and doctrines important for moral formation. To teach out loud required a relationship between a student and a catechist (Luther advocated it between parents and children), a relationship that was central to the Reformers' educational method — for like all languages, the Christian vocabulary must be learned from someone who speaks it.

Unfortunately, rote memorization of abstract doctrinal questions *did* come to define much of Christian curriculum, helped in part by the American Sunday School movement in which nineteenth-century Protestants substituted a stripped-down version of Christian schooling for more relational models of Christian discipleship. Originally established to teach reading, writing, and arithmetic to poor children forced to work in the factories every day but Sunday, the "Sunday Schools" soon abandoned the "three R's" in favor of religious instruction as child labor laws and the expansion of public schools made education more available to poor children.[12] In this transition, a new industry was born: church curriculum production. Readily available printed educational literature soon supplanted

---

11. The concept of *didache* is hauntingly depicted — from an entirely different cultural vantage point — in the movie *Crouching Tiger, Hidden Dragon* (Sony, 2000), in which Jen, the Chinese bride-to-be who is a teenage prodigy in ancient swordplay, is brilliantly skilled but forever disadvantaged because a relationship with a teacher she can trust has eluded her.

12. To be sure, reformers have always noted an important link between reading, writing, and Christian faith; for the Scriptures to be accessible, one must know how to read. Thus, from the earliest days of the church, catechesis and reading have always been closely linked, with the Bible serving as the most frequent text.

teaching "by word of mouth" — a development that pushed the mentor/ student relationship aside and divested the educational process of much of its moral force.

For adolescents, the diminished role of the teacher proved to be a critical loss. Removing the relationship between catechist and catechumen from the center of the church's teaching not only dismissed the moral example necessary for teaching purgative practices; it unhinged religious instruction's potential for reaching adolescents, for whom truth is always incarnational. The most significant curriculum for any adolescent is the *person who teaches*. Learning correlates directly with teacher "immediacy" — students' perception that the teacher wants to interact with them — which makes adult and peer leaders far more important than printed curriculum in determining how much and what kind of education takes place.[13] For teenagers, revelation takes human form — which does not minimize the importance of doctrine, but explains why doctrine conveyed in the absence of trustworthy love falls on deaf ears. Plenty of perfectly sound Christian curriculum has rolled off the backs of teenagers not because they rejected its content but because they failed to identify with the person espousing it. The brutal truth is this: When the teaching ministry fails with teenagers, it does not normally fail because of inadequate resources or poor materials or deficient teaching methods, but because the church has failed to "be there" sufficiently with young people to establish the fidelity that makes curriculum credible.

For young people, credibility comes in the form of a person who "gets it" — someone whose concern for the adolescent's well-being translates into sympathy for her worldview, validation of her interests, and acknowledgment of her struggles. Because the adolescent deems this person to be trustworthy, competent, and dynamic, this adult holds moral sway.[14]

13. See Roger Sensenbaugh, "How Effective Communication Can Enhance Teaching at the College Level," available at http://www.indiana.edu/~eric_red/ieo/digests/d102.html; accessed October 23, 2000; Anne Frances Freitas, Scott Meyers, and Theodore Avtgis, "Student Perceptions of Instructor Immediacy in Conventional and Distributed Learning Classrooms," *Communication Education* 47 (October 1998): 366-72; R. Powell and B. Harville, "Instructional Outcomes: An Intercultural Assessment," *Communication Education* 39 (1990): 369-79; Kristi Schaller and Sue DeWine, "The Development of a Communication-Based Model of Teacher Efficacy" (paper presented at the Annual Meeting of the Speech Communication Association, Miami, Florida, November 18-21, 1993), available at http:// ericae.net/ericdb/ED362928.htm; J. Anderson, "Teacher Immediacy as a Predictor of Teaching Effectiveness," in D. Nimmo, ed., *Communication Yearbook* 3 (New Brunswick, N.J.: Transaction Books, 1979), 543-59.

14. Competence, trustworthiness, and dynamism are the basic dimensions of credi-

Young people identify with those they consider true to them, a position of influence that advertisers cultivate and celebrities covet, but that parents underestimate and churches tend to ignore. On the one hand, the adolescent desire to identify with someone true to them is to the church's advantage, since Jesus really *is* true to teenagers, and since imitating Christ really *is* the route to fidelity. On the other hand, unless Christ's radical fidelity is *incarnated* by those of us who teach, young people dismiss us quickly — and correctly — as hypocrites.

"Being There" through Exhortation: The Dragon Gym Philosophy

When Brendan was five, our pediatrician recommended karate lessons to address some of his stomachaches. I was dubious; after all, for five years I had valiantly fought to keep toy guns and Ninja Turtles out of our house, and now I was going to pay someone to teach my son to kick his friends in the head. But we signed on with Grand Master Goh at the Dragon Gym anyway, and for the next three years — until Brendan got his black belt — I hovered in the balcony with the other nervous parents as we watched our children mutate into small Jackie Chans.

At the first lesson, nobody got hit. They learned to bow and to take their shoes off when they entered the gym and to address their teachers by shouting, "Sir!" or "Ma'am!" At the second lesson, nobody got kicked. The teacher brought an apple that he cut into slices for the children while lecturing them on "Dragon Gym Philosophy" of self-care and healthy eating habits.

I began to notice that the lessons, stratified according to belt color, involved children of all ages, as well as a few teenagers and parents. Everyone pitched in to set up the equipment, and to adjust it for taller or shorter class members. The teachers were assisted by youth in the upper belt levels, because "teaching others" was part of the Dragon Gym Philosophy. On test days — the one day you could count on hitting and kicking — children who did not successfully master a move were met by thunderous applause and a gym full of children chanting their name to encourage them until they tried again — all part of Dragon Gym Philosophy. When Brendan earned his blue belt, halfway to the black belt goal, Grand Master Goh held

---

bility; see Michael Z. Hackman and Craig E. Johnson, *Leadership: A Communication Perspective,* 2nd ed. (Prospect Heights, Ill.: Waveland Press, 1986), 125-26.

a Korean tea ceremony for his class "in secret" (no parents). Brendan might as well have had tea with the Queen of England. He recounted the Dragon Gym Philosophy of tea drinking in excruciating detail — how they sat around the table, how they used candles, how they held the cup, how they spoke to one another with great respect, and how a room full of seven-year-olds all agreed that Korean tea tastes fabulous.

I decided karate might not be so bad.

Before Brendan earned his black belt, he had indeed learned to kick people in the head, take down attackers, smash through boards and cement blocks with his bare hands, and handle an arsenal of weapons that made toy guns and Ninja Turtles look positively benign. At the same time, he had also learned some traditional Asian values: respect for elders, group solidarity, and mutual encouragement. But this formation did not come from Grand Master Goh alone, although the Grand Master was clearly the gym's spiritual leader. Dragon Gym Philosophy was quite intentionally a program of mutual exhortation, and it was contagious. Soon I was caught up in Dragon Gym Philosophy too, as children nudged me when I forgot to take off my shoes and other parents taught me how to bow properly. Encouraged and admonished by one another, Dragon Gym members shaped one another in an identity appropriate to the distinctive ethos of a Korean karate school.

The word "exhort" means to urge or encourage, and implies concern for another's well-being. "Exhortation" is the term Paul used (and classical rhetorical tradition used) for the art of "being there" through the encouragement, admonishment, and truth-telling that guides the moral formation of communities. Ministry with youth has a stake in shaping one another in an identity appropriate for Christians, just as Dragon Gym Philosophy created a culture appropriate for karate. In the classical world, exhortation was for newcomers to a way of life. Senior members of the community exhorted those entering a new stage of life or role in the *polis* to acquire behaviors appropriate to the new position.[15] For Paul, exhortation focused on the practices of Christian life that "build up" the community in love. Paul used "word of mouth" teaching to encourage young charges like Timothy to develop a moral *habitus* patterned on the suffering love of Jesus Christ.

The goal of this exhortation was to loosen believers' grip on their former identities and guide them toward action that explicitly identified them

15. Leo G. Perdue, "The Social Character of Paraenesis and Paranetic Literature," *Semeia* 50 (Atlanta: Scholars Press, 1990), 6, 19.

as followers of Jesus.[16] As Richard R. Osmer points out, Paul gave special attention to relationships in the community as a source of moral formation, pointing to lives of faith (like his own) that believers could reliably imitate to distinguish between their former worldly selves and the "new creation" available to them in Jesus Christ.[17] In other words, exhortation depended upon relationships that modeled the cruciform pattern of self-giving love. By identifying with trusted mentors who sought to conform their own lives to the template of Christ's life, death, and resurrection, young people entered into practices alongside their teachers that cultivated prayerful receptivity to the Holy Spirit and that aligned them with the Passion of Jesus Christ.

Contemporary young people recognize the exhorter as a coach, someone gifted in the art of truth-telling who guides young people's actions from a position of concern, skill, and experience. The ultimate exhorter, of course, is the Holy Spirit; we are the Spirit's human assistants who engage young people in spiritual conditioning through exercises and disciplines that stretch and strengthen them for "the ancient relay of faith."[18] While no Christian "grows out" of the need for exhortation, exhortation is still common among newcomers to the faith. It aims at establishing an ethic in which our "oddity" as Christians stands out against a backdrop of self-fulfillment. While exhortation includes preparatory instruction about the life of faith, the real faith curriculum (derived from the French *courir,* meaning "to run a course") lies in the race itself. Exhortation's enduring gift to young people is not familiarity with the moral me-

---

16. In the Pauline letters, exhortations share several features: (1) personal concern on the part of the teacher toward the learner; (2) moral counsel that relates human experience to the Word of God; and (3) reference to Jesus Christ as the power behind Christian ethics. Similarly, Hebrews (not a Pauline letter) was written as "a word of exhortation" (13:22) — the writer urges Jewish Christians to go "outside the camp" to Jesus (13:13), making a clear break from their former Jewish practices to Christianity, which the book presents as a different, higher order of Judaism.

17. Richard R. Osmer argues that the three tasks of Christian teaching are catechesis, discernment, and exhortation. Osmer helpfully distinguishes between moral *formation,* the informal "building up" of the community through identification with moral exemplars who participate in the patterns, practices, and norms of a community's shared life, and moral *education,* which is formal moral instruction of the congregation. I am focusing primarily on the first dimension of exhortation, recognizing that purgative practices require, at points, explicit moral instruction in the context of informal educational forms. Richard Osmer, *The Teaching Ministry of Congregations* (Louisville: Westminster/John Knox, 2003).

18. Barbara Brown Taylor, *Gospel Medicine* (Cambridge, Mass.: Cowley Publications, 1995), 8.

chanics of Christian life, but the assurance of fidelity that gives them the knowledge that others are "for" them, running alongside them, even when it hurts, even when it rains, even when the finish line seems impossibly far away. In being loved sacrificially, young people discover God's fidelity in a community that emboldens them to "be there" for one another.

Christian exhortation has a chameleon quality that allows it to be expressed in many contexts: studying the Scriptures, singing the songs of faith, serving the poor, and parenting a child, to name a few. In youth ministry, two forms of exhortation have recurring significance: the explicit, mutual exhortation available through what John Wesley called practices of *Christian conference,* and the implicit exhortation of the Holy Spirit evoked by practices of *Christian caretaking* that extend God's fidelity to others. The practice of Christian conference, which Wesley intended for corporate spiritual direction, involves young people in spiritual "huddles" where "teammates" practice the sacred solidarity of Christian life together and urge each other's passionate faithfulness despite the frenetic demands of self-fulfilling culture. The practice of Christian caretaking, on the other hand, extends this sacred solidarity beyond the huddle, and shapes youth through acts of compassion that allow teenagers to experience self-giving love directly, and that encourage them to "be there" for others.

Practicing Fidelity	
PASSIONATE PURPOSE	Enacting fidelity
EXAMPLE OF PRACTICE	Exhortation
FORMS OF PRACTICE with recurring significance for young people	Christian conference
	Caretaking
STREAM OF TRADITION	Didache

Exhortation through Christian Conference

Long before football arrived on the scene, Christianity employed "huddles" — small monastic communities (sometimes involving monks or nuns) that self-consciously cultivated a distinctive way of being in the world based on the imitation of Christ. As the monastic movement took hold in the early Middle Ages, people headed into the desert not only to avoid "worldly" distractions, but also to embrace a community's rule, designed to aid members in shedding the identities assigned to them by rank, family, or circumstance so they could freely adopt a new identity conformed to the life, death, and resurrection of Jesus Christ.

Devotion to a rule gave monastic communities a radical reputation; medieval history abounds with tales of determined young people who dramatically escaped the social roles proscribed for them (usually a dreaded career or marriage) by fleeing to the liberating arms of the church.[19] Most contemporary young people can barely conceive of their congregations in such terms. Yet for much of Christian history, monasticism represented freedom and opportunity, and it shaped passionate Christians who, despite their countercultural ethic, often flourished in the world they critiqued by providing energy and direction for massive social and ecclesial reforms.[20]

While the central role young people played in these radical cells of faith throughout history ought not be overlooked, monasticism's larger gift to youth ministry is the proof that small communities of belonging can serve as "petri dishes" hospitable to an alternative ethic to the dominant culture. Although the first monastic on record, twenty-year-old Anthony of Egypt (c. 270), *did* try to leave the world behind by selling his possessions and heading to the desert for a life of solitude, this proved impractical and psychologically dangerous for most people (and in the end even Anthony found himself relating to a community). By the fourth century, desert ascetics had gathered their followers into communities of chastity, poverty, common prayer, and obedience to a spiritual abbot. As Europe descended into the "dark ages," these early monastic communities kept learning alive and provided the primary voice of reform in the church. Their calling card was fidelity — a life-and-death commitment to Jesus Christ — that relied upon small communities of mutual exhortation to encourage one another in the passionate pursuit of God.

---

19. In the eighteenth century, seminary provided an alternative identity to that of dutiful son or farmer for young men, while the nineteenth-century missionary movement offered an "escape hatch" (especially for young women) who hoped for a future that included more than marriage and children. See Joseph Kett, *Rites of Passage* (New York: Basic Books, 1977), 70-75.

20. This pattern was not without its tensions. Especially as monasticism became equated with mysticism, community life also included strong interior, individualistic dimensions. Cf. Mark A. McIntosh, *Mystical Theology* (Oxford: Blackwell, 1998), 68-69.

Christian Conferences: Just Another Small Group?

Despite their external similarities, Christian conferences have a markedly different ethos than "small groups," popularly conceived. For one thing, while Christian conferences' sole purpose is to foster fidelity to the cruciform pattern of divine love, most small groups are relatively impotent in the practice of passion. Sociologists point out that, no matter how "family-like" they appear, small groups typically stop short of real (read: financial) sacrifice for one another, and they eliminate tension in the direction of group maintenance — people who think or act differently either conform or quit.[21] Instead of providing a context where young people may safely question and wrestle with faith and with one another, small groups — like youth groups and churches as whole — tend to operate under a veneer of niceness that makes the kind of honesty to which Christians are called decidedly unwelcome. When theology conflicts with group norms, small groups normally recast doctrine to suit the group rather than adjust the group to conform to doctrine.[22]

Small groups also lack the Christian conference's integral connection to a worshipping community. In fact, many Christian small groups — some youth groups included — meet as *alternatives* to worshipping congregations, a development that gave rise to the so-called "one-eared Mickey Mouse" model of youth ministry that still dominates mainline Protestant churches' approach to teenagers. Yet when we shield young people from the intergenerational witness of a congregation, remove them from the interpretive lens of the broader Christian community, and separate them from the fidelity of potential adult role models, we provide an idiosyncratic experience of community that exists nowhere but the youth group. The practices of Christian conference, on the other hand, make a mutant out of Mickey, for every Christian conference simultaneously preserves teenagers' critical association with a peer group while anchoring them in Christian tradition through the historic practice of exhortation (figures 6 and 7, on p. 187).

A glance at the Methodist societies of the late eighteenth and early nineteenth centuries dramatically illustrates the distinctive character of the Christian conference. The Methodist societies met "to pray together, to receive the Word of Exhortation, and to watch over one another in Love,

21. See Robert Wuthnow, *Sharing the Journey: Support Groups and America's New Quest for Community* (New York: The Free Press, 1994).

22. Wuthnow, *Sharing the Journey,* 255.

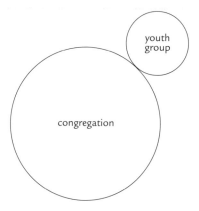

Figure 6. The One-Eared Mickey Mouse Model of Ministry[23]

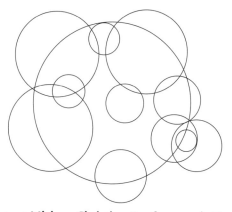

Figure 7. Mutant Mickey: Christian Conferences in Youth Ministry

that they may help each other to work out their Salvation."[24] Each society (small congregations of sixty or so people) was divided into subgroups called "class meetings" or (smaller still) "bands." In these "Christian conferences," members held each other accountable to mutually agreed upon standards of spiritual and ethical behavior (a "covenant"), much as an ab-

23. Stuart Cummings-Bond, "The One-Eared Mickey Mouse," *Youthworker* 6 (Fall 1989): 76. In a personal conversation, James B. Notkin noted that megachurches built on a small group model lack "Mickey's face" — ministries common to the whole congregation. The small group emphasis tends to make these communities "all ears," which is quite different from the "mutant Mickey" model of spiritual huddles.

24. John Wesley, "Rules, &c. of the United Societies," cited in David Lowes Watson, *The Early Methodist Class Meeting* (Nashville: Discipleship Resources, 1985), 204.

bot watched over the moral formation of monks in his care with an eye toward "building up" the community in love.

However, a significant difference separated the abbot's exhortation from the Methodists'. Monks vowed obedience to an abbot in the bounded world of the monastery; Methodists promised to watch over one another's moral formation in the thick of daily life. Class rosters listed each member by occupation: farmer, seamstress, spinner, yeoman, gentleman, etc. (When Methodists began ordaining clergy, preachers met annually for Christian conference in order to report on one another's spiritual growth and pastoral effectiveness — the precursor of today's Methodist "annual conferences," where exhortation has largely devolved into parliamentary procedure.) Before joining a Methodist band, the prospective member was interrogated by a class leader (who we may assume was cut of stiffer cloth than his or her present-day small group counterpart), using a standard list of questions that had all the appeal of a bad game of "Truth or Dare." For example:

- Do you desire to be told all your faults?
- Do you desire that every one of us should tell you, from time to time, whatsoever is in his heart concerning you?
- Do you desire that, in doing this, we should come as close as possible, that we should cut to the quick, and search your heart to the bottom?
- Is it your desire and design to be on this, and all other occasions, entirely open, so as to speak everything that is in your heart without exception, without disguise, and without reserve?[25]

Fidelity to What?

As you might expect, adapting such questions for youth ministry has not had extraordinary success. "Accountability" frequently eclipses "fidelity" as the goal of such groups, making exhortation seem like a trip to the principal's office. For instance, covenant discipleship groups (a form of the Wesleyan class meeting that has been adapted for teenagers) often make adhering to

25. Five questions were subsequently asked at every meeting of the band societies: (1) What known sins have you committed since our last meeting? (2) What temptations have you met with? (3) How were you delivered? (4) What have you thought, said, or done, of which you doubt whether it be sin or not? (5) Have you nothing you desire to keep secret? "Rules of the Band Societies Drawn Up December 25, 1738," cited by Watson, *The Early Methodist Class Meeting*, 200-201.

the covenant unnaturally significant, which tends to cause exhortation to fall victim to its own mechanics.[26] In the fifteen years in which I have used covenant discipleship groups with young people, one pattern consistently emerges: when youth perceive the goal of the covenant group to be remaining faithful to *one another,* the group succeeds, and when they perceive the goal to be remaining faithful to *the covenant,* the group ultimately fails.

The idea, of course, is to remain faithful to *Christ* in these practices — not to group members or a covenant. Christian conferences create a community of solidarity in which members are similarly committed to "be there" for one another, and in so doing they make visible the faithfulness of Christ. For many young people, the practice of Christian conference provides their first inkling that their presence *matters* — an awareness so mind-boggling that some youth test it, abandoning the group to see if anyone notices (an occasion for swift encouragement and loving admonition on the part of other group members). Enacting suffering love in small, face-to-face communities occasions a gentle ministry of noticing — a ministry to which every teenager is called, for which every teenager is equipped, and through which every teenager glimpses Christ's fidelity to *them.* In the Christian conference's web of encouragement, honesty, and trust, the church earns the right to be heard as a trustworthy guardian of passion, a community of people who "get it."[27]

Exhortation through Christian Caretaking: Forced Starts

Maybe this ad came across your desk. It announces World Vision's "30 Hour Famine" program that "hypes" famine by appealing to young people's desire for transcendence:

> Make your mark through the planet's coolest event! More than 600,000 young people in the U.S. will be part of it. Twenty-one other countries will do it. It's a gathering of global proportions! It's World Vision's 30 Hour Famine — the worldwide event you and your group won't want to miss. It's fun. It's free. And best of all, the 30 Hour Fam-

26. I must take partial responsibility for some of these adaptations; see Kim Hauenstein-Mallet and Kenda Creasy Dean, *Covenants on Campus* (Nashville: Discipleship Resources, 1990). The position I am extending here is more explicit in emphasizing fidelity.

27. This phrase is borrowed from the philosophy of Young Life, where it is used to justify the parachurch ministry's relationship-centered strategies.

ine lets you make your mark on a world that's seriously hungry. So hungry that 33,000 kids die every single day from hunger and hunger-related causes. Kids you and your group can help save. How? When your group goes without food for 30 hours to raise money for hungry kids, you will save kids' lives! That's what makes the 30 Hour Famine a cool event.... Don't miss out on the fun. You can make a difference — you can save kids' lives.

Put aside, for a moment, the fact that the ad confuses a famine with a fast; famines are neither self-imposed nor "cool," and they are certainly not "fun." Exhortation in youth ministry also comes in the form of Christian caretaking, whose fruit is the Holy Spirit's pique of conscience. While recognizing the power of solidarity around an activity like the "30 Hour Famine" to mobilize young people for a cause (the package comes with materials to help churches integrate the weekend youth activities into the broader worshipping life of the congregation, if churches choose to use them), Christian educator Michael Warren wonders aloud if there might be another way to encourage young people to feed the hungry — one that might be "less manipulative and truer to [young people's larger] capacities."[28]

By way of contrast, Warren offers the story of a part-time youth minister, who — owing to his former experience as a restaurateur, merchant seaman, butcher, and bouncer — invited teenagers from his parish to help him cook and serve at a soup kitchen. The youth minister explained that Jesus called his followers to feed the hungry, and that's what they will be doing:

> When they meet the next week to cook, he doesn't need any ice breakers or group building activities. They set to work cooking. . . . When they finish about two hours later, they sit for a moment of prayer. Two days later . . . during the forty-five minute van trip [to the soup kitchen] he details what it will be like and what they will do. Basically, he answers their questions. . . . On the trip back to suburbia, [he explains] — in response to their questions — how it happens in their area that such a large group of people come to the soup kitchen to eat. They also sing songs and tell favorite jokes. In subsequent trips, the group doubles and triples as more young people want to cook and serve. Parents have to

28. Michael Warren, "Youth Ministry's Bottom Line Conviction: Self-Esteem" (paper presented at the Association of Professors and Researchers in Religious Education, Orlando, November 1999), 11.

volunteer their vehicles and their own service as drivers. On arriving back at the church, they always spend a few minutes in prayer for those they met that day.[29]

Embedded in the miles of driving and the hours of conversation, observes Warren, are theological questions about who our neighbors are, what worshipping people do in the days between times of worship, the purpose of a life, discipleship, and what it means to take Jesus' proposals seriously.[30]

Christian caretaking has long been a support beam for mainline Protestant youth ministry, extending God's fidelity to those whom Jesus exhorts us "to suffer alongside" *(com + passio)* as we share one another's burdens. In this sense, Christian caretaking is also an act of pilgrimage that stretches youth beyond their comfort zones, as we will discuss in Chapter Eight. Yet for most of us, extending ourselves on behalf of others — bearing one another's burdens, especially for people we have never met — does not come naturally. So a significant part of moral formation entails planting the seeds of compassion at an early age. We engage young people in Christian caretaking for the same reason gardeners plant peat pots in February: they are "forced starts" that enable generosity to take root in the protected setting of a caring community while providing a fertile environment in which young people can put down deep enough roots to risk reaching out to others on their own.[31]

The question, of course, is how Christian caretaking can create a community of mutual exhortation without "using" compassion for instrumental ends. Whether adults encourage practices of Christian caretaking among teenagers as a route to transformation, or merely as a means of behavioral modification, is often difficult to discern. Clearly youth ministry is capable of creating communities of mutual exhortation around moral issues. In 1881, when "isolationism" was official national policy, women could not vote, and "separate but equal" was the law of the land, the Society for Christian Endeavor's explicitly international, ecumenical, interracial, and coeducational charter exhorted mainstream denominations to follow suit.[32] Nearly a century later, student activist groups from Freedom

---

29. Warren, "Youth Ministry's Bottom Line Conviction," 12.

30. Warren, "Youth Ministry's Bottom Line Conviction," 12.

31. I have developed this metaphor further in relationship to *diakonia* with Ron Foster in *The Godbearing Life* (Nashville: Upper Room, 1998), chapter nine.

32. Mary-Ruth Marshall, "Precedents and Accomplishments: An Analytical Study of the Presbyterian Youth Fellowship of the Presbyterian Church in the United States, 1943-1958" (unpublished Ph.D. dissertation, Presbyterian School of Christian Education, 1993).

Riders to the Students' Non-Violent Coordinating Committee, organized primarily by youth and widely supported by churches, spread the Civil Rights Movement across the South, exhorting adults to join in the cause. Not all youthful activism, obviously, is so freely chosen, as military conscription and terrorist cells around the world illustrate. The unformed self's vulnerability to sweeping ideological visions makes adolescents malleable mouthpieces for adult agendas, and sometimes adults marshal young people's idealism in support of self-serving political and social ends.[33]

The acid test for *Christian* caretaking, then, is its contribution to the moral formation of adolescents *as well as* to the moral transformation of society. In 1991, the Carnegie Council on Adolescent Development identified "other-directedness" as one of the five most important ways religious youth organizations contribute to adolescent development.[34] Nine out of ten youth leaders identify mission trips as one of their two most effective strategies for involving hard-to-reach adolescents (the other is camping).[35] Since the 1970s, adolescent enrollment in traditional "church camps" declined dramatically while adolescent participation in service projects surged forward, with nationally-networked "work camps" filling up more than a year in advance. College admissions officers report that one of the most common essays written on college applications today is composed around the theme: "How a church mission trip changed my life."[36]

Beyond Christian Parachuting

The risk, always, is that if we serve others for our sake instead of for their sake — or for God's sake — compassion easily becomes Christian "parachuting," a decontextualized "dropping in" to a needy situation just long

33. Robin Maas calls this the "Pied Piper" syndrome in youth ministry. See "Piper or Prophet?" in *Christ and the Adolescent: A Theological Approach to Youth Ministry — 1996 Princeton Lectures on Youth, Church and Culture* (Princeton, N.J.: Princeton Theological Seminary, 1997), 35-47.

34. Kenda Creasy Dean, "A Synthesis of the Research on, and a Descriptive Overview of Protestant, Catholic, and Jewish Religious Youth Programs in the United States" (Washington, D.C.: Carnegie Council on Adolescent Development, 1991), 99-100, 171.

35. Eugene Roehlkepartain and Peter Scales, *Youth Development in Congregations: An Exploration of the Potential and Barriers* (Minneapolis: Search Institute, 1995), 72.

36. Ed Trimmer, reported in an unpublished paper presented at the Youth Ministry Educators' national meeting, Nashville, Tenn., October 1998. Confirmed anecdotally in personal correspondence, December 8, 2002.

enough to distribute beneficial goods that sometimes places unwanted stress on a beleaguered community. Such efforts offer temporary satiation, but not fidelity; they rely on sightseeing instead of "being there" in an authentic relationship with the other. True compassion requires young people's identification with Jesus that allows them to take on another's burdens as their own.

Yet it is also true that, in the early stages of faith, most young people — indeed, most adults — simply cannot do this. This does not cheapen Christian caretaking; it merely recognizes that adolescents typically lack the cognitive capacities and, in most cases, the spiritual maturity to approach practices of compassion in a deeper way. In the early stages of faith, when purgative practices eclipse unitive ones, we serve others not out of a desire to identify with Christ's suffering, and not because it makes us "feel good" to help others, but *because Jesus told us to.* In adolescence, we lack what cognitive psychologist Robert Kegan calls "third-order consciousness" that enables us to take into account another's point of view as we construct the self or the other.[37] As Kegan observes, adolescents basically think like sociopaths: they have the ability to provide others with the sense that they understand the needs of others, while their intent is to pursue their own goals and purposes.[38]

For a young person still in second-order consciousness — let's call him Justin — that is simply what helping others looks like. Justin really does not see how building a house for Habitat for Humanity possibly makes a difference to him (although he does recognize it makes a difference to the people who live there). Justin thinks helping others is good insofar as he gets something out of it. He participates in his church's youth mission trip not out of a desire to ameliorate suffering in Christ's name, but because it will be fun. He gleans a number of "goods" from the experience: adventure, friendships, a sense of accomplishment (not to mention thirty service hours to count towards graduation). To Justin, this makes perfect sense; why else would he spend eight hours in a van headed to West Virginia? To Justin's parents, however, and maybe to his youth leaders, these reasons look selfish, callous, even deceptive. (All of these adults encourage his participation, however, because they hope he *will* get something out of it — namely, a slightly expanded worldview.)

---

37. Robert Kegan, *In Over Our Heads: The Mental Demands of Modern Life* (Cambridge, Mass.: Harvard University Press, 1994), 39-40.

38. Kegan, *In Over Our Heads,* 39.

Hope and Humility

Of course, Justin *does* get something out of Christian caretaking, whether he undertakes it across town or across the country — though what he gleans may not be what he expects. Practices of Christian caretaking create communities of mutual exhortation in part because the encounter with "otherness" holds a mirror up to the developing self, exposing once-hidden seams in the adolescent's sense of identity. As globalization sweeps the world, contemporary young people encounter "otherness" in ways unimagined by previous generations that potentially threaten the fragile adolescent ego. Many youth are unprepared for such exposure, which they know will un-do them in some way. Bethel Temple — which supports a thriving youth ministry in a distressed Latino neighborhood in Philadelphia — installed a recording studio where teenagers can produce and record their own CDs to give them a constructive "voice" in their beleaguered and sometimes violent community. Yet when the youth pastor arranged a mission trip for youth to repair a church in a middle-class suburb of Baltimore (on the assumption that Christian caretaking is a two-way street), no one signed up. When the youth pastor finally asked why, one streetwise teen finally blurted out: "Are you crazy? I'm *afraid* to go into those neighborhoods!"[39]

In fact, Christian caretaking exhorts young people to confront otherness in ways that are *necessary* for both Justin and the youth at Bethel Temple to move beyond second-order consciousness towards a cognitive schema marked by the Christian virtue of humility. Humility is the ability to discern who is God and who is not, what is "other" and what is "me," and to hold these poles together in love. It is safe to say that humility does not rank high on the list of virtues promoted by a culture of self-fulfillment, for humility is a passionate virtue, a form of suffering in which one allows oneself to be vulnerable to another. Christian humility approaches human relationships through *pathos* — a position that, because it risks being overtaken, inverts the ethic of self-fulfillment. Humility enables young people to approach the other as a gift instead of a threat. In the *pathos* of Christian caretaking, the other becomes a companion *(com + panis),* literally someone with whom we break bread, which always reveals Christ to us in new ways.

39. Reported by Cazden Minter, unpublished case study conducted for the Princeton Project on Globalization, Youth, and the Church, presented at research team meeting, Princeton Theological Seminary, September 2000.

Rowing Across the River:
We're All in the Same Boat

A proverb says, "When you row someone across a river, you get there your-self." Clearly we need the exhortation of young people as much as they need ours. Practices of mutual exhortation are ways in which people in the Christian community row one another across the river, "being there" for each another in a sacred solidarity even as we draw strength from those who live in solidarity with us. Participating in the mutual exhortation of Christian conferences holds us accountable as well as teenagers; the Holy Spirit shapes us through Christian caretaking as well as our youth. Only when we proclaim a fidelity beyond our own is our witness credible, when the solidarity we practice is with Christ, whose "being there" for us trans-lates into our "being there" for one another as we urge one another on in the passionate pursuit of God.

When young people practice their faith in the company of others, Je-sus is revealed in those who will "be there" for them in Christian commu-nity, and who therefore serve as icons of divine fidelity. But practicing fi-delity does not stop here. When adolescents extend this sacred solidarity to others, *they* become icons of fidelity, people who make Jesus visible in acts of self-giving love that assure others that we are all in the same boat, rowing toward Christ.

Chapter Eight

THE ART OF AWE

Pilgrimage as a Practice of Transcendence

*If you can't go to church and, for at least a moment, be given
transcendence; if you can't go to church and pass briefly from
this life into the next; then I can't see why anyone should go.
Just a brief moment of transcendence can cause you to come
out of church a changed person.*

Garrison Keillor[1]

*Royal Academy of Ballet Judge (to Billy Elliott, the son of a
    coal miner, at his audition): Just one more question, Billy.
    What does it feel like when you're dancing?*
*Billy: (Pause.) Dunno. (Stops.) It sorta feels good. I start stiff
    and all that, but once I get goin' I forget everythin'. It starts
    to disappear. It starts to disappear, like, I feel a change in
    me whole body. I get this fire in me body. Just fire — flyin'
    — like a bird. Like electricity — Yeah. Electricity.*

From the movie *Billy Elliott*

*If you could understand a single grain of wheat, you would die
of wonder.*

Martin Luther[2]

---

1. Garrison Keillor, quoted in Ken Gire, *Windows of the Soul: Experiencing God in New Ways* (Grand Rapids: Zondervan, 1996), 120.
2. Quoted by Kathleen Norris, *Amazing Grace* (New York: Riverhead, 1998), 244-45.

W hen the courts ordered the Alexandria (Virginia) Public Schools to
integrate in 1971, the school board created T. C. Williams High
School by merging two existing schools — one white and one black — and
hired African American coach Herman Boone to create a winning football
team (or else). The pre-season looked grim: Boone endured threats to his
family, an embattled training camp, and his young team's struggle to overcome the racial fears their parents taught them. In *Remember the Titans,* the
movie that dramatizes his story, Coach Boone steals a private moment beneath the lights of the empty stadium before the season's opening game.
As he steps out onto the field, his demeanor changes. His shoulders
straighten. He stands a little taller, inhales a little more deeply and savors
the stadium's silence, thick with promise. He muses softly: "This is my
sanctuary, right here. All this hatred and turmoil is swirling around us —
but this, *this* is always right."

The world of sport — like the world of faith — is a decidedly different
universe from the one most of us live in.[3] Where I grew up, the Ohio State
Buckeyes drew people out of the fields and factories into a shared, transcendent mystery of artificial turf and time. The holy ground of the stadium, the
ritualized rules of the game, the pilgrimages to Columbus on holy days
(football Saturdays), the liturgical colors of the high priests (black and white)
and the worshippers (scarlet and gray) generated fervor among the faithful;
flags flew at half-mast the day Coach Woody Hayes died. American parents
routinely catechize their children into the sacred truths of their sport of
choice, adding to the millions of teenagers who know what passion means
not because they learned about it in church, but because they have suffered
for the love of a game, and willingly submitted to its discipline, practices,
even injuries. To be a "good sport" as either player or disciple means temporarily surrendering to the sport's momentum and allowing oneself to be
overtaken by its anguish and its ecstasy — something ABC's "Wide World of
Sports" described for years as "the thrill of victory, and the agony of defeat."

Compare this to a game suggested for youth groups that I ran across
recently in a youth ministry magazine:

SPARROW FLIGHT:
Players crouch down and grab their ankles, remaining in this hunched
position throughout the game. If they let go of their ankles, they're

---

3. See Joseph L. Price, "An American Apotheosis: Sports as Popular Religion," in *Religion and Popular Culture in America,* ed. Bruce David Forbes and Jeffrey H. Mahan (Berkeley: University of California Press, 2000), 201-18. Thanks to Ron Foster, who originally
pointed out the connection between religion and sports to me.

eliminated. Participants hop around holding their ankles and moving their elbows (wings) like a bird. The goal is to knock over other players without losing their balance. If they're knocked over, they're eliminated. The last person "standing" is the winner. . . . This is a fun game to watch as well as to play.[4]

Let me detour long enough to insert a caveat about this last line: If a game is fun to watch as well as to play, the fun had better not depend on laughing at a few unwitting people made to look ridiculous. Every youth group is full of phantom members who came — and left — when they realized that the group's "fun" quotient depended on being laughed at. Most self-respecting teenagers observe these antics and ask themselves two questions we ought to ask as well: (1) If they made that person look ridiculous this week, will I be next? And (2) What does this have to do with Jesus?

I received this magazine in the mail the week of September 11, 2001 — the week that made every silly game we have ever played in the name of youth ministry look ludicrously out of touch. Even gifted teachers — the ones who can root metaphors out of silly games like truffles, evoking an intuitive grasp of a larger truth (a teaching method educators call "synectics") — tread a fine line between the trite and true in youth ministry. Fun is good; triviality is deadly. The word "fun" has its origins in the word "fool"; one of Paul's strangest assertions is that Christians are called to be "fools for Christ" (1 Cor. 4:10). When fun leads to the foolishness of the cross, ecstasy flows from God's triumph over death and defeat. This is the tremendous mystery of faith that Christians celebrate: that joy springs from anguish, that love abounds in passion, that life comes from death, that hope hallows despair.

Weirdness Reconsidered

In the early twenty-first century, awe, affect, and mystery are launching a visible comeback. As always, Hollywood was the first to read the tea leaves; by the 1990s, prime time television shows like "The X-Files," "Buffy the Vampire Slayer," and "Touched by an Angel" had made the mysterious commonplace, while in the 2000s "reality" shows made ordinariness look weird, banking on that ultimate oxymoron, vicarious primary experience. William H. Willimon, dean of the chapel at Duke University,

---

4. Les Christie, "Hot Games," *Group*, September 10, 2001, 27.

describes a different approach to "the weird" among today's college students than he remembers from his own days as a student in the 1950s. "When *we* looked at 'weird,'" remembers Willimon, "we wanted to take it apart, figure it out, explain it. When today's kids look at 'weird,' they want to *enjoy* it."[5]

One explanation may be that, fifty years ago, modern young people understood their world by cracking it open, exposing its beams, dissecting its "mystery" in order to see what it was made of. Modern youth tended to view mystery as a threat to be disarmed, an ambiguity to be explained, a problem to be solved. They believed reality could be best understood by breaking it down and scrutinizing its component parts. So young people like Willimon became skilled deconstructionists, growing up to conceive such modern notions as form criticism, outcome-based education, and the Jesus Seminar. Today's young people, on the other hand — youth who have inherited modernity's component parts — tend to try to understand the world by putting it back together again. Postmodern youth view mystery as a possibility to be explored, a totality to be experienced. They understand reality by interacting with it, seeking connections with it, probing its dynamic potential. Consequently, postmodern youth study quantum physics, holistic medicine, the Green Movement. They conspire not to dissect mystery but to experience it, and to let it move them to a new place.

Holy Weirdness: The High of the *Mysterium Tremendum*

A curriculum of passion includes sustained opportunities for young people to practice transcendence, acts of witness that cultivate awe and prepare youth for the possibility of encountering the divine in concrete acts of worship, praise, and lament. For contemporary adolescents, the tremendous mystery of faith is less about the divine grandeur that makes God "other" than about the passion in which God condescended to be one of them. In the Passion of Christ, love crossed the chasm between heaven and earth, spilling onto mortals like pixie dust, moving us to hope, wonder, and reverence. As teenagers share in the momentum of the Holy Spirit that

5. A written version of this story appears in William H. Willimon, "Imitating Christ in a Postmodern World: Young Disciples Today," *Growing Up Postmodern — Imitating Christ in the Age of "Whatever" — 1998 Princeton Lectures on Youth, Church and Culture* (Princeton, N.J.: Princeton Theological Seminary, 1999), 82. I have paraphrased the oral presentation of the story, delivered at Princeton Theological Seminary, April 1998.

moves through the Christian community, they are led toward an expanded awareness of what God has done, is doing, and will do.

"Being moved" is God's work, not ours. God condescends to address young people where they are. At the same time, "being moved" depends on a willing vulnerability, a susceptibility to holy heat. Transcendent practices strive for an appropriate humility in the presence of the Holy Spirit that gives young people a readiness to catch fire in the nearness of God. Practices of transcendence focus less on forging new identities in Christ than on sustaining and intensifying the sense that God has called young people to be set apart by the "oddity" of self-giving love. This sense of "oddity" — we might think of it as holy weirdness — requires an ongoing sense of dislocation from the pulse of popular culture, along with an increased attunement to the rhythms of God.

Transcendent practices lead to boundary-breaking experiences as they invite us to reach beyond our comfort zones into the new and mysterious world of the "other." They may be literal acts of reaching out, as in practices of Christian caretaking, or more liturgical expressions of the cultic life *(leitourgia)* of the Christian community.[6] Originating in Christian asceticism, the church regards these practices as "means to the end of a renewed and intensified religious experience," and often turns to the image of the spiritual "pilgrimage" to explain their power.[7] Worship, of course, is the church's premiere form of pilgrimage, punctuating life with holy interruptions that gather us and send us forth to enact the cruciform pattern of self-giving love in the world. By interrupting and changing the habits of daily life, youth become more alert to the *mysterium tremendum* and gain new energy for living "odd" lives of faith among their peers. The effects of these adolescent awakenings seldom last long without other faith practices that support the dehabituated worldview. But transcendent prac-

---

6. "Liturgy leaves room within itself for those spontaneous or extemporaneous forms of worship which some Protestants favour as an alternative to what they class as 'liturgical.' If the word liturgy is allowed to retain from its etymology the sense of 'the work of the people', it hints at the focal place and function which I ascribe to worship in the Christian life as a whole. Into the liturgy the people bring their entire existence so that it may be gathered up in praise. From the liturgy the people depart with a renewed sense of the value-patterns of God's kingdom, by the more effective practice of which they intend to glorify God in whole life." Geoffrey Wainwright, *Doxology: The Praise of God in Worship, Doctrine and Life — A Systematic Theology* (New York: Oxford University Press, 1980), 3.

7. Margaret Miles calls ascetic practice "one of the currently least understood and most universally rejected features of historical Christianity." Margaret Miles, *Practicing Christianity: Critical Perspectives for an Embodied Spirituality* (New York: Crossroad, 1988), 94, 51.

tices tend to leave deep and enduring impressions: while the shimmering vision of divine ecstasy may fade, a track has been laid that once led to a holy place, leaving open the possibility of our return.

Mainline Protestants harbor justifiable suspicion of ascetic practices; we know them for their extremes and abuses, and less for their potential in forming Christian identity. We are painfully aware of the adolescent penchant for excess, and we worry about connections between asceticism and self-mutilation and humiliation. As a result, we often treat transcendent practices as masochistic curiosities instead of opportunities to help young people reset the spiritual metronomes of their lives.[8] A theology of passion has an undeniably ascetic side to it — not because it requires suffering for its own sake, but because suffering love renounces all that diverts us from our beloved in order to liberate the self from the psyche's agenda:

> [In ascetic practices], a consciously chosen self was created by the strategy of systematically dismantling the self automatically created by socialization. The real point of ascetic practices, then, was not to "give up" objects, but to reconstruct the self. . . . Ascetic practices can break the bondage of the senses to the psyche's agenda, a form of habituation in which any stimulus that does not relate directly to physical and psychic protection is ignored.[9]

The key to these practices, easily lost on American individualists, is the discerning presence of the larger faith community, in order to distinguish moments in which we encounter God from other kinds of ecstatic experiences, say, like being at a rock concert when "the bass kicks in."[10] Ascetic practices may jolt young people from spiritual complacency, but they re-

8. Throughout Christian history, teachers have warned against the abuse of asceticism, when the practice ceased to be a tool and became an end in itself, much the way dieting in vulnerable people quickly devolves into anorexia. These leaders considered ascetic practices useful only if "carefully chosen and individually tailored to address a particular person's compulsive behavior, addictions, or destructive thought patterns" (Miles, *Practicing Christianity,* 94). Christianity, however, implies an inherent connection between doctrines of creation, Incarnation, and resurrection that celebrates the permanent integrity of the body. Centuries of practices that have disparaged the body have also eclipsed the doctrinal defense of the body's integrity in the minds of most modern Christians. Therefore, the contemporary church's most common solution has been to abandon ascetic practice altogether, without critically examining its potential for dehabituation.

9. Miles, *Practicing Christianity,* 97.

10. Phrase attributed to Rich Mullins, explaining the power of his concerts. Thanks to Joshua and Amy Sunderland for sharing this story.

quire the interpretive framework of the Christian community to avoid being seduced by the inescapable pulse of self-fulfillment. When a fast becomes a diet, a Sabbath becomes a vacation, a praise service becomes a youth rally, or a pilgrimage becomes a trip to the mall, the practice of passion turns into a caricature of Christian life — weird, perhaps, but hardly holy.[11]

Resisting Gravity:
Pilgrimage as Spiritual Dehabituation

When Jessica was fourteen, she moved out of an abusive family situation to live with her aunt and uncle in New Jersey.[12] They loved Jessica deeply, but they were at wits' end when they called her youth minister to join them in sessions with the principal, the therapist, and the juvenile court judge. Through it all, Jessica remained silent and bitter, a "hard" kid. Forced to come to youth group by her aunt and uncle, Jessica made no effort to get to know other girls her age, and by all accounts was a pain in the neck.

I found out about Jessica because her youth pastor, Pam, was one of my students. Pam had started training that semester for "extreme" rock climbing — an arduous course for anyone, and as far as I knew Pam had never done anything remotely like this. I cornered her and asked what was going on. "I decided to take Jessica rock climbing in Colorado," Pam told me. "We leave in October for a week in the Rockies."

"You're taking a youth group from New Jersey rock climbing to the Rockies?" I asked, incredulous.

---

11. Fasting, for example, can be a powerful practice of dehabituation; yet in the absence of the faith community's hermeneutic, fasting can quickly be derailed by culturally-driven agendas about body image. Like all Christian practices, fasting is primarily for the sake of the Body of Christ — not the body of the participant. Yet for American girls who internalize media messages about thinness, fasting without a Christian view of passion poses real risks for eating disorders. Fasting remains a time-honored form of holy "weirdness," but the "little deaths" involved in Christian practices require a theological tradition in which self-denial operates out of love, not disapproval — divine or human. Unless adolescent fasting takes place in a community that balances asceticism with other practices like prayer, praise, and stewardship of God's gifts (including the body), fasting can play into the values of the dominant culture, which of course is not only dangerous but also fails to be "odd" by the standards of self-fulfillment. Instead of helping youth celebrate their oddity as people "set apart" by the Passion of Christ, the practice could become abusive and deteriorate into a dangerous form of enculturation.

12. Not her real name.

"Not the youth group," said Pam. "Just Jessica and me. It's a wilderness program for at-risk kids. Her aunt and uncle have agreed, and I think it might help Jessica find out something new about herself."

I admired Pam's determination, but I thought she was crazy. All the usual concerns went through my mind: safety, competence, liability, supervision, stamina, time missed from school — well, not that Jessica was attending much school — and of course, the general awkwardness of spending a strenuous week with a fifteen-year-old who hates you. But Pam did her homework, signed on with a reputable program, and the time together had the effect Pam hoped for. She and Jessica formed a partnership, a friendship, and a tentative new beginning that grew out of shared prayer and wet sleeping bags, forgiveness and trust, put to the test scaling purple mountains' majesty three thousand feet up. Jessica came home with hope and purpose; Pam came home with a broken ankle, euphoric.

Sometimes we need a sacred shove in the right direction. Transcendent practices give faith momentum by following the logic of pilgrimage, a logic that asserts that physical movement to a new location can produce an altered, or more alert and sensitive, consciousness.[13] As a result, pilgrimages — both the existential and the literal kind — have a force that other practices assume only over time. For this reason, practicing transcendence calls for guides more than coaches, people who have traveled this route before. God's transcendence can never be mastered; it can only be navigated by someone who knows where it leads. Although every practice of self-giving love seems "odd" in a culture of self-fulfillment, some practices of the church are *for the sake of* jarring us out of sinful complacency and steering us back toward the Passion of Christ. These practices "dehabituate" us — break us out of old habits, awaken the soul from inertia, renew spiritual energy and insight, redefine us as people who live "awed" lives.[14] Transcendent practices help us escape the gravitational pull of earthly pursuits with an impetus only passion can provide.

The Art of Awe: "Thinning the Membranes" between Sacred and Profane

Pigrimages are journeying practices; they are designed to traverse new territory both within and without in order to move us closer to the cross. Every

13. Miles, *Practicing Christianity*, 51.
14. Margaret Miles, "The Recovery of Asceticism," *Commonweal*, January 28, 1983, 41.

pilgrimage, therefore, leads to Jerusalem in either literal or metaphorical ways. The allure of this trek, notes Martin Robinson, is its liminality; pilgrimages lead to a special location "where the membrane between this world and a reality beyond is especially thin, where a transcendent reality impinges on the immanent."[15] In medieval Europe, the pilgrimage physically extracted the pilgrim (a word that means "stranger") from his daily hardships and placed him literally on the road to Jerusalem or to some other sacred destination so he could imitate Christ's suffering, receive healing from relics, or obtain forgiveness from sins.[16] All was strange on the pilgrimage: work, locale, relationships, food. Because the journey was dangerous (bandits, illness, and death were common), the pilgrimage dramatically enacted the diverse landscapes of the soul and the brevity of life.[17]

Pilgrimages were never undertaken for the sake of the journey itself. Pilgrims traveled with a destination in mind — union with God, symbolized by a liminal experience of "arriving" at a sacred spot. Once arriving, the medieval pilgrim could grasp Christ's Passion emotionally as well as intellectually, having re-imagined Jesus' journey to the cross in order to become a living symbol of Christ's sacrificial love. Then as now, pilgrimages held special appeal for people in transition (especially for those moving from sin to absolution, but also for people in life cycle transitions like adolescence, middle age, or retirement). The spiritual pilgrimage "moved" these people, quite literally, to explore the profound questions that typically arise in these periods, acknowledging transition itself as part of imitating Christ.[18] Even Christ's transfiguration — literally, a "mountaintop experience" — took place at the fulcrum of his ministry, when Jesus "set his face to go to Jerusalem" (Luke 9:51).

We immediately recognize, in both form and purpose, similarities between a pilgrimage and the youth retreat, summer camp, conference, or mission trip, as well as in lesser forms of "movement" that change our spir-

15. Martin Robinson, *Sacred Places, Pilgrim Paths: An Anthology of Pilgrimage* (London: Marshall Pickering, 1997), 2.

16. Norman Housley, "Western European Pilgrimages," in *Dictionary of the Middle Ages,* ed. Joseph R. Strayer, vol. 9 (New York: Charles Scribner's Sons, 1987), 654-61. Thanks to my colleague Paul Rorem for alerting me to the possibilities of pilgrimage.

17. Not until the late Middle Ages did pilgrimages become a form of "tourism," thanks to a safer political climate and better amenities for the traveler (who by this time could obtain guides, overnight accommodations, souvenirs, and travelogues). These developments lessened pilgrimages' spiritual value but increased their tourist appeal. Thus Chaucer's pilgrims could enjoy the road to Canterbury, and travel books became popular reading. See Housley, "Western European Pilgrimages," 660.

18. Robinson, *Sacred Places, Pilgrim Paths,* 1.

itual vantage point, and therefore our perception of God. Miles admits, "There is nothing particular to Christianity in the recognition that practices of asceticism — from mild disciplines to body-damaging practices — change consciousness."[19] Twelve-step programs designed to eliminate addictive behavior and wilderness education programs like Outward Bound also function as programs of asceticism rooted in practices of pilgrimage. Jewish youth work identifies the pilgrimage to Israel as its most important educational strategy — virtually every Jewish-affiliated youth organization in the United States sponsors the "trip to Israel" in some form — because it helps adolescents re-imagine themselves, with the literal help of geography, as children of Abraham.[20] Not far behind in importance is the Jewish camp, "the most potent expression of Jewishness most teenagers ever experience."[21] Because Jewish educators understand "Jewishness" as a counter-identity to those available in the dominant culture, Jewish youth work relies heavily on temporarily removing young people from their accustomed environments in order to steep them in the practices and traditions of Jewish life.

It is telling that, while we acknowledge the value of "getting kids away from distractions" for the purpose of rigorous religious formation,[22] most mainline Protestants do not consider dehabituating practices essential to Christian identity — a position that belies a numbing level of enculturation. Intuitively, youth leaders do rely on such tempo-changing practices in the form of cross-cultural mission opportunities, experimental forms of prayer and worship, proclamation through the arts, and so on — though we are prone to seeing them as "methodologies" that hold interest more than as practices that change consciousness. Without an awareness of

19. Miles, *Practicing Christianity,* 95.

20. "Nothing is more critical to Jewish identity than spending time in Israel," notes Sandra Kilstein of the Board of Jewish Education of Greater New York. "It is a very emotional experience for a Jewish teenager to walk on Biblical soil, to feel the continuity of his people." Cited in Kenda Creasy Dean, *A Synthesis of the Literature on, and a Descriptive Overview of, Protestant, Catholic, and Jewish Religious Youth Organizations in the U.S.* (Washington, D.C.: Carnegie Council on Adolescent Development, 1991), 48.

21. Asher Melzer, director of camping for the United Jewish Association-Federation. Cited in Dean, *Synthesis and Overview,* 47.

22. Some youth events (like the Catholic World Youth Day), and some faith communities (like the brothers of Taize, France) are organized entirely around pilgrimages (not only do youth "make pilgrimage" in order to come to Taize, but every weekend is treated as the liturgical equivalent of Good Friday, Holy Saturday, and Easter). Recent lifecycle curriculum series (the Episcopalian "Journey to Adulthood," for example) have included "pilgrimages" as marker events for transitions in adolescent life.

transcendent practices' power to relocate the self (not to mention some degree of educational intentionality on our part), these practices can fall prey to manipulation, "moving" youth with pragmatic techniques that "work" by evoking emotion, instead of creating space for the movement of God.

Cultivating the art of awe depends upon liminal spaces — intermediate areas that, to use D. W. Winnicott's phrase, serve as "resting places" in the emerging self's struggle to keep inner and outer reality separate but related. Religious educator Jerome Berryman proposes Christian liturgy itself as such a space, an overlapping area of experience between "me" and "not me," I and Thou.[23] In ways analogous to a retreat or physical pilgrimage, youth trudge after Jesus when they imitate Christ in the Eucharist, or when they follow the Advent-to-Easter movement of the Christian year. Liturgy allows youth to participate in the momentum of the Christian community's journey toward Jerusalem, fully partaking in the journey's ups and downs, fits and spurts, dry spells and lavish celebrations.

Young people readily participate in such symbolic pilgrimages and attend closely to their rhythms. Ordinary time in the Christian year is peak season for adolescent pilgrimages of ascent, as young people flock to spiritual "mountaintop experiences" provided by summer mission trips, camps, and service projects. Lent occasions psalms of descent. Mennonite teenagers at a church I know in Ontario sponsor "media fasts" during Lent in which they swear off television, music, movies, video games, and the Internet (unless required for homework) as a way to renounce media images that may impede their journey to the cross, while Presbyterian youth in California give away "stuff" — forty items, to be exact — in hopes that living with less will clear the clogged arteries between them and Jesus.[24] From the standpoint of self-fulfilling culture, such practices are "weird" indeed. But by renouncing some of consumerism's shackles, they also help teenagers transcend popular attempts to define them as less than they are.

Despite the pilgrimage's emphasis on movement, transcendent practices tether young people securely to the community of faith rather than remove them from it. This is because the movement that matters in the pilgrimage is God's movement, not ours; we "go somewhere" in practices of pilgrimage only to dislodge our complacency and to make us more alert to the movement of the Holy Spirit in the world. Two practices of pilgrimage

---

23. Jerome W. Berryman, *Godly Play: A Way of Religious Education* (San Francisco: HarperSanFrancisco, 1991), 10.

24. See Mark Yaconelli, "Stuff," in *Way to Live,* ed. Dorothy C. Bass and Don C. Richter (Nashville: Upper Room, 2002), 47-64.

come to mind as natural "fits" for youth ministry — practices of play, and practices of praise and lament — that move young people to ecstatically reach beyond themselves toward God as they discern God's movement toward them. Practices of play, praise, and lament find specific expression in worship, but are also critical dimensions of discipleship generally. By providing liminal spaces that can serve as "destinations" for a spiritual pilgrimage, practices of play, praise, and lament in youth ministry move adolescents away from the din of daily life so they can hear more clearly the Holy Spirit nudging them toward the passion of God.

Practicing Transcendence	
PASSIONATE PURPOSE	Enacting transcendence
EXAMPLE OF PRACTICE	Pilgrimage
FORMS OF PRACTICE with recurring significance for young people	Play Praise and lament
STREAM OF TRADITION	Leitourgia

Snowboarding for Jesus: Changing Tempo through Play

In the focus groups conducted as part of this project, a group of young adolescent boys told us that the most important practice of adolescence — the practice that, as middle-school boys, they prized most highly, cultivated most assiduously, followed most rigorously and sought never to violate — was the practice of "not being serious." They proceeded to illustrate their commitment to this principle for the remainder of the interview (to the point that I finally turned off the recorder).

They were, of course, doing more than "not being serious." They were playing hide and seek, dodging my questions while at the same time peeking out from behind them, inviting me to come find them — on their terms, not on mine. Playing is always more than "not being serious." As any sports fan knows, playing can be extremely serious. All the world seems to admire a "serious" skier or a "serious" tennis player. L. L. Bean sells parkas good for playing in minus-40-degree temperatures (as if). When I went shopping for my son's birthday dream, I was quickly disabused of the idea that one could just own a snowboard; one must *become a snowboarder*. The twenty-something salesclerk who looked like Shaggy on "Scooby Doo" reprimanded me for even *thinking* that Brendan might snowboard on the hill in our neighborhood instead of going to a ski resort: "He'll use it when he drives up to the resort with his friends," he told me.

"But he's twelve. His friends don't drive to ski resorts. His friends don't *drive*," I said.

"Well, I guess you'll go with them."

"What if they just want to get together, or if I don't have $100 to drop on a twelve-year-old's good time?"

"Listen, lady," said Shaggy, hushing me before other customers caught on. "Snowboarding is a *serious* sport. This is not a toy. This is *serious*. You're going to spend *a lot of money* on this."

I eyed him suspiciously. "How much money?"

"Three hundred, four hundred bucks to start."

"*Three hundred bucks* for a kid to learn to snowboard? What if he hates it?"

"If he hates it, he can't be a serious snowboarder."

I left. My mom found Brendan a snowboard for $50, and yes, it has a gash in the bottom of it from a rock in our backyard.

Of all transcendent practices, young people are most passionately faithful to the practice of play. Sometimes play produces an altered consciousness by shifting physical location, but usually the change in consciousness comes from an imaginative relocation that invites absorption, a devotion that "passes into rapture and, temporarily at least, completely abolishes that troublesome feeling" that we are "only" pretending.[25] Like all forms of passion, play kneads us, engaging us while overtaking us. Play seeks surrender, self-abandonment — giving ourselves over to a good game of basketball, "getting lost" in deep conversation, allowing a dance or a book or a creative project to overtake us. "Play is not a mood," warns theologian Robert E. Neale, who goes so far as to describe the crucifixion as God's "non-anxious play." "It is a condition which encompasses many moods, including the 'negative' ones of fear, anger, and grief. Christ suffered such moods, yet his suffering was undergirded, not by anxiety, but by delight."[26] The passion of play seizes us, therefore, not by force, but by ec-

---

25. Johann Huizinga, *Homo Ludens: A Study of the Play-Element in Culture* (Boston: Beacon Press, 1950), 8.

26. Robert E. Neale, "The Crucifixion as Play," cited in Jürgen Moltmann, *Theology of Play* (New York: Harper & Row, 1972), 84.

statically drawing us beyond our present reality into an alternative, non-anxious, delighted consciousness determined by God.

Playing accentuates the alternative sense of time inherent in transcendent practices. It has structure, rules, and boundaries, but also a "back-and-forth," give-and-take relationship between partners (who need not be human, as dogs and video games illustrate). Play is its own objective, and symbolically represents a higher-order reality that we may or may not acknowledge.[27] Philosopher Johann Huizinga writes, "In play there is something 'at play' which transcends the immediate needs of life and imparts meaning to the action. All play means something."[28]

As a result, play contributes to the serious business of constructing the self. As we identify with the reality play represents, we internalize its representation, making it part of the basis for our identities.[29] Play becomes a template for our values, behaviors, and expectations. Children take in gender roles they see played out around them. Americans love football partly because of the hometown team, but also because the game dramatizes basic (if flawed) assumptions about American culture: success belongs, not to stature or birthright, but to practice, strategy, a willingness to tackle your opponents and, above all, the ability to get up and keep going after they have tackled you. Play's reward comes from the deep satisfaction of losing ourselves in it, the moment of self-abandonment when the reality we glimpse but cannot grasp somehow grasps us.

Yet when we play in the Christian community, we internalize a distinctive template: a reality inverted by Christ, a cruciform pattern of human relationships in which the last shall be first and the first shall be last. All play connotes freedom, but in the Christian community, play liberates rather than tranquilizes, awakens rather than anesthetizes.[30] The word "win" means to struggle, but it also means desire; the word "lose" means to release or set free. So in the economy of God, the gospel is for losers: to

27. "The *fun* of playing resists all analysis, all logical interpretation. As a concept, it cannot be reduced to any other mental category. No other modern language . . . has the exact equivalent of the English 'fun.' . . . Nevertheless it is precisely this fun-element that categorizes the essence of play. . . . We may well call play a 'totality' in the modern sense of the word, and it is as a totality that we must try to understand and evaluate it." Huizinga, *Homo Ludens*, 3.

28. Huizinga, *Homo Ludens*, 1.

29. D. W. Winnicott observes that relaxation — allowed by trust — is required for play to take place; but the creative, physical, and mental activity manifested in play forms the experiences that are the basis of the self. D. W. Winnicott, *Playing and Reality* (London: Routledge, 1971), 56.

30. Jürgen Moltmann, *Theology of Play*, 113.

win is to lose, and to lose is to win. When this playful inversion breaks into our daily routines, it transforms our sense of give and take between human beings. In losing, we are resurrected. In Christ's Passion we find God's redemption.

One of youth ministry's most important responsibilities is to sound the call to deep play and recreation (re-creation) for the church and for the world. As Scottish runner and Olympic gold medalist Eric Liddell explains in a famous line from the movie *Chariots of Fire,* "When I run, I feel God's pleasure."[31] Youth long to feel God's pleasure in all of Christian life, although the weirdest, and most playful, ways we do this as Christians are to gather weekly for worship and keep Sabbath. The existential surrender and non-defensiveness of playful worship engenders the kind of authenticity that adolescents prize, for when we play our defenses are down. But at the same time, this playfulness reminds us that we cannot re-create ourselves, which means Sabbath is required. Only a playful God can re-create us, accepting our participation as we are but also presenting us in a larger vision of who we could become. Adolescents insist on playful — i.e., interactive, relational, and self-forgetting — worship, just as they insist (sometimes rebelliously) on Sabbaths, times set aside for God to play *in* us, turning our human rules for winning and losing inside out.

Play and Sabbath: Recreational Ministry

Play is imitation. It is not "real" life; it is a "stepping out" of real life into a temporary sphere of activity with a reality all its own. Despite the seriousness with which we take our faith, there is no imitation of Christ, and no Christian identity, without play. According to the tradition of the saints, even God plays; the ecstatic nature of the Trinity issues in a perichoretic dance in which the Father's delight in the Son overflows into all creation.[32]

---

31. Liddell won the Olympic gold for Britain in the Paris 1924 Olympics, but became inadvertently famous for refusing to run on Sundays because he felt it compromised his Christian faith. Liddell became a missionary to China, where he died in an internment camp during World War II. In the internment camp he served as an unofficial youth minister, according to Langdon Gilkey, who wrote about the internment in *Shantung Compound: The Story of Men and Women under Pressure* (New York: Harper & Row, 1966), 192. According to Gilkey, who referred to him incorrectly as Eric Ridley, under his guidance the youth in the camp ran a lot of track.

32. Hugo Rahner points out that before the fourth century, when scholars rushed to close loopholes for Arianism, which denied that the Father and Son were of the same nature,

Christian theology, therefore, is a playful enterprise. God did not need creation; God made the world to enjoy it, and made us to enjoy God. As Moltmann (and Augustine) point out, only when we stop making God useful — when we "cease using God as helper in need, stopgap, and problem solver" — can we really do liturgy playfully, not because God needs our work, but because we long to delight in God.[33]

Christ, therefore, calls the church to play. The most playful Christians of all were the mystics, lovers of Christ given to seeing through the material world into an inexpressible reality where they freely approached God. African martyrs Perpetua and Felicitas (d. 203) reportedly had a vision of their entry into paradise, in which God met them, stroked their cheeks, and told them "Go and play!"[34] Mechtild of Magdeburg (1207?-1282) begged Jesus to "open to her the flood that plays within the Trinity by which alone the soul can live." And she heard God respond, "The soul shall experience my blessedness . . . if it will lay itself trustfully in my divine arms, so that I must play with it."[35] Therese of Lisieux (1873-1897) desired to be Jesus' plaything, "a toy of no value — a ball say — such as a child might throw on the ground or leave lying in a corner, or press to his heart if he feels that way about it."[36]

Historically, of course, terms like "Sabbath" and "play" were seldom spoken in the same breath. Yet the distinguishing feature of playfulness is its regenerative potential, which is also the purpose of keeping Sabbath. Sabbath means "to rest"; technically, it starts at sundown the night before, to acknowledge that God's renewal begins in our sleep. Every pilgrimage requires rest along the way — a good night's slumber, a satisfying meal, the unhurried company of friends as we literally lose track of time with them. Sabbath accentuates the countercultural rhythm of the pilgrimage; it dislodges the pilgrim from the relentless onward march of linear time *(chronos)* and attunes us to God's unhurried time *(chairos)* instead.

---

translators of Proverbs likened Divine Wisdom to a playful child. In one early translation, Proverbs 8:27-31 reads: "When he established the heavens, I was there, . . . when he marked out the foundations of the earth, then I was beside him, like a little child; and I was daily his delight, rejoicing before him always, rejoicing in his inhabited world and delighting in the sons of men." Rahner, *Man at Play* (New York: Herder and Herder, 1967), 19.

33. Liturgy means "the work of the people" in Latin; like teenagers, Moltmann considers this serendipitous, not ironic. Moltmann, *Theology of Play*, 63-64.

34. Rahner, *Man at Play*, 61.

35. *The Revelations of Mechtild of Magdeburg (1210-1297); or, The Flowing Light of the Godhead*, trans. Lucy Menzies, IV, 12, p. 105 and V, 25, p. 152. Cited in Rahner, *Man at Play*, 55.

36. Therese of Lisieux, *Autobiography of a Saint*, trans. Ronald Knox (London: The Harvill Press, 1958), 171.

The problem with Sabbath, of course, is that we don't have time for it — and neither do teenagers. Economist Juliet Schor reports that between 1968 and 1988, the average American worker added 164 hours to the work year — an additional month of labor.[37] According to one national survey, free time for children (the time remaining after time allotted for school, meals, and rest) between 1981 and 1997 declined by twelve hours a week, while time spent *in* school increased by eight hours a week. Participation in organized sports nearly doubled during the same period; churchgoing declined by 40 percent. Outdoor activities declined by about 50 percent, household conversations by 10 percent, and the amount of time families spent eating together declined by an hour a week.[38] It's not that teenagers haven't noticed. In one survey, 21 percent of young adolescents listed "spending more time with family" as their biggest concern, and 73 percent of thirteen- to nineteen-year-olds told *Newsweek* that "parents don't spend enough time with their children."[39]

In short, playful regeneration may have been fine for mystics and nuns, but young people, not to mention their parents and youth ministers, are just about drowning in *chronos.* As one rabbi advised, it is good to observe the twenty-four hours of the Sabbath; but if your life is too busy, then you are encouraged to observe twelve hours of Sabbath; but if your life is too busy, then observe six hours of Sabbath time; but if your life is too busy still, then observe one hour of Sabbath; and if you can't observe even one hour of Sabbath, then at least want to.[40] Yet as Dorothy Bass points out, Sabbath means that we see time not as something that controls us, but as God's first gift, as the medium of God's presence and activity, so we "begin to sway to a beat that runs counter to some of the other rhythms of our busy lives."[41] Biblically speaking, God ordained the Sabbath both as a sign of obedience (God rested on the seventh day) and of freedom (slaves are

37. Juliet Schor, *The Overworked American,* cited in Dorothy Bass, *Receiving the Day: Christian Practices for Opening the Gift of Time* (San Francisco: Jossey-Bass, 2000), 59-60.

38. See Sandra Hofferth, *Changes in American Children's Time, 1981-1997* (Ann Arbor: Institute for Social Research, University of Michigan, 2000), available at http://www.ethno.isr.umich.edu/papers/ceel013.00.pdf; accessed 16 December 2002. Teens who eat dinner with a parent six or seven days a week or more are less likely to smoke, use alcohol or marijuana, or have sex, according to a study by the president's Council of Economic Advisors (May 2, 2000).

39. Francine Kiefer, "Teenagers Want More ... Family Time?" *Christian Science Monitor* (May 3, 2000), available at www.csmonitor.com/durable/2000/05/03/p1s3.htm.

40. Recounted on the United Church of Canada Family Ministries web page, www.uccan.org/familyministries/articles/020601.htm.

41. See Bass, *Receiving the Day,* 11-12.

not permitted to rest). Bass suggests several kinds of Sabbaths that playfully punctuate the journey to Jerusalem, for adolescents as well as the rest of us. To offer young people a rest from commerce, a rest from worry, a rest *for* creation and creativity, as well as a rest from work helps adolescents counter the culture of self-fulfillment by setting before them the alternative possibility of self-giving love.[42]

Play and Worship: Experiencing God's Immediacy[43]

Most of us learned early on that playing in worship is off limits (as is playing on Sundays generally, in some strict Christian sects). Besides distracting the folks in the pew behind us, playing risks trivializing what we have come to celebrate in worship in the first place: the life, death, and resurrection of Jesus Christ, undertaken on our behalf. Church nurseries (a telling development in twentieth-century liturgical life) were conceived so playing children could be extracted from the sanctuary until they reached the age of reason — namely, when they became old enough to know *not* to play in church, and thus they were permitted to "worship."

The irony, of course, is that worship constitutes the oldest form of play known to humankind. Human beings have always engaged in "sacred games," and originally offered worship as a form of theatre to please the gods.[44] The cataclysmic error of some so-called "contemporary" worship innovations was not that they pandered to adolescent taste by making worship playful, but that they directed the performance of worship to humans instead of to God. Theologically, this meant heresy; practically, it made the church an also-ran "competitor" with the entertainment media for Sunday morning programming. Since theatre traces its origins to religion, it is ironic indeed to find the church borrowing from popular culture what popular culture has, for centuries, been borrowing from the church — namely, play itself. No wonder many of our early efforts at renewed worship seemed like a bad fax of entertainment genres. Congregations (or

42. Bass, *Receiving the Day*, 66-70.

43. Portions of this section appeared in expanded form in "Moshing for Jesus: Adolescence as a Cultural Context for Worship," in *Making Room at the Table: An Invitation to Multicultural Worship*, ed. B. Blount and L. Tisdale (Louisville: Westminster/John Knox, 2000).

44. See Huizinga, *Homo Ludens*; Adolf E. Jensen, *Myth and Cult Among Primitive Peoples*, trans. M. T. Choldin and W. Weissleder (Chicago: University of Chicago, 1963). The intrinsic relationality of play is described in Winnicott, *Playing and Reality*.

were they audiences?) had little choice but to evaluate worship according to the criteria of the performances we sought to imitate: not the Passion of Christ, but Hollywood, Motown, MTV.

Experiencing God's immediacy in worship is crucial for adolescents, regardless of the style of worship. Despite impressive statistics suggesting otherwise, God's presence during worship — even dismal worship — is never in question. What *is* in question is our ability to *perceive* God's presence. Playful worship aims for Jerusalem by tuning our perceptual skills to God's movement, engaging God's give-and-take with the material world (through candles, oil, water, wine, ashes, fire, as well as other symbolic objects); moving people physically (inspiring clapping, dancing, or postures of humility); participating in sacraments that dramatically reenact Christ's life, death, and resurrection. All of these acts of worship intensify the perception of God's presence in the present while at the same time releasing young people from needing to "feel God" emotionally in order to have a spiritually significant experience. Even the so-called "traditional" elements of worship (the order of service, the presence of Scripture, prayer, proclamation, musical intercession, and so on) serve as scaffolding for the spiritual journey, sacred "dots" to be connected by leaps of faith invited by God's playfulness, affection, and grace.

Worship with adolescents never reduces to issues of style. Young people desire a subjective encounter with the Passion of Christ, a sense of divine immediacy that is mediated through God's majesty and mystery as often as through interpersonal identification with Jesus Christ. By emphasizing divine immediacy, teenagers call us to reclaim subjective aspects of faith that were often undervalued by the modern church. Playful worship is re-creational — which is not the same thing as saying it is trivial, light-hearted, or even exciting. Youth have their fill of frivolity elsewhere, and the church neither can nor should out-entertain the entertainment industry. Playing in worship means relinquishing control to God, who transports us into a new reality regardless of the "style" of the service. Young people converting to Eastern Orthodoxy — and their numbers are increasing — often say they are drawn to its ecstatic ritual and sensual liturgy that assaults the worshipper with visual, aural, aromatic, gustatory, and tactile experience, making worship almost trance-like. On the other end of the liturgical spectrum, worship in some Pentecostal churches — where membership among the young is also on the rise — means self-abandoning practices like *glossolalia,* being "slain in the Spirit," or "quaking" (a permissible dance because feet don't leave the floor).

What stands behind the so-called "worship wars" in contemporary

Protestant churches, I think, is not really our dissatisfaction with style — we know God doesn't care about style — but our sense of losing touch with worship's playfulness.[45] Without the ability to point beyond itself, to convey God's give-and-take with creation, worship lacks the power to engender an existential surrender, a moment in which we joyfully "lose ourselves" to an other who passionately overtakes us. It is too simple to reduce concerns about worship and adolescents to marketing: What will appeal to the youth? How will we get them to come? What should we avoid so they won't leave once they get here? Hundreds of resources are produced each year to answer such questions, all of them obsolete within a week. Media-saturated, information-overloaded, advertising-savvy adolescents don't really care what we do to attract them, or how we do it. They care that when they worship, God is present, and that something "happens" because God is there.

Partying on the Road to Jerusalem:
Changing Tempo through Praise and Lament

If God uses practices of play to condescend to us and "meet us where we are," God employs ecstatic practices like praise and lament to transport us into a state of being in which we glimpse ourselves and others, however briefly, as new creations in Jesus Christ. True ecstatic ritual seeks an altered state of consciousness in which the worshipper experiences something extraordinary, something different, something to be identified with the divine reality.[46] These experiences are short-lived but profoundly liberating. Practices of ecstasy issue in a range of affective experiences, from a pleasant sense of release to trances and speaking in tongues. They free us of our self-consciousness so we may fall into the embrace of the Divine Lover, whose love for us overflows into all creation.

Praise is the culmination of Christian life, as well as an ecstatic practice of gratitude for God's grace and mercy, a feasting spirit best described by teenagers as "partying." Partying is a universal ritual among adolescents, often accompanied by everything a parent dreads: alcohol, drugs, cigarettes, sex. In a supreme example of co-opted human passion, adoles-

---

45. See Thomas Long, *Beyond the Worship Wars* (Washington, D.C.: Alban Institute, 2001).

46. Bernhard Lang, *Sacred Games: A History of Christian Worship* (New Haven: Yale University Press, 1997), 371.

cent "feasting" often takes the forms of binge drinking or getting high, which can look disturbingly like ecstatic spiritual experience as well. Consequently, like cautious parents overseeing their child's first serious crush, mainline Protestants historically have viewed ecstatic practices askance. Ecstatic ritual, according to anthropological research, "is often practiced by the lowly and the oppressed for whom participation produces a temporary respite from the pressures of life. People whose lives are given little structure because they have been denied participation in well-defined, socially acknowledged roles seem to be especially prone to experiences of trance and possession."[47] Given the lack of well-defined, socially acknowledged roles available to youth in American culture, their interest in ecstatic ritual is hardly surprising.

Meanwhile, adolescents also universally (and sometimes simultaneously) practice lament. The "high" of the party is matched by the "lows" of anxiety, abandonment, and invisibility. In the poetry of hip-hop, the scarification of tattoos, the dance of the mosh pit, adolescents lose themselves in lament as often as they find themselves in praise. Sandy Miller, editor of the teen devotional magazine *DevoZine,* which solicits teen contributions, observed that her files are bulging with adolescent submissions of lament, but to get contributions from teenagers on subjects like joy, humor, or happiness "is like pulling teeth."[48] The road to Jerusalem is not a sunny stroll for youth any more than it is for adults.

The Christian Party and the Christian Protest: Acts of Praise and Lament

In mainline Protestant circles, ecstatic practice is most often associated with praise. The objective of this ecstasy — and of every practice of Christian life — is doxology. The first question and answer of the Westminster Shorter Catechism (1647) famously states:

> What is the chief end of man?
> Man's chief end is to glorify God, and to enjoy him forever.

Although praise has an affective dimension, it cannot be reduced to naked emotionalism. Contemporary young people recognize emotional manipu-

---

47. Lang, *Sacred Games,* 369-70.
48. Sandy Miller, personal conversation, 16 January 2002.

lation even when they play into it; they are, after all, the first generation raised on cable TV and omnipresent advertising, where emotional excess has made them wary consumers of advertising even while making them lavish consumers of everything else.[49] Affect simply acknowledges the subjective side of God's gift of faith, the "religious affections" — variously named — important in the theology of Martin Luther, Jonathan Edwards, John and Charles Wesley, and others for whom religious experience (despite charges to the contrary) had less to do with outward "enthusiasm" than with an inward conviction of love toward God and neighbor that issued in social generosity.[50]

In the Christian community, celebration is impossible without praise. Worship historian Bernhard Lang notes that biblical languages developed no concept of "thanking" apart from praise, and Lang claims its primacy over other forms of prayer.[51] King David's loud dance in his underwear before the ark of the covenant — and wife Michal's disgusted reaction (2 Sam. 6:15-16) — sounds like a scene straight out of the fraternity house. Christian praise offers ecstatic thanksgiving to God that is normally shared with others in the faith community. Youth sometimes describe exhilarating praise as a "spiritual high," an ecstatic release accompanied by visionary clarity and lingering euphoria. Inspired by alternative worship movements in Britain and Australia aimed primarily at Baby Boomers and their progeny, "praise services" have become a *modus operandi* for many mainline Protestant churches in the United States (whose idea of "alternative," as it turns out, is quite conventional compared to "alternative" worship outside the U.S.) that hope to attract young people to worship.

Yet praise is meaningless in the absence of lament. The suffering love of Christ means that practicing passion entails waiting by the cross on Good Friday as well as running from the tomb on Easter. Transcendent practices not only transport us to places where our cups runneth over, but also through the valley of the shadow of death. Just as Christian

49. See Matthew McAllister, *The Commercialization of American Culture: New Advertising, Control and Democracy* (London, New Delhi, Thousand Oaks: Sage, 1996).

50. See Rex D. Matthews, "With the Eyes of Faith: Spiritual Experience and the Knowledge of God in the Theology of John Wesley," *Wesleyan Theology Today,* ed. Theodore Runyan (Nashville: United Methodist Publishing House, 1985), 406-15; Martin Luther, "Preface to the Romans," in *Martin Luther: Selections from His Writings,* ed. John Dillenberger (Chicago: Quadrangle Books, 1961), 24; Jonathan Edwards, "A Treatise Concerning Religious Affections," in *The Works of President Edwards* 4 (New York: Burt Franklin, 1968).

51. Lang, *Sacred Games,* 10, 13.

praise is more than divine flattery, Christian lament is more than sanctified whining. Laments are protests — rages, really — born out of horror and grief: God seems to have allowed something to occur that is unthinkably out of character for a compassionate God who loves us.[52] Lament's ability to give voice to grief, complaint, and anger is necessary to surviving calamity, says Old Testament scholar F. W. Dobbs-Allsopp. But he points to a fourth element that is equally powerful. By directing a lament toward God, its author implies a stubborn allegiance to Yahweh in spite of other encroaching deities. "Fidelity to God," writes Dobbs-Allsopp, "remains the driving force behind these poems, and it does so fully aware of the terrible nature of God's violence and the pain of God's abandonment."[53]

Despite the teenage emphasis on celebration, lament is the *lingua franca* of adolescence, as young people's grief, disappointment, and rage sometimes explicitly, and often implicitly, becomes directed toward an unknown god (Acts 17:23). Song is generally the genre of choice; lament wends its way through car radio speakers, lingers in conversations among friends, and creeps into the adolescent vocabulary to express internal bleeding. Some songs do, of course, simply whine; not every adolescent gripe is a lament. Yet because suffering defies explanation, the scent of pain is frequently captured nondiscursively — positively, for instance, in art, or negatively through "acting out." The "universal language" of music is often cited as a boundary-breaking medium, and the explosion of the Christian contemporary music industry since the 1970s suggests an important place for explicitly religious music in the adolescent vocabulary. But since music is a subjective medium, lyrics often play a secondary role to a song's beat, tone, or "texture" in determining a song's sacred significance for teenagers. Increasingly, so-called "Christian" groups "cross over" into mainstream markets, and youth continue to ascribe sacred significance to secular music — expressions that move them towards transcendence as they grope for a language of redemption.

A few years ago, I invited my junior high Sunday School class, which was overwhelmingly populated by unimpressed seventh- and eighth-grade boys, to bring their favorite compact discs to class. Besides giving them a "hook" for showing up, the idea was to see where we could, and couldn't, discern God's voice in the music of popular culture. From what I could tell,

52. Patrick D. Miller, *They Cried to the Lord: The Form and Theology of Biblical Prayer* (Minneapolis: Fortress, 1994), 71.

53. F. W. Dobbs-Allsopp, *Lamentations* (Louisville: John Knox Press, 2002), 41.

most of them were there under protest (Sunday School was a confirmation requirement). That included Kevin, a sullen athlete with long blond hair who gave me the silent treatment unless we talked about Korn, his favorite band. When Kevin's week to share his CD came, I knew I was in over my head. Understanding Korn through a lens of faith (actually, understanding Korn at all) was a lost cause, so I printed out the lyrics online and wondered why this otherwise wholesome teenager was so committed to this band. Unable to find a single redemptive song on the CD Kevin had loaned me, I reverted to genre. I showed them where the Book of Lamentations was in the Bible (fairly certain they hadn't seen it before) and hoped they would somehow connect a groaning metal band to the fact that God's people groan sometimes too.

At the end of class, I played one of the songs on the CD, stopped it midway, and asked them to compose their own ending, turning it into a personal lament to God. The class's signature chaos ceased, and the floodgates opened. Everyone had something to hurl at heaven — disappointment at home, injustice at school, a grandparent's death, theodicy — and after a few minutes, we closed ranks around a candle and read the laments (which turned out to be extremely moving). Kevin's lament was especially eloquent, filled with cadences of longing and regret. Then it occurred to me: we sounded a lot like a Korn album. Young people who had great difficulty discerning God's presence in popular culture had no trouble at all experiencing what they took to be God's absence. No wonder they felt out of place in church; everything we did as a congregation assumed the *presence* of God, when what these boys knew best from the vicissitudes of junior high was the hiddenness of God, the silence of God, the death of the kindly, bespectacled Yahweh they had come to expect from Sunday School. And their grief stung them. Some of them complained, some grumbled, and some raged — *but they did not doubt.* Just like their bodies, their childhood theology had grown gangly and unseemly. As their God-capacities expanded along with their bones and their hormones, they ached from growing pains. All this left me with a question: Can our congregation offer these young teenagers a God who is big enough to transcend the stretch marks, or will they leave the church having outgrown these too-tight Sunday clothes?

Sacrifice and Praise

Christian liturgy tangibly links suffering and love, anguish and ecstasy, self-denial and self-giving. The bishops of the early church urged Christians to practice transcendence by offering God, the source of their existence, "sacrifice and praise." The link between sacrifice and praise was a uniquely Christian connection, celebrated in a new ritual instituted by Jesus to honor God. This ritual honestly acknowledges Jesus' suffering while giving thanks for all that we have received. Christians called this ritual *eucharistia,* the Greek term for thanksgiving.[54] In creating a substitute for blood sacrifice in the Temple, Jesus continued the already well-established tradition of joyous meals — parties, if you will — shared with large crowds, publicans and sinners, wealthy sponsors, and sometimes his closest circle of friends.[55] Though we often approach the Last Supper as the final meal of the condemned, the Eucharist actually came about through celebrations; Jesus introduced these joyful meals with an unprecedented ritual of thanksgiving. Even today we "celebrate" the Eucharist — language that is not lost on teenagers, no matter how somber the meal turns out to be.

Not every praise celebration is a high-voltage, high-octane event, and not every lament leads to tears of repentance. But practices of praise and lament reach out for the awesome nearness of God, even while they surround young people with a profound sense of belonging in a community of grace. In the experience of the Eucharist, for example, "the distance between the human and the divine disappears."[56] Rather than recoiling from the divine mystery of God's passion for us, adolescents embrace it, especially in sacramental acts that embody the strength and the mystery of love that is "to die for."

Dancing to Zion

Practicing transcendence never depends on the *form* of our praise, but on the *object* of our praise. We do not create transcendence; as Karl Rahner reminded us, human self-transcendence is grounded in and oriented toward divine Transcendence as its source and term.[57] The holiest, weirdest fact of our faith is God's Incarnation and death on the cross out of self-giving love — a story of passion whose "strangeness" is embodied in its telling and in its sacraments, in which generations of Christians have prac-

54. Lang, *Sacred Games,* 226-27.
55. Lang, *Sacred Games,* 226-27.
56. Lang, *Sacred Games,* 431.
57. Wainwright, *Doxology,* 15.

ticed the art of awe. The suffering of desire is fulfilled in the ecstasy of communion shared and extended into the world through the Christian community. Passionate faith, then, knows ecstasy because of agony, joy because of suffering, release because of bondage. Communities of people who have known real anguish and oppression — including the young — often find praising God easier than the rest of us. Having known suffering, they also know a party when they see one.

Chapter Nine

THE ART OF INTIMACY

Spiritual Friendship as a Practice of Communion

Adolescents in America are ultimately left with little guidance or example in the area where they need it most: human relationships. Busy with their battles over propaganda and prophylactics, adults aren't addressing young people's yearning for intimacy, for contact, for connections that prove they matter.

Nell Bernstein[1]

It is impossible to find truth without being in love. Love itself is knowledge; the more one loves the more one knows.

St. Gregory[2]

And did you get what you wanted from this life even so?
I did.
And what did you want?
To call myself beloved, to feel myself beloved on the earth.

Raymond Carver[3]

---

1. Nell Bernstein, "Learning to Love," *Mother Jones,* October 30, 2001, 3; available at www.motherjones.com/mother_jones/JF95/bernstein.html.

2. Cited in Parker Palmer, *To Know as We Are Known: A Spirituality of Education* (San Francisco: Harper & Row, 1983).

3. Cited in Anne Lamott, *Traveling Mercies: Some Thoughts on Faith* (New York: Pantheon Books, 1999), 89.

Jorge, a sixteen-year-old in one of our focus groups, told us why he can't go to his girlfriend's house anymore:[4]

> Me and my girlfriend kind of got caught having sex, and her dad didn't like that too much. So I'm not allowed to see her no more till I become a man. I guess by becoming a man he means "set a future," so that I will do. . . . I want to be married to her one day. Only the Lord knows really how much I love her. She's like the big inspiration in my life, and that's why I feel that marriage is an important thing. And I know she would be a great wife, and I know marriage with her would be happy, and very fulfilling and, you know, wonderful. . . . I guess I kind of messed up my life in a way [by getting kicked out of school]. . . . But if all works out well, I'll marry her and we'll have beautiful kids, and I'll go to college too, while I'm in the National Guard. . . . I want my kids to have everything, unlike myself. Basically why I want to be married so much is to correct the wrongs that my father made. . . . I just want to be the father I never had for myself.

Maybe I should have expected it, but when I talked to youth about practices that mattered to them, I heard more about marriage than I did about sex. Perhaps the presence of an adult interviewer inhibited their candor on the subject (although that didn't seem to bother Jorge). Or maybe sex simply was not the "big deal" that marriage seemed to be. Whatever the reason, marriage interested every group of teenagers we talked to, regardless of age, gender, or social background.[5] In spite of the fragmentation of fami-

---

4. Not his real name.

5. After conducting three pilot focus groups of mixed ages and socio-economic backgrounds (total: 26 youth), Blair Bertrand and I officially interviewed 22 teenagers in five focus groups. These interviews were not conducted to obtain scientifically reliable data, but to provide "reality checks" for my thinking on adolescent practices, and to solicit teenagers' reactions to my hypotheses. We wanted to know how they "practiced passion" apart from the church: what ongoing activities do adolescents engage in for the sake of attaining fidelity, transcendence, and communion in the normal course of their lives as teenagers? Our primary organizing principles were age (two groups of young adolescents, two groups of middle adolescents, and one group of older adolescents), and, for the young adolescents, gender. Other demographic features included ethnicity (one group was entirely Hispanic, one group was a mix of African Americans and whites, and three were white) and risk factors (one group was composed of youth who were economically at risk, one was composed of youth who were academically at risk, and one was composed of youth identified as academically gifted). Each discussion was recorded, and all but one (due to a technical malfunction) was videotaped. We also scheduled "casual" time with the teenagers in order to maximize their comfort with the camera and the facilitator.

lies, social institutions, and general culture surrounding them — or maybe because of these things — these youth steadfastly hoped for a happy marriage with the perfect partner who would know them intimately and love them unconditionally.

Sociologist John Gagnon, co-author of the University of Chicago's "Sex in America" study that surveyed 24,000 eighteen- to fifty-nine-year-olds, is astounded by adolescents' sentimental view of sex: "The degree to which adolescents believe in being in love is absolutely extraordinary," says Gagnon.[6] Surveys show that the vast majority of young people want to marry and raise children with a spouse. Journalist Nell Bernstein notes, "Unlike children of the sixties — for whom the fear of ending up like one's parents manifested itself as a terror of being old, married, and bored — today's teens fear ending up old and alone."[7] A number of recent studies challenge the assumption that all teen pregnancies are "unwanted." About four in ten girls in the United States get pregnant at least once before they turn twenty, and some of these pregnancies (some studies estimate between 15 and 22 percent)[8] are rationally planned as a way to guarantee unconditional love, to have "an achievement,"[9] to advance themselves economically,[10] or to beat "weathering," the pervasive belief among disadvantaged teenagers that their lives will be cut short.[11] One pregnant eighteen-year-old told Bernstein that she had always planned to have a baby right after high school, "to make a person all her own, who would

6. Cited in Bernstein, "Learning to Love," 3. Also see Edward Laumann, John Gagnon et al., *The Social Organization of Sexuality: Sexual Practices in the United States* (Chicago: University of Chicago Press, 1994), 475-508.

7. Bernstein, "Learning to Love," 3.

8. For example, Health Initiatives for Youth (2002) report that approximately 86 percent of teen pregnancies are unintended (available at www.hify.org). The National Campaign to Prevent Teen Pregnancy puts the figure at 78 percent (*Not Just Another Thing to Do: Teens Talk about Sex, Regret, and the Influence of Their Parents,* available at www .teenpregnancy.org/resources/data/pdf/teenwant.pdf). Statistic on the frequency of teen pregnancy in the United States is from the same report. Both accessed 16 December 2002.

9. Leon Dash, "When Children Want Children," *Washington Post,* cited by Sarah Schiltz, *The Daily Illini Online,* 10/04/00, www.dailyillini.com/oct00/oct04/news/printer/news.06.shtml.

10. Cecilia A. Conrad, cited in Emory Thomas, "Is Pregnancy a Rational Choice for Poor Teenagers?" *Wall Street Journal,* November 25, 2002, available at http://home.fuse.net/mllwyd/teen_pregnancy.html. Accessed 16 December 2002. Thomas notes that teenagers themselves offer an array of reasons for becoming pregnant, including peer pressure, lack of birth control, and fear of losing a boyfriend.

11. See Arline T. Geronimus, "What Teen Mothers Know," *Human Nature: An Interdisciplinary Biosocial Perspective* 7 (1996): 323-52.

love her and not leave." She had no illusions that any man would step into the role of the father.[12]

The most powerful form of self-transcendence for adolescents is also the most intimate: the oneness of being truly known by another, the unconditional love promised by friendship, the ecstatic intimacy that transforms "me" into "we." To describe love worthy of suffering as merely loyal, longsuffering, or steadfast is insufficient, for passion is also deeply personal, familiar to the point of knowing us better than we know ourselves. In practicing communion (the word means "one with"), the church embodies the passion of God by extending the tender trust of knowing and being known. We take part in the intimacy of the triune God, expressed by Jesus toward the Father in the words "Abba, Father" (Mark 14:36).[13]

Knowing as We Are Known

A curriculum of passion requires a deep investment in practices of communion, starting with the specific practice of spiritual friendship. Communion connotes the intimacy of being known, the personal truth that educator Parker Palmer contrasts with truth as "object." "All truth is known through personal relationships," writes Palmer. Truth "involves a vulnerable, faithful, and risk-filled interpenetration of the knower and the known."[14] Palmer argues that, in addition to knowledge gleaned for its own sake (curiosity) and knowledge garnered for practical ends (control), the example of Jesus calls us to a third kind of knowing, rooted in Godly passion:

> Another kind of knowledge is available to us, one that begins in a different passion and is drawn toward other ends. This knowledge can contain as much sound fact and theory as the knowledge we now possess, but because it springs from a truer passion it works toward truer ends. This is a knowledge that originates not in curiosity or control but in compassion, or love — a source celebrated not in our intellectual tradition but in our spiritual heritage. The goal of a knowledge arising

12. Bernstein, "Learning to Love," 3.

13. In *The Message*, Eugene Peterson paraphrases the text: "Papa, Father, you can — can't you? — get me out of this. Take this cup away from me. But please, not what I want — what do *you* want?" (Mark 14).

14. Parker Palmer, *To Know As We Are Known* (New York: HarperCollins, 1993), 83.

from love is the reunification and reconstruction of broken selves and worlds.[15]

When we practice communion, we enjoy and extend the friendship of God. Unlike interpersonal practices of community, practices of communion enact God's relationality more than ours. In contrast to classical treatments of divine transcendence that equate God's "otherness" with God's distance, the concept of the friendship of Jesus is "a notion of Christ which is near to the people."[16] Theologian Elisabeth Moltmann-Wendel calls the Last Supper a "meal of friendship" that has as its center the self-surrender of John 15:13: "Greater love has no man than this, that he lays down his life for his friends."[17]

Practices of communion involve willing surrender for someone else — what we might call the sacrament of one another. If we lay down our lives for our friends, it is not because we can, but because we abide in Jesus who already has. In the sacrament of one another, we are known in the true biblical sense, which is to say we are known intimately, personally, and with

15. Palmer, *To Know As We Are Known*, 7.

16. Elisabeth Moltmann-Wendel, *Rediscovering Friendship*, trans. John Bowden (London: SCM Press, 2000), 39. Moltmann-Wendel notes that African theology is more helpful on this subject than Western feminism. Mercy Oduyoye says the Christ of African women is "above all a friend and companion who meets them in their daily life, conquers the powers of death which destroy life, and frees women from the burden of patriarchal prejudices and oppressive cultural customs" (40).

17. Moltmann-Wendel, *Rediscovering Friendship,* 46. Moltmann-Wendel, who shares Rene Girard's view that the Gospels do not speak of sacrifice "except to exclude it," distinguishes self-surrender from sacrifice: "A sacrifice usually presupposes guilt and damage . . . [but] self-surrender is an act of one's own free will; it is bound up with responsibility and love, and is interested in the preservation of life." She argues that Jesus' total loving self-surrender — to the Father and to us — changes the concept of sacrifice in Christianity to mean a kind of self-giving that takes place out of self-affirmation, not out of self-denial or a desire for sacrifice. On this last point I agree, although to excise sacrificial language from Christian tradition on the basis of modern semantics seems unrealistic. My position here has been to define passion in terms of self-giving; the sacrifice or self-denial associated with passion — because they are acts of love — may be considered "self-surrender" in the sense Moltmann-Wendel uses it, a willing act of one's own free will. Moltmann-Wendel's theological anthropology fails to distinguish between the "social" self shaped by social practices, and a transformed "religious self" that is shaped by the Holy Spirit in sacramental practices of the church. The "social" self in adolescence is unformed, and therefore cannot be surrendered — save through God's gift of sanctifying grace that transforms the disparate passions of the social self with the Passion of Christ. The transformed self that is conformed to Christ can be "given" in acts of passion, or self-giving love, because it is a subject, a positive self that can be "surrendered."

the vulnerability called forth by true love. Palmer, like his biblical fore-bears, turns to the language of sexuality to describe this kind of intimate knowledge. When knowing seeks the oneness of communion, "knowing is an act of love, the act of entering and embracing the reality of the other, of allowing the other to enter and embrace our own."[18] What is at stake in biblical intimacy is not merely solidarity but identification; not being one "of" the community of faith, but being one, period: one with Christ, one with one another, and one with all creation.

First Comes Love: Marriage as the Archetype of Sacramental Intimacy

Because communion represents ("makes present again") the passionate love of God, Christians throughout the centuries have often described communion in terms of marriage, and specifically in terms of the sexual intimacy implied by marriage. Although men as well as women drew upon sexual metaphors, spiritually elite women in the Middle Ages — primarily nuns and mystics — are most often associated with describing personal union with Christ in terms of sex and marriage. Benedictine abbess Hildegard of Bingen (1098-1179) dressed her nuns as brides on feast days when they went forward, sick with love, to take the Eucharist; by the nineteenth century, the practice had extended to young girls who wore white dresses in order to take their First Communion (a practice that spawned an industry of its own among children's clothing manufacturers in the twentieth century).

Mystical theology viewed the Eucharist as a symbolic beginning for an erotic encounter with Christ, the first step in a full-blown encounter with spiritual intimacy. In the early thirteenth century, Flemish beguine Hadewijch had visions of communion with Christ that makes moderns blush. First, Hadewijch reported, "[Jesus] gave himself to me in the shape of the sacrament, in its outward form, as the custom is." But then "he came himself to me, took me entirely in his arms, and pressed me to him, and all my members felt his in full felicity."[19] The visions of Hadewijch's contemporary, Gertrude of Helfta, were even more explicit. Buoyed by the promise of spiritual pregnancy, Gertrude envisioned a Mass said by Christ him-

18. Palmer, *To Know As We Are Known*, 8.

19. See Bernhard Lang, *Sacred Games: A History of Christian Worship* (New Haven: Yale University Press, 1997), 343.

self instead of by a priest. In her vision, when the time came for communion Christ embraced Gertrude, and she felt his "caresses," his "penetration," and "influx." Normal communion thereafter entailed a similar intimate union with the Lord as Gertrude experienced Christ's "most affectionate embrace" and "sweet kiss of peace."[20]

It is tempting to attribute such spiritual eroticism to some mysterious alchemy between sexual repression and Catholic mysticism, but Protestants — Jeremy Taylor in England (1613-1667), Count Nicholas Ludwig von Zinzendorf in Germany (1700-1760), and Jonathan Edwards in America (1703-1758) among them — also described communion with God in terms of marital intimacy. Here is Jonathan Edwards explaining communion to his congregants:

> Our taking the bread and wine is as much a professing to accept of Christ, at least as a woman's taking a ring of the bridegroom in her marriage is a profession and seal of her taking him for her husband. The sacramental elements in the Lord's supper represent Christ as a party in covenant, as truly as a proxy represents a prince to a foreign lady in her marriage, and our taking those elements is as truly a professing to accept of Christ, as in the other case the lady's taking the proxy is her professing to accept the prince as her husband. . . . It is as if a prince should send an ambassador to a woman in a foreign land, proposing marriage, and by his ambassador should send her his picture, and should desire her to manifest her acceptance of his suit, not only by professing her acceptance in words to his ambassador, but in token of her sincerity openly take or accept that picture.[21]

Though Edwards was satisfied to view the relationship between marriage and communion symbolically, in Germany some pietists recommended sexual intercourse in wedlock not for the sake of begetting children, but for the sake of celebrating "communion" with Christ, "just as in the Lord's Supper."[22]

At the root of these comparisons is the rhetorical nature of passion: Passion communicates itself. For all of its steamy connotations, *eros* is primarily a communicative impulse, not a sexual one. The objective of inter-

20. Lang, *Sacred Games,* 343-44.

21. Jonathan Edwards, "An Humble Enquiry into the Rules of the Word of God," Part 2, section 9, available at www.jonathanedwards.com/text/Communion/Communion%20Part2.htm; accessed 16 December 2002.

22. Lang, *Sacred Games,* 345.

course is the communion of souls, which may or may not be complemented by sexual intimacy. Eroticism expresses our longing for mutual association, and communication is the way humans seek intercourse with others — people who "commune" with us, a community. Practices of communion hold out the promise of "being known" in the true biblical sense — which is to say, they represent the ways we seek to know God as intimately as God knows us.

The Art of "Being Known": The Foundation of Spiritual Intercourse

Sociology of religion has long maintained that "attachments lie at the heart of conversion"; across religious lines, conversions tend to proceed along the lines of interpersonal social networks.[23] Youth ministers, therefore, strive to "earn the right to be heard" — that is, to earn young people's friendship so they will trust what we say to them. The issue is not manipulation, but credibility; friends possess unparalleled credibility for adolescents, especially adult friends who, because they are both scarce and powerful, serve as significant resources for adolescent identity formation. Young people who "find Jesus" typically trace this discovery to a trustworthy other, usually an adult, who illuminates Jesus' presence in the "here and now" of his or her own life, and who invites the teenager to share in this relationship. Yet because Christianity teaches that the object of human passion is God Incarnate — not just another human being — theology reinterprets sociology by making the attachment necessary for conversion a relationship with the person of Jesus Christ. This allows for considerably more diversity in the Christian community than interpersonal social networks permit, since the primary attachment is to Christ and all other attachments ultimately proceed from him.[24]

---

23. Rodney Stark and Roger Finke, *Acts of Faith: Explaining the Human Side of Religion* (Berkeley: University of California Press, 2000), 118.

24. Christian solidarity, therefore, follows the three-dimensional pattern described in Chapter Five. Let's say that Nick shares his identification with Jesus Christ with his family and friends. Other youth who wish to identify with Nick may proceed to identify with Jesus as well (a fact that makes peer-to-peer Christian witness far and away the most potent form of teen evangelism). At the same time, youth who know nothing about Nick but who identify with Jesus suddenly find themselves in communion with Nick as well, expanding the notion of Christian solidarity to the entire church community. For this reason, "relational ministry" — a staple in all missionary endeavors — is endemic to Christian youth work. Since all prac-

What adolescents need, and what spiritual friendship offers, is a transitional ground for *eros* in which adolescents may explore the pleasure of intimacy in ways that acknowledge the deep connection between sexuality and spirituality, body and soul, without doing violence to either one. Spiritual friendship need not be limited to the "formal" relationship of a spiritual director and directee; in youth ministry it simply means the distinctive quality of friendship that stems from grounding human relationships in the relationality of God. Spiritual friends' primary relationship with Jesus Christ defines their kinship with one another; drawing closer to Jesus, they become closer to each other as well. Since spiritual friendships recognize many ways in which passion communicates itself, they offer a context in which young people can explore intimacy's range. This "holding environment" for the emerging sexual and spiritual self serves as what cognitive psychologist Robert Kegan calls "an evolutionary bridge, a context for crossing over" into the adult world of intimate attachments.[25] In contrast to popular culture, spiritual friendship does not reduce this intimacy to sex, but it does acknowledge adolescents' desire to be deeply known by an "other." Friends hold out the promise of "being known," not through orgasm but through communion, first with God and, through God, with one another.

In a world where adolescents experience profound abandonment, teenagers long for intercourse with people who "know" them. The murders at Columbine High School were the treacherous result of two "unknown" teenagers: unknown by classmates (who described Dylan Harris and Eric Klebold as students "you just didn't notice"), unknown by parents (who had no inkling of the pipe-bomb manufacture going on in the garage), unknown by teachers and juvenile authorities (who failed to take seriously the violence described in class projects and web sites). Only one motive was ever found, and this thanks to a videotape in which these two unknown boys declared their intent: they wanted to be known. Incredibly, as a spate of school shootings in the past decade have demonstrated, youth often perceive violence as a vehicle to "being known," confusing notoriety on the evening news with the deep satisfaction of social intercourse with people who love them.

Most young people navigate sexual intimacy by bouncing back and

tices point to the Passion of Jesus, Christian testimony requires transparency in order to point beyond the personal witness of the believer to the person of Jesus Christ.

25. Holding environments foster developmental transformation by providing a safe space that is at once challenging and supportive. Robert Kegan, *In Over Our Heads: The Mental Demands of Modern Life* (Cambridge: Harvard University Press, 1994), 39.

forth between the entertainment media, which overwhelmingly portrays sexual passion as potentially pleasurable (true), and panicked parents who overwhelmingly portray sexual passion as potentially dangerous (also true). Consequently, teenagers tend to develop a dualistic view of sexual intimacy: there is "hands off" and there is "all the way" — and nothing in between. In truth, there is quite a bit in between, and "being known" provides a helpful metaphor for exploring the distance. Holy friends reflect the spectrum of intimacy. Even life partners are not equally intimate at all points on this spectrum, and churches step up to the prophetic plate by modeling alternatives to Hollywood's one-size-fits-all view of intercourse.

In most ways, teenagers are masters of the art of friendship; they have far more resources for "being known" and for knowing others than they have for addressing sexual passion. When the church helps young people explore different ways of "being known" by offering varied routes to communion with God and others, we go a long way in helping teenagers "map" appropriate steps to sexual intimacy as well. Spiritual friendships offer young people a repertoire of practices that invite vulnerability patterned after the self-giving Passion of Christ rather than after the self-destructive passions of consumerism.[26] Above all, spiritual friendships incarnate the nature of God's intimacy with us, allowing teenagers to perceive Christ in every human relationship.

Practicing Communion through the Art of Spiritual Friendship

Christians have struggled over the centuries to discern the proper place of human friendship alongside the communion of God. Believing that preferential relationships violated a Christian's duty to love all people equally, the desert *abbas* and *ammas* of the Eastern church discouraged friendships among Christians, except with a spiritual mentor. As monasticism became institutionalized in the West, spiritual leaders in the high middle ages also grew suspicious of special friendships, and worried about their corrosive effects on the religious community. Teresa of Avila, for instance, advised her nuns to avoid preferential friendships, except in very large convents. In the typical convent of twelve or thirteen nuns, Teresa urged the sisters to

26. The classical term for this redirection of passion is *sublimation,* in which sexual energy is refocused on the Divine and often finds expression in doing "God's work" instead of being suppressed as undesirable.

"refrain from making individual friendships, however holy, for even among brothers and sisters such things are apt to be poisonous and I can see no advantage in them."[27]

For the most part, however, Western teachers viewed spiritual friendship as basic to our understanding of God, and they encouraged friendship as a fundamental expression of Christian life. Augustine set the stage by viewing human friendship as a metaphor for, and conduit to, life with God.[28] By the sixth century Pope Gregory the Great proclaimed the friend a "the guardian of the soul,"[29] and for a while much of Western monasticism followed suit. One historian dubbed the twelfth century the "age of friendship" in Western Europe, encouraged by reform-minded Cistercians like Bernard of Clairvaux, who, not surprisingly, entered monastic life accompanied by a host of friends and relatives.

Aelred of Rievaulx (1109-1167), whose *Spiritual Friendship* became the most important of the monastic treatises on friendship, saw virtue in the fact that friends draw each other beyond themselves toward God. Aelred set out to unite Christian devotion with classical conceptions of friendship, and defined spiritual friendship as the joining together of two souls in Christ, acknowledging true friendship as "a path to the love and knowledge of God."[30] While Aelred believed that male friendships enriched the spiritual life, he maintained that close bonds between the sexes inevitably provoked sexual sin. Many monastic communities, however, defended male-female spiritual friendships and practiced them — a position that, thanks to the Ciceronian premise that friendship can only exist among equals, had the effect of according men and women a degree of equality unusual for the period.[31]

---

27. She makes an exception in this rule for the relationship between a nun and her confessor. Teresa of Avila, *The Way of Perfection,* trans. and ed. E. Allison Peers (New York: Image Books, 1964), 55, 63.

28. See Augustine, *Confessions,* trans. Henry Chadwick (Oxford: Oxford University Press, 1991), 98-110.

29. Brian Patrick McGuire, *Friendship and Community: The Monastic Experience 350-1250* (Kalamazoo: Cistercian Publications, 1988), xv.

30. Aelred of Rievaulx, *Spiritual Friendship,* trans. Mark F. Williams (Scranton: University of Scranton Press), 1994. See Mark F. Williams, prologue to Aelred, 19.

31. An eleventh-century collection includes a letter from the Bishop of Worms written to a superior of a women's monastery in which he defends spiritual love among men and women (McGuire, *Friendship and Community,* 188). By the twelfth century, concern for the spiritual direction of religious women used the prototype of Christ and Mary Magdalene to justify spiritual friendship between a subordinate woman and a male superior (McGuire, *Friendship and Community,* 390). By the thirteenth century, a new attitude toward women

Despite conflicting opinions on the subject, spiritual friendship persists as a basic feature of Christian community, and as a practice of communion it bears enormous significance for youth ministry. Two forms of this practice serve as "templates" for spiritual friendship among adolescents: chastity and prayer. Before going further, let me admit that the church seldom classifies either chastity or prayer as a practice of friendship. Chastity sounds quaint, like chamomile tea, conjuring up memories of medieval prophylactics and Victorian sexual ethics. Prayer, on the other hand, sounds ethereal and far removed from the daily terrain of physical relationships. Yet both chastity and prayer are basic to the art of intimacy among adolescents; they are fundamental to the *koinonia* itself. Whether directed to God or to another young person, friendship unites adolescents' passion for others with the holy passion for God. The particularity of friendship gives the urge to know and be known concrete embodiment that acknowledges but transcends sexuality as intimacy's only shape.

Practicing Communion	
PASSIONATE PURPOSE	Enacting communion
EXAMPLE OF PRACTICE	Spiritual friendship
FORMS OF PRACTICE with recurring significance for young people	Chastity Prayer
STREAM OF TRADITION	Koinonia

True Love Dates:
Spiritual Friendship through Chastity

I learned about chastity from "The Sonny and Cher Show." Somewhere back in the dark recesses of the 1970s, Sonny and Cher introduced their cherubic blond toddler named Chastity to a national television audience.

---

encouraged by Dominic and Francis led to more egalitarian, and more familiar, spiritual friendships between monastic men and women (McGuire, *Friendship and Community,* 394). Correspondence of the Dominican Jordan of Saxony to the nun Diana of Andalo between the 1220s and 1230s, for instance, consistently describes the sisters as "spouses of Christ," while the friars are given the status of friends of the spouse.

"Chastity?" my mother sniffed. "That's not a name. That's what you do so you won't have a baby to introduce on national TV."

To say that chastity is a means to spiritual intercourse sounds counterintuitive, until we remember that chastity is not really a synonym for sexual abstinence (which, by the way, I am all for among teenagers). From the Latin *castus* ("to be without"), chastity is the art of incremental intimacy. Chastity seeks communion, not abstinence, and in this light it is more about "saying yes" than "saying no." Communion is predicated on the self-giving love of passion, not the need-love of self-fulfillment. For adolescents to "give" themselves to others, sexually or emotionally, is not possible; psychologically, teenagers have no self to give, since the development of selfhood concludes adolescence. Yet there is an exception: when a young person seeks to imitate Christ, she becomes conformed to Christ's Passion, and she discovers that her true self has already been given by God. Though this God-given identity has been shattered by sin, her participation in the self-giving love of Jesus opens her to the divine transformation of the ego. This young person *can* explore love as self-giving, because the self she has to give is the Christ who dwells within her. Love that imitates Christ is passionate love that willingly submits to "little deaths" of self-denial, guided by vows the Christian communion intended for joy: baptism, vows taken in a religious community, ordination, marriage.[32] For this reason, passion counters promiscuity, for true passion fixes its gaze upon a life-giving other for whom sacrifice — "to be without" — is a glad expression of love, not a reluctant act of self-deprivation.

Saying No: Renouncing Neediness

"To be without" represents a fundamental condition for Christian friendship, not just romantic love. The spiritual life is about letting go, not grab-

---

32. A number of traditions expand upon these vows, so that ordination or religious life might include vows of poverty, obedience, and celibacy; some traditions offer liturgies to offer the benefit of public vows in the context of a faith community to gay or lesbian partners who are not married (these vows serve important pastoral functions but lack the normative status of vows more widely recognized by the church). The point is that "the vowed life" has the weight of the Christian community behind it, giving Christians a social context of support for seeing these vows through. Regardless of other vows a particular Christian community supports, baptism, ordination, and marriage have been acknowledged by the majority of Christians over time as ecclesial practices, and therefore offer the greatest likelihood for fidelity.

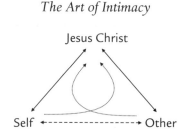

Figure 8. The Dynamics of Chastity

bing on, for renunciation is the primary condition for freedom — and friends are free. Friendships based on self-fulfillment are not passionate friendships that give us permission to be ourselves; they are needy relationships that force us to be the person the other requires (or vice versa). Passionate friendships, on the other hand, free us for incremental intimacy, a joyous self-giving marked by willing self-restraint. Rather than flood the emerging self with immediate gratification (sexual, emotional, or intellectual), chastity seeks joy through restraint. Because it is grounded in self-giving rather than "need-love," chastity avoids relationships based solely on personal gratification and rules out patterns of interaction in which we use others for our own gain. The freedom acquired through incremental intimacy stems from the ability to be fully human as our true identities unfold before one another. Our journey toward the cross draws us to each other. As we gradually identify with Christ's Passion in the practices of faith, we find ourselves increasingly identified with others who are travelling toward the cross as well.

Because chastity explores the range of intimacy, it has the effect of both stretching and restraining the usual gamut of adolescent friendship. Befriending others on the basis of chastity means youth learn to "be without" a circle of friends made up exclusively of people who are like them. Since chastity's objective is communion with Christ, youth find themselves intimately connected with others who may be nothing like them, save their common desire for union with God. Chastity also means young people learn to "be without" destructive relational patterns: gossipy conversations that enhance one friendship while degrading another, behavior calculated to control someone else, and other forms of emotional manipulation that are standard issue in the human interpersonal repertoire but that grow larger-than-life in the high school hallways ("If I say hi to that geek, people will think that I like him").

Saying Yes: Cultivating Mutual Vulnerability

Perhaps the primary benefit of re-introducing chastity to adolescents is that it *does* have sexual connotations and therefore acknowledges the embodied nature of human relationships. This enables Christians to recognize the role of sexuality in human attraction (male and female), which factors into all friendships and needs some latitude to develop. Teenage girls go to the restroom in packs and teenage boys bond in the locker room because, in these inner sanctums, youth ritualize both their friendship and their emerging sexuality. Same-gender friends develop strong bonds from shared experiences around gender roles in a given culture. The desire for God is a desire for otherness, and the otherness of friendship is part of its allure, whether immediately apparent (say, in male-female attraction) or gradually ascertained (in the case of same-gender soulmates). To deny the sexual dynamics of friendship, whether or not romance is involved, is to court disaster. Sexual desire demands its due, and while acknowledged sexuality calls our attention to the ways we are drawn to "otherness" and ultimately to God, unacknowledged sexuality is famous for exploding under the covers.

The art of incremental intimacy gives spiritual friends ways to practice creative fidelity that equates eroticism, the self-communicating impulse of passion, with communion instead of with orgasm. By privileging intercourse with God over all other forms of intimacy, chastity means rejecting sexual intercourse as the *primary* basis for human communion, but it also means saying yes to relationships in which passion's self-communicating impulse is mediated in other ways.

Chastity operates on the principle of divine accommodation — the idea that God's passion is so overwhelming that no human relationship can embody it "full strength" — and so even in passion God reveals the divine self incrementally, according to our level of trust and vulnerability. Authentic intimacy unwraps us by degrees, exposing us layer by layer to one another. Spiritual friends unbandage us; they reveal us to ourselves. But this is not to be feared, for they also pull us toward Christ. As we are exposed, such friends stand ready to bathe us in grace, to flush out old wounds with tears and trust. In the end, it is chastity, not promiscuity, that disrobes us before one another. Thanks to the passion of spiritual friendship, we stand naked and vulnerable — without defense or pretext — before the Passion of Christ.

Chastity, then, cultivates a mutual vulnerability that supercedes the kind available in the parents' bedroom after school.[33] Teenagers learn to

---

33. The family home of the boy is the most common place that youth 16-18 first have

"say yes" to one another, to trust one another, and to risk for one another through conversation and mutual generosity, physical and intellectual play, creative expression and shared introspection. Chastity creates a "holding environment" that honors both the acute sexuality and the innate spirituality of the adolescent life. Holding environments cultivate communion by encircling young people in an environment in which they can safely test intimacy through adults who model fidelity, concrete opportunities to suffer love on behalf of others at a variety of risk levels, the development of trust-building skills that invite grace-filled connections between people, and ample time and opportunity to fail and succeed in relationships in a setting where communion does not depend on us. This, of course, is the point of the Eucharist. Chastity requires passion, for "to be without" requires something of value to renounce. But the holding environment of spiritual friendship leaves an important margin of error (altogether absent in a popular culture) in which young people can recover from their relational mistakes, experience forgiveness, and start again in a community of love.

Holding Environments That Cultivate Communion

1. Include adults who model fidelity
2. Offer concrete opportunities for sacrificial love at varying risk levels
3. Develop trust-building skills in teenagers
4. Provide time and opportunity for teenagers to safely fail and succeed at relationships

   Maybe more because of than in spite of our sexually charged popular culture, teenagers often greet chastity with a sense of relief, and they find it less of a stretch than we might imagine. Saying "yes" to spiritual friendship gives sexual resistance positive content, whereas saying "no" to sexual pressure leaves a vacuum to be filled by other greedy passions. Because teenagers possess highly developed skills of friendship, youth ministry is a natural place to cultivate an ecology of mutual care that supports the practice of chastity. Chastity takes place in a community in which we are called

---

sex, normally between 10 p.m. and 7 a.m. The second most common timeframe is in the evening between 6 and 10 p.m. Child Trends, National Longitudinal Survey of Youth (Washington, D.C.: U.S. Bureau of Labor Statistics, 2000); Brooke Adams, "Home Is Where the Teen Sex Is," *Salt Lake Tribune,* Tuesday, October 8, 2002; available at www.sltrib.com/2002/oct/10082002/tuesday/5079.htm.

to lay down our lives for one another, making the ultimate act of communion self-denial, not self-fulfillment — death, not sex. This is why, in the church, sexual intercourse is accompanied by sacred vows: in the Christian community, passion is a relationship of communion, which means that every act of intercourse is with Jesus as well as with one another.

By itself, sex — as the youth in our focus groups continually reminded us — is not a big deal to many teenagers. Girls in each of our focus groups consistently rated getting their driver's license ahead of losing their virginity in terms of "what mattered more." A number of girls stated that they were actually relieved when they lost their virginity because "it got it over with." Intimacy, on the other hand — the authentic intimacy of being known and unconditionally accepted by an idealized spouse, or by unborn children — was a very big deal, a distant but desperately hoped-for possibility. Adultery shatters intimacy because it compromises a relationship's three-dimensionality; the church classifies adultery as sin because adulterous relationships omit God. This means that, technically, even marital relationships can be adulterous, though the community's support of the marriage vows makes this far more difficult. Two-dimensional relationships do not acknowledge God's participation and therefore lack the cruciform pattern that defines passion. In the absence of a community of faith that enacts the cruciform pattern of self-giving love, intimacy easily succumbs to violence or infidelity in search of the fulfillment and stability offered by three-dimensional relationships that acknowledge Christ as a participating partner. Christian marriage ritualizes communion by embodying the passion of union with another through God.[34]

Communicating Passion:
Spiritual Intercourse through Prayer

The primary friendship to which we are called is with the Triune God who has befriended us — a friendship as life-giving as sexual intimacy, as transformative as falling in love. Since all communion begins with God's self-communication, prayer is also an indispensable practice of spiritual friendship, a basic form of God's self-communicating passion. All prayer begins in desire: our suffering for what we do not have and God's desire

34. In some traditions, vows of holy union between same-sex partners may also be understood in the context of communion. Because these unions are not always considered legally binding, they often lack the public support that benefits most marriages.

for communion with us. The communicative impulse of passion, therefore, prepares us for the life of prayer, which — like sexuality — seeks intercourse with the beloved. The vast majority of American teenagers (80 to 89 percent) say they pray, and two out of five say they pray daily (though they are not always certain who they pray *to*).[35] Jewish, mainline Protestant, Catholic, Baha'i, Buddhist, and Quaker youth tend to pray less frequently than Christian teenagers from theologically conservative, Pentecostal, or sectarian traditions.[36] When it comes to public prayer, young people are noticeably more pro-prayer than adults; 69 percent of teenagers polled by a University of California-Berkeley survey said they favored prayer in schools, compared with 59 percent of adults.[37]

Prayer is "primary speech," the most profound form of intercourse we know.[38] It is both intimate and expansive, personal and outward-reaching, a means by which we know and become known — which makes prayer a vital contributor to the teenager's developing identity. In prayer, we begin to hear our true selves emerge from what Ann and Barry Ulanov call "our counterfeit selves." But even more important, in prayer we begin to know God:

> Prayer to God, to the source of being, gives us more being, more self. But that is not the primary point of prayer; it is almost a by-product. The primary point is the other, the one we are seeking in our speech. The only way we know anything about God . . . is through praying. That is the mode of consciousness in which the object, God, appears to the subject, us.[39]

Whether in the form of thanksgiving or confession, intercession or supplication, prayer enlarges us by making us conscious of God, which in turn makes us more deeply and authentically conscious of our own being. But

---

35. George Barna, "Teenagers," *Barna Research Online* November 25, 2002; available at www.barna.org/cgi-bin/PageCategory.asp. Barna (2002) reports 89 percent of teenagers say they pray, but the National Longitudinal Survey of Adolescent Health (1995) offers a more conservative statistic: 80 percent (cited by National Study of Youth and Religion, available at www.youthandreligion.org).

36. National Longitudinal Survey of Adolescent Health, 1995; cited by National Study of Youth and Religion, www.youthandreligion.org.

37. University of California-Berkeley, press release, 24 September 2002; available at http://www.berkeley.edu/news/media/releases/2002/09/24_youth.html.

38. We cannot lie when we pray. See Ann and Barry Ulanov, *Primary Speech: A Psychology of Prayer* (Atlanta: John Knox, 1982).

39. Ann and Barry Ulanov, *Primary Speech*, 2, 8.

being known in prayer is also a two-way street. In prayer we reach for God, but God also reaches for us. If desire primes us for a life of prayer, the hormonal heat of adolescence makes teenagers more than ready for this form of intercourse.

Embodied Prayers: Helping Adolescents Reach for God

Lacking fluency in the language of intimacy, young people often find talking to adults about prayer like talking to adults about sex: awkward and invasive. When desire begs expression but lacks a way to communicate itself, it intensifies both the urgency and the ambiguity of desire. So teenagers seek ways to concretize their desire for intimacy by embodying it in human relationships. Similarly, adolescents look for ways to convey their desire for God concretely as well. Frequently they turn to the material world for tangible tokens of God's friendship with them, and they look for ways to express their friendship concretely in return.

Mediating prayer through embodied forms of expression relieves young people of needing a language that perfectly describes the depths of their desire for intimacy. If the sages and the poets have yet to come up with words to describe these longings in the human heart, asking young people to put prayers into words — spontaneously, out loud, in public, and at church — is a recipe for noncompliance. And no wonder, given the stripped-down vulnerability of the prayer encounter. Even saying grace before meals is difficult, since most young people's public prayer repertoire consists of little more than "God is great" or "Now I lay me down to sleep" and (maybe) "The Lord's Prayer" — period. These are the only prayers many mainline Protestant young people have ever been asked to pray aloud — and for their friends who do not come from religious homes, the range is smaller still.

Yet these same youth often willingly pray when they can express their friendship with God physically, either through their own bodies or through some aspect of the material world. During a communion service I attended recently — where the loaf of bread was swaddled and laid in a manger before it was broken for the sacrament, and where large rough nails were distributed after the bread and wine — two middle school boys behind me fingered the nails and whistled under their breath: "Man, that would hurt!" Since teenagers still hover between concrete and formal operational thought, the revelation that God, the Holy Other, works in and through the material world is both startling and convincing. Material symbols serve as "transitional objects" that help teenagers navigate the transition from concrete operational to formal operational thought, and from the tangible world of human experience to more abstract levels of spiritual reflection.

Unconsciously, we often engage young people in embodied prayer by focusing on prayer's physical dynamics, expressing God's intimacy by hugging, holding hands, maintaining close interpersonal space, and using direct and sustained eye contact as we listen to one another.[40] Physical prayer is a time-honored means of introducing young people to healthy, affirming touch; Christian tradition contains a wide repertoire of strenuous body prayers ranging from prostrate to ecstatic prayer positions, and in this regard the church has much to offer adolescents' experience of physical intimacy with God. But if this is the *only* form of embodied prayer young people experience, it can "set them up" to confuse sexual and spiritual intimacy, especially in conference or retreat settings where youth live in close physical proximity to each other while participating in activities designed to heighten their awareness of each other.

Physical prayers, like embodied relationships, should reflect intimacy's range, and therefore prayer should also express various dimensions of friendship with God, from the casual to the erotic. In an increasingly image-driven society, nonverbal prayers can assume extraordinary significance. Typically, Christian youth events employ rudimentary forms of embodied prayer that quickly devolve into event "souvenirs," but these can also be nurtured into more sustained forms of contemplation. Prayers of confession written on the last day of camp and tossed ritually into a fire; hopes written on cards and nailed to a cross; intercessory "ribbons" tied to a gate or a tree as memories of those they have prayed for — these are all concrete expressions of our friendship with God and can symbolize God's friendship with us. Sometimes intimacy is evoked by physical space as well — a silent glen or a demarcated labyrinth — or it slips out in song drenched in reverence or joy. In all cases, embodied prayers take their cues from Christian sacraments, in which prayers over water, oil, bread, and wine invite young people into an experience that imitates the Passion of Christ and invites them to share this experience with others.

40. In Western cultures, direct eye contact (especially among women) is interpreted as deeply truthful, while in Asian cultures (and in Asian American subcultures) it can be interpreted as a sign of disrespect.

Holy Listening: When God Reaches for Us

Relationships require mutual communication; research on self-disclosure indicates that one person's disclosure evokes a similar disclosure from the other, and if one party discloses and the other does not, the relationship suffers imbalance and falters.[41] Love seeks to know the beloved down to the smallest details, which is why celebrity magazines flourish and why a school crush spawns platoons of friendly spies whose sole mission is to lurk around corners listening for clues about the one who is secretly adored. Knowing Jesus through prayer requires holy listening as well as sacred speech. It involves practices that filter out the static of daily life in order to hear God's personal address to us.

Like infatuated teenagers, Protestants approach holy listening in both direct and indirect ways. The Word of God is spoken through Scripture as well as through those who help us discern Jesus' voice in daily life. "Searching the Scriptures" — John Wesley's phrase for reading the Bible with the prayerful expectation that God will meet us there — aims at the personal knowledge of the lover, not just at intellectual understanding of a text, though both, obviously, are optimal. Searching the Scriptures seeks communion more than comprehension. As in other practices of spiritual friendship, searching the Scriptures means submitting ourselves to them, seeking the word God intends us to hear. While Bible study focuses on understanding, searching the Scriptures implies listening to a text, not analyzing it, and focuses on God's Word addressed to us rather than on our address to God. While prayer and Bible study undergird all Christian practices, searching the Scriptures calls for a specific kind of appropriation, asking the Spirit to speak through the text and to assist us in prayerfully internalizing it, so that we can live the gospel from within.

Holy listening, therefore, has direct forms (*lectio divina,* guided meditations, and certain kinds of Bible study that privilege deep reflection on the text) as well as indirect forms like mentoring, in which we rely on another person to frame how we listen for God. Mentoring is a kind of "interpretive eavesdropping" in which a more experienced disciple helps a less experienced one listen more intently to the promptings of the Holy Spirit. The mentor's primary job is to listen in on the relationship between a

---

41. Known as the "dyadic effect," when one person discloses something about himself or herself to another, he or she tends to elicit a reciprocal level of openness in the other person. Stewart Tubbs and Sylvia Moss, *Human Communication,* 5th ed. (New York: Random House, 1987), 214.

young person and God, to notice and reflect back to the adolescent patterns that the mentor observes. Mentoring is a form of spiritual apprenticeship in which an experienced Christian prepares a young person for a life of discipleship and ministry in his or her own right — something akin to the relationship Elizabeth had with Mary, or Paul had with Timothy. Elizabeth interpreted her own baby's leap in the womb as God's sign that Mary was indeed called to bear Christ; Paul reassured Timothy that, in spite of his youth, he must not doubt God's call to set an example for the believers in thought, word, and deed (1 Tim. 4:12).

Significantly, neither of these mentors spent much face-to-face time with their budding disciples. Mentors do not hover; it's hard to imagine Mary or Timothy complaining about attention from Elizabeth or Paul. Still, spiritual "parenting" can shape young people as much as biological parenting. The presence of an adult guarantor in faith is cited repeatedly as the most important factor in a young person's decision to claim faith as her own.[42] Often, it is through a significant adult that we first recognize that Christ's transformation is available to us as we practice the passion of God. This makes mentoring both threatening and demanding for youth ministry: threatening because legal guardians and biological parents often envy the visible influence other well-meaning adults assume in their children's unfolding identities, and demanding because youth idealize their mentors much as they idealize their parents — and suffer the same disappointment when we fail to live up to their expectations. Mentoring, notes W. Paul Jones, "requires models who have 'been there' and yet have not fallen, experienced but not succumbed, suffered but gained wisdom through it all, and have so much by wanting so little."[43]

No wonder mentors are hard to come by. Yet Jones is not suggesting that mentors are perfect any more than parents are perfect. Youth may pattern part of their emerging identities after adult faith mentors, yet the goal of mentoring is not for young people to replicate an adult's faith but to acquire a life in God of similar substance. Mentoring does remind us, however, that — like it or not — we may be the only window to Christ many young people ever have, a responsibility that requires excruciating honesty on our part, as well as a transparency that is possible only when *we* practice

42. Kenda Creasy Dean, *A Synthesis of the Literature on, and a Descriptive Overview of, Protestant, Catholic, and Jewish Religious Youth Organizations in the United States* (Washington, D.C.: Carnegie Council on Adolescent Development, 1991), 51.

43. W. Paul Jones, *The Art of Spiritual Direction: Giving and Receiving Spiritual Guidance* (Nashville: Upper Room, 2002), 17-18.

Christ's Passion as well.[44] This transparency to Christ allows parents to remain primary in their children's identifications, and it protects young people from confusing us with idealized versions of ourselves. Tilden Edwards's image of the spiritual director as physician is instructive, for the physician does nothing more than "cleanse the wound, align the sundered parts, and give it a rest. That's all. The physician does not heal. He or she provides an environment for the natural process of healing to take its course."[45] Ultimately, this means that the Holy Spirit — not the adult leader — is the true mentor, and the human relationship serves simply as a vessel for revelation and grace.

Sacramental Intercourse

Like video games, every form of intimacy comes with various difficulty levels, and young people must have enough exposure to multiple practices of spiritual friendship to learn the range of skills intimacy requires. While some youth readily practice chastity as incremental intimacy, others form more halting relationships, unable to risk trust until someone risks for them first. Likewise, some youth easily pray at an altar rail or through art forms like dance, music, or video (all public, high-stakes ventures), while others can barely acknowledge that they know the youth pastor who visits the school, unable to take the social risks associated with going to church. But very few of us spout full sentences as toddlers. Passion communicates itself, but only awkwardly and partially at first. Practices of communion require a rhythm of risk and encouragement, with plenty of chances to go back and start again, as we acquire a language of faith that can frame every relationship, and not just our relationship with God.

And so the church keeps going back, day after day, week after week, worship after worship, to the only instruction Jesus gave to his followers regarding communion: "Do this." He gave them an embodied, material way to remember him. Keeping company with one another, they prayed

---

44. Spiritual directors are a specific kind of mentor, whose formal roles are often absent in youth ministry — a fact that may hurt youth leaders more than young people themselves. Mentoring and spiritual direction specifically need serious reconsideration among Protestants, especially those in youth ministry. See Jones, *The Art of Spiritual Direction,* and Eugene H. Peterson, *Working the Angles: The Shape of Pastoral Integrity* (Grand Rapids: Eerdmans, 1987), 188-92.

45. Tilden Edwards, *Spiritual Friend* (New York: Paulist, 1980), 172. Thanks to Greg Rohde for pointing out this image to me.

over material things like bread and wine, and they remembered Jesus. But something else happened as well: Jesus came to the meal, too. No relationship need be adulterous again, Jesus told them, for wherever two or three of you gather in my name, I am in your midst. Invariably, Jesus reveals himself in the company of spiritual friends, people who practice communion, the three-dimensional intimacy of God.

And so, again and again, we "do this." Spiritual friendship is obviously not just for teenagers; it is the way the *church* practices communion — if only we would. One of youth ministry's legacies to the mainstream church is the adolescent insistence that intimacy matters, and that practices like chastity and prayer give substance to relationships that sanitized versions of "fellowship" cannot muster. Jesus raises the stakes on intimacy considerably, calling us to lay down our lives for our friends. No two-dimensional relationship is capable of this. Only three-dimensional communion is marked by passion, making unselfish love possible — not because of the self young people have to offer, but because of the self Christ has offered them.

THE PASSION OF MARTYRDOM

Why Youth Ministry Needs Theology

I look at the sky. I look at the people.

> Arien Ahmed, 20-year-old Palestinian student, on the
> moment she decided not to detonate the bomb she
> had carried in her backpack to a pedestrian mall
> in Israeli city Rishon de Zion[1]

*The secret of man's being is not only to live but to have some-
thing to live for. Without a stable conception of the object of
life, man would not consent to go on living.*

> Fyodor Dostoyevsky[2]

Only a suffering God can help.

> Dietrich Bonhoeffer[3]

1. "Perspectives," *Newsweek,* July 1, 2002, 21.
2. Fyodor Dostoyevsky, "The Grand Inquisitor," *The Brothers Karamozov,* available at www.ccel.org/d/dostoyevsky/karamozov/htm05/chapter05.html.
3. Dietrich Bonhoeffer, *Letters and Papers from Prison,* ed. E. Bethge, trans. R. Fuller (New York: Macmillan, 1962), 218.

Some people have cautioned me during the course of this project, "It almost sounds as if you think young people should be ready to die for their faith." That is not true. I think *all* Christians should be ready to die for their faith — it's just that teenagers are simply more likely than the rest of us to actually do it. This is both because of their youthful enthusiasm and because we send them to die in our stead, co-opting their passion, their ideological openness, and their desire to invest in something meaningful in order to send them to do scapegoating's dirty work. It is easy for us to point accusing fingers at the deployment of teenagers as suicide bombers, or at the training of young pilots for terrorist attacks.[4] But every society participates. Geneva Convention protocol prohibits recruiting or deploying soldiers younger than eighteen, but human rights organizations have documented the use of child militants (some as young as eight years old) in thirty-three recent armed conflicts around the world.[5] Of those countries known to impose the death penalty on juvenile offenders — Congo, Iran, Nigeria, and the United States — the U.S. has executed eight adolescents since 1998, far more than any other country.[6]

An unexpected thing has happened between the start of this project six years ago and now. Martyrdom has gone mainstream among young people around the world. Young people *are* dying for their faith, in alarming numbers, and it has fallen to those of us in the church to ask, "Faith in what?" Although American teenagers trace it to a school library in Littleton, Colorado, elsewhere in the world — especially in regions where globalization is perceived as a threat to local culture, and where the population

---

4. The Qur'an forbids suicide, but it encourages the destruction of Allah's enemies. Those who lose their life in the cause of destroying Allah's enemies *(jihad)* are viewed as martyrs, not suicides. See Br. Abu Ruquiyah, trans. Br. Hussein El-Chamy, "The Islamic Legitimacy of the 'Martyrdom Operations,'" *Nida'ul Islam*, December-January 1996-97, available at www.islam.org.au; accessed December 16, 2002.

5. See "Afghanistan," *Child Soldiers' Global Report 2001* (London: Coalition to Stop the Use of Child Soldiers), available at www.child-soldiers.org; accessed December 16, 2002. The same report noted that 23 percent of recruits in the United States armed services are seventeen at the time they sign their enlistment contracts, though less than one-quarter of one percent are actually assigned to units before they are eighteen.

6. "Virginia Governor Urged to Halt Execution of Juvenile Offender" (New York: Human Rights Watch, 1999), available at www.hrw.org/press/1999/jun/virginia699.htm; accessed December 16, 2002. As I write this, another juvenile, seventeen-year-old John Malvo, is being tried for his role in sniper shootings including those in Washington, D.C. U.S. Attorney General John Ashcroft selected Virginia as the site of the first trial specifically because Virginia offers the death penalty for juvenile offenders.

is disproportionately young and unemployed[7] — adolescence and the rhetoric of martyrdom go hand in hand. Sam George, an Indian youth pastor who helps network and train persons for youth ministry in regions that he calls "terrorcultures," observes, "To many young men who have lived their entire lives under humiliating conditions, commitment to martyrdom is a final act of power, stemming from desperation."[8] If George is correct, then we can expect to see more of these desperate commitments in the near future. The United Nations estimates that 85 percent of the world's youth population lives in developing nations, expected to reach 89 percent in 2020. Teenagers in China alone outnumber the entire population of the United States, and more than half (55 percent) of the world's Islamic population is under the age of thirty.[9]

Christianity, Judaism, and Islam all share histories of persecution, and all accord the rank of the martyr to those who are killed in the name of faith. But most of what the press (and the perpetrators) call martyrdom is a far cry from Christian passion. In Christianity, passion means clinging to the Christ we love in the face of death — never imposing death on others. Jesus chose to follow the course of perfect love — a path that led to the cross — but he did not crucify himself. Christian passion, in fact, inverts the usual formula for violence. Locating Christian passion in a love worth dying for means precisely that we will not kill for our faith. This does not, however, prevent others from killing us.

7. Some social scientists link a bulge in the male youth population with an increase in violence; these correlations are speculative, since corroborating factors such as poverty, unemployment, religious ideology, and education also play a role. Cf. Samuel Huntington, *The Clash of Civilizations and the Remaking of World Order* (New York: Simon and Schuster, 1996), 265.

8. Sam George, "TerrorCulture: Worth Living for or Worth Dying for," in Taylor et al., eds., *One World or Many: The Challenge of Globalization in World Missions* (World Evangelical Alliance, forthcoming).

9. The United Nations defines youth as people ages 15-24; available at www.un.org/esa/socdev/unyin/qanda.htm; accessed December 16, 2002. In Iran, where two-thirds of the population is under thirty, youth are called "the angry generation, longing for jobs, more freedom, and power." See Amy Waldman, "In Iran, an Angry Generation Longs for Jobs, More Freedom and Power," *The New York Times,* December 7, 2001. I am grateful to Sam George for pointing out these statistics.

Taking It All the Way:
The Unequivocal Call to Martyrdom

There is no escaping the logical conclusion of the imitation of Christ. From the earliest days of the church, many believers considered the most excellent and most perfect way to imitate the Lord's Passion to be literal death, or "complete" martyrdom. In response to Roman persecution, early church leaders proposed an intimate union between Christ and the martyr who "participates in the passion of Christ and bears the Savior's wounds in his own body."[10] Martyrs were considered so intimate with Jesus that Christ "possessed" them; when the witness suffered, it was said, "it is no longer he or she who suffers, but Christ who suffers in them."[11] Christian theology teaches that, in the imitation of Christ, Christ's death becomes our death, and Christ's life becomes our life. So the passion of Christian faith does, in fact, imply a complex but undeniable connection to martyrdom; as Bonhoeffer pointed out, "When Christ calls a man, he bids him come and die."[12]

The word *marturia* means "witness," a term borrowed from the Greek courts, where a martyr was someone who gave testimony or evidence in a court of law. Witnesses proclaim the truth of Christ with their lives and not only their words. Since early Christians — coerced into either dying for Jesus or denying him — chose death over apostasy, the church came to view martyrs as people who testified for Jesus not only in life, but in death.

Ultimately, martyrdom reveals the human desire to testify to that which gives us hope, to bear witness to whatever we deem worthy of our dreams, our trust, our lives. The adolescent search for "something to die for" is always a quest for something to *live* for — and this quest escalates whenever reservoirs of hope run low. In the bloody Israeli spring of 2002,

10. Cyprian of Carthage, *The Concept of Martyrdom According to St. Cyprian of Carthage,* ed. Edelhard L. Hummel, *The Catholic University of America Studies in Christian Antiquity,* ed. Johannes Quasten (Washington, D.C.: Catholic University of America Press, 1946), 97.

11. Lang cites Cyprian's account of the martyrdom of the pregnant slave Felicitas by way of example, who was killed in Carthage in 203. While she was imprisoned, Felicitas went into labor; one of the prison guards said to her, "You suffer so much now — what will you do when you are tossed to the beasts?" "What I am suffering now," she replied, "I suffer by myself. But then Another will be inside me who will suffer for me, for I shall be suffering for him." "The Passion of Perpetua and Felicitas," cited by Lang, 256.

12. Dietrich Bonhoeffer, *The Cost of Discipleship* (New York: Simon and Schuster, 1995), p. 89.

an elementary school principal in a Palestinian refugee camp lamented to a *Newsweek* reporter that his students "want to be martyrs even if they don't know the meaning of the word. They see the images on TV, the posters in the streets, the honor of the martyrs' families, and they want that kind of honor for themselves, for their families."[13] In Gaza City, signs on the walls of Hamas-run kindergartens read, "The children of the kindergarten are the shaheeds (holy martyrs) of tomorrow." Slogans in the classrooms at Al-Naja University in the West Bank and Gaza City's Islamic University read: "Israel has nuclear bombs, we have human bombs."[14] An online document called "The Palestinian Authority School Books and Teachers' Guide" instructs eighth graders to learn by heart: "The Muslim sacrifices himself for his faith and fights a Jihad for Allah. He does not know cowardice because he understands that the time of his death is already ordained and that his dying as a Martyr on the field of battle is preferable to dying in bed."[15]

It is chilling rhetoric — but before we congratulate ourselves on having a more enlightened approach to child rearing, we should remind ourselves our difference lies in Christ alone, and not in any moral judgment we might hasten to proclaim. The church has also promised martyrs glory in heaven, and Christian history is littered with youth who prayed for a martyr's death, some of whom got their wish.[16] For adolescents resisting social pressure to suppress their *pathos,* the life of the martyr fascinates — not because they want to share martyrs' grisly suffering, but because young people envy their passion, their purpose, their brazen determination, their utter commitment to an ideology. To quote youth minister Sam George, "Ministry [to youth] in terrorculture will call for a *radical* discipleship."[17]

In fact, ministry to youth in *any* culture calls for a radical discipleship, for Christian witness also grows out of an unshakable conviction:

13. Muhammad Abu Rukbah, cited by Christopher Dickey, "Inside Suicide, Inc.," *Newsweek,* April 27, 2002, 27.

14. Jack Kelley, "Devotion, Desire Drive Youths to 'Martyrdom,'" *USA Today,* July 5, 2001, available at www.usatoday.com/news/world/june01/2001-06-26-suicide-usat.htm; accessed December 16, 2002.

15. The Palestinian Authority School Books and Teacher's Guide, Islamic Education for Eighth Grade #576, p. 176, available at www.edume.org/reports/1/11.htm; accessed on December 16, 2002.

16. Martyrdom was believed to effect salvation by God's grace in the "baptism of blood," substituting for the baptism of water and guaranteeing immediate entry into heaven. Cf. Cyprian, *Concept of Martyrdom,* 108-28. The martyr's death is the "perfection of every virtue" that is rewarded immediately by God with "the crown of life," 132.

17. George, "Terror Culture."

that Jesus loves us enough to die for us and calls us to love in equal measure. This is how adolescents want to love and to be loved; they yearn for the utter fidelity, the all-surpassing transcendence, the total communion that promises "till death do us part." No passion — personal, political, or religious — overrides Christ's ability to make good on this promise, for the life, death, and resurrection of Jesus reveal God's indefatigable mercy, immeasurable purpose, and undefeatable love.

What Witness Is — and Is Not

A witness is a martyr, theologically as well as etymologically: someone who stakes her life on something or someone worth dying for, who views faith as a life and death proposition — someone who is, in other words, very much like a teenager. This is exactly what unnerves us. If the logical extension of the practice of passion is martyrdom, then what business do we have advocating passion as a starting point for youth ministry? What if young people actually *did* do what Jesus did? What if they *do* imitate Christ in his life and death? What if they *would* lay down their lives for their friends — for their faith — as though these things mattered? Does the oddity maintained by Christian practices tempt yet another form of pathological extremism? In a world where young people with radical views of holiness commit suicide and murder as a "witness" to their gods, what prevents the practice of passion from degenerating into *jihad*?

In the church, the witness's testimony is not simply that Christ has died, but that Christ is risen; not only that Christ suffers, but that in Jesus Christ God trumps death. Thomas Long reminds us that participating in Christian practices, therefore, requires both a sense of mystery (only God can mock death!) and a sense of humor (because God has mocked death, we are free to lighten up a little ourselves).[18] As a result, for Christians the preeminent form of witness is not physical martyrdom, but worship. Every Christian practice is an act of worship that leads to doxology; in every act of witness, we race from the tomb to tell those who have heard and those who have not that the Lord is risen, and is among us. In the practices of discipleship, whether acts of piety or acts of mercy, we testify to God's self-communicating passion, and we open ourselves to the divine grace that makes Christian witness possible.

18. Thomas G. Long, *The Witness of Preaching* (Louisville: Westminster/John Knox Press, 1989), 15-16.

Like most people, I remain convinced that God seeks the life of witness over the witness of death. If the invitation to follow Jesus, as Bonhoeffer claimed, is an invitation to come and die, it must also be remembered at whose hands we are slain. Humans choose violence, not God — whether in the Roman Coliseum or in a Jerusalem grocery store where young girls carry out suicide bombings. The referent for Christian passion is a person, not a righteous "cause" or sacred artifact. Therefore Christian *marturia* preserves the essential humanity of both the other and the self. Sometimes this requires a conscious act of resistance, choosing to identify with Christ's suffering instead of accepting the role of a victim. One of the striking features of 1 Peter, an epistle of encouragement written to potential martyrs in Asia Minor at the end of the first century, is its insistence on imitating Christ's "active passivity." Self-restraint constitutes the active posture of a subject, not the passive posture of a victim. Given the likelihood of religious persecution during this period, the "submission" urged by the author of 1 Peter for slaves, wives, and other marginalized members of the Christian community (in stark contrast to the death-to-the-enemy rhetoric of extremist fundamentalism) should be taken as the words of a pastor hoping to empower his flock by preserving their human agency in the face of insufferable cruelty, and not as a bid to maintain existing social inequalities:

> If you suffer for doing good and you endure it, this is commendable before God. To this you were called, because Christ suffered for you, leaving you an example, that you should follow in his steps. . . . When they hurled their insults at him, he did not retaliate; when he suffered, he made no threats. Instead, he entrusted himself to God who judges justly. He himself bore our sins in his body on the tree, so that we might die to sins and live for righteousness; by his wounds you have been healed. (1 Pet. 2:20b-24)

Fortunately, even at the height of persecution in the early church, physical martyrdom remained the exception. Meanwhile, the church grappled with what it meant to be incorporated into Christ's Passion if physical martyrdom was not required. Paul happily anticipated meeting Christ in heaven, but he found ego "death" an acceptable form of self-giving for Christians who were spared physical martyrdom. Paul described his own witness in these terms: "I have been crucified with Christ and I no longer live, but Christ lives in me" (Gal. 2:20). In the early days of the church, the term "martyr" had not yet acquired the narrow connotation it bears today.

Even the Bishop of Carthage Cyprian (himself martyred in 258) — who did not shrink from advocating "complete" martyrdom involving torture and death — also approved of "unbloody or spiritual martyrdom" in which Christ lives in the believer and is communicated in the believer's *life*, provided the believer was willing and prepared to die as a martyr, should he be called to do so.[19]

Youth Ministry as a Theological Enterprise

Youth ministry, as mainline Protestants have come to know it, seldom calls young people to martyrdom — to lives that bear witness to the Christ who lives in young people and who reveals himself in practices that point to the passion of God. For more than a century, youth ministry has been considered a subdiscipline of Christian education, a place where educational insights are "applied" to young people like sunscreen. Yet good youth ministry is good *ministry,* and vice versa. When we approach youth ministry as practical theology, it belongs to a much broader discussion than Christian education alone. Youth ministry becomes a vehicle for understanding ministry with *all* people, forcing the church to reckon with the fact that Christian identity is the consequence of grace enacted in the practices of Christian community, and is not the result of "educational programs."

Understanding adolescents through a lens of Christian passion rather than through youth ministry's usual viewfinders (namely, educational, psychological, and social theory) suggests a very different course of action for the church if we hope to ignite faith and not just cheer wholesomeness. One such a course of action, grounded in the "practices of passion" unique to the Christian community, has been outlined in this book. Utilizing passion as a theological starting point for youth ministry, however, has also unearthed our culpability in mainline Protestantism's current ecclesial identity crisis. When the "to die for" core of Christian theology, the Passion of Christ, became muted in the mainline church, youth searching for passion inevitably looked elsewhere. It simply never occurred to them (or, quite frankly, to us) that they should look for passion *in church.* The fragmented identity of adolescents echoes our own personal and institutional fragmentation. Young people are dying for something, someone, to live for — *but so are we.* And the love we seek, the Love who will not let us go, who will not let us down, and who will not go away, is Je-

---

19. Cyprian, *Concept of Martyrdom,* 21-23.

sus. *He* is "to die for." And if the church bears witness to anything else, we are not martyrs, but fools.

Immersing adolescents in the practices that participate in the life, death, and resurrection of Jesus Christ does not just turn them into nice people who help others; it shapes them into subversives and prophets, forever marked by their identification with Jesus Christ and set apart by grace for lives of holy service. Practicing passion does something else as well: it gives teenagers wise mentors and concrete venues through which they can critique, and begin to change, the church. Unencumbered by fully developed ideological systems, young people share what Abraham Heschel thought was the prophet's signature trait: a heightened sensitivity to *pathos,* that psychic "heat-seeking" device that allows prophets and teenagers to notice holy fire, where it is and where it is not.[20] While Christian young people have a prophetic role to play in the world as a whole, perhaps their most important message is to the church itself. If young people detect an absence of passion in the mainstream church in spite of our relentless enthusiasm, perhaps it is time to take notice.

The Wild Card of Divine Grace

The adolescent social self is neither formed nor embedded in the psyche, and it therefore begs participation in practices that construct identity. Participating in the life of God through the practices of the Christian community forges a distinct kind of identity — a Trinitarian self that reflects the *imago dei* — in adolescents who lack the developmental sophistication and human support systems that engender integrated, socially constructed identities. Christian practices present the developing self with a formidable "wild card": God's infusion of divine grace into the world through practices that enact the life, death, and resurrection of Christ. The social self is constructed by restricting passions, and it encourages "facsimiles" of passion designed to maintain existing social systems. But by participating in the Passion of Christ, the adolescent takes on *God's* suffering love as the core of her identity, the very Passion that most threatens a society based on self-fulfillment. Cultural pressure not to "overdo it" cannot contain the passion of God. The adolescent transformed by God's passion cannot suppress it or "tone it down" without compromising the ecstatic reach of the Holy Spirit. This young person discovers that Christ has made

20. Abraham Heschel, *The Prophets,* vol. 1 (New York: Harper & Row, 1955), 26.

her into someone capable of toppling some of society's most cherished ideals, beyond the Christian community and even within it.

Conformity, therefore, is never the outcome of Christian practice; *oddity* is the outcome of Christian practice. Youth ministry is not about the corporate mimicry of Jesus. It is about incorporating young people into the self-giving love of God that is loose in the world. Anchoring youth ministry in the life, death, and resurrection of Christ suggests an approach to youth ministry that relies less on the order of human development and more on the order of salvation. In communities that enact divine passion — communities where God's steadfast, ecstatic, and intimate love is given human form — young people take part in the life of God that bears Christ's transforming grace beyond the walls of the church building.

All this makes a curriculum of Christian practice a notoriously unreliable way to ensure the perpetuation of the church, if by "church" we mean the congregation at hand. A curriculum of passion is fraught with surprise, for the practices that imitate Christ enable youth to critique the church as well as take part in it. Indeed, practice-based youth ministry is dedicated to the formation of "out of control" teenagers — out from under the control of the culture of consumption — by relocating the self's governing ideology in the freedom of the cross. And so, yes: Christianity seeks "martyrs," — people who know the way to the cross and who can accompany others there, people reconstructed by grace in practices that reveal the fidelity, transcendence, and communion of God.

Life as an Oyster

W. Paul Jones writes, "Deep within our souls, actually as proof that we have a soul, is a profound something that will not be quieted" — an *obsessio,* the pain we most crave to alleviate, the question we most ache to answer, the dilemma by which we are most defined.[21] While an *obsessio* takes many forms and is easily corrupted, its answering *epiphania* is the suffering love of Jesus Christ, which — to use Jones's image — works like an oyster, enfolding our *obsessio* in grace like a pearl envelops a grain of sand, making the grating particle both bearable and beautiful.[22]

The divine grace imparted in the practices of passion transform our *obsessios* by answering them with the *epiphania* of the cross. As Christian

---

21. W. Paul Jones, *The Art of Spiritual Direction* (Nashville: Upper Room, 2002), I, 48.
22. Jones, *The Art of Spiritual Direction*, 49.

practices enact the cruciform pattern of self-giving love, they guarantee the church's "oddity" in a culture of self-fulfillment. Sacrificial love is a distinctly countercultural virtue in the context of consumerism, for communities that practice it erode the support beams of a self-fulfilling culture. Anchoring youth ministry in the self-giving love of God, therefore, requires adult faith to be nurtured in acts of Christian witness as well. Young people unabashedly test God's faithfulness through our own, and in a world known for dashed hopes, youth demand that we, the church, act as God's surrogates by becoming the Love that will not disappoint. But we do disappoint them, always. And fidelity-starved adolescents, ever in search of a love worth dying for, easily conclude that Jesus isn't.

What we do have at our disposal is a reservoir of practices that point beyond our own fallibility to the wide arms of God. They are icons, not portraits; they make Jesus visible, but we never capture Jesus in them. Practices provide a holy toolbox for creating communities proficient at the art of being there, the art of awe, and the art of intimacy — the well-worn paths that centuries of Christians have used to journey into the passion of God.

So here is a practical proposal: What if the church exegeted the ways adolescents search for fidelity, transcendence, and communion in secular culture to listen in on young people's search for a love worth dying for — which is to say, their hope for a love worth living for?[23] And what if the church connected these hopes to practices that echo the Passion of Jesus Christ? Could we show young people a Passion that exceeds their own, a church that takes their desires seriously, and a way of life that presupposes divine passion as the normative pattern for every relationship? Could we give young people an *epiphania* that surpasses their *obsessio,* and surround them with grace that utterly transforms them — and the church as well?

Centuries of Christians have thought so. In the historic practices of Christian community, the restless human longing for a love that will not disappoint finds its home in the utter fidelity of God on the cross. The insistent adolescent desire for a love so tremendous that it cannot be contained is at last met by the never-to-be-contained mystery of the life, death, and resurrection of Jesus Christ. The profound human hunger to be known intimately and truly finally rests in the source of all communion. In

23. I am grateful to Ray Owens, who introduced me to Anthony Pinn's concept of "nitty gritty hermeneutics" for youth ministry and Christian ethics. See Anthony B. Pinn, *Why Lord? Suffering and Evil in Black Theology* (New York: Continuum, 1995). For Pinn, "nitty gritty hermeneutics" represents a form of interpretation that "takes the material of life that goes unspoken and hidden, and expresses it" (p. 117).

the practices of suffering love, Christ draws young people to himself little by little, until his Passion becomes their passion, his will becomes their will, his love becomes their love.

If the question, as Jürgen Moltmann raises it, is how to form the church as a community of passion, the answer is through those practices that bring us face-to-face with the Passion of Christ. In the quest for a passionate church, young people prod us to be more than we have become. They ask only that we be who we say we are: people of Passion, who live for a love that is "to die for," and who ask them to do the same. Youth ministry so conceived transforms young people — but it also transforms the church.

INDEX